HEBREW
VOCABULARY

FOR ENGLISH SPEAKERS

ENGLISH-HEBREW

The most useful words
To expand your lexicon and sharpen
your language skills

7000 words

Hebrew vocabulary for English speakers - 7000 words

By Andrey Taranov

T&P Books vocabularies are intended for helping you learn, memorize and review foreign words. The dictionary is divided into themes, covering all major spheres of everyday activities, business, science, culture, etc.

The process of learning words using T&P Books' theme-based dictionaries gives you the following advantages:

- Correctly grouped source information predetermines success at subsequent stages of word memorization
- Availability of words derived from the same root allowing memorization of word units (rather than separate words)
- Small units of words facilitate the process of establishing associative links needed for consolidation of vocabulary
- Level of language knowledge can be estimated by the number of learned words

T&P Books Publishing
www.tpbooks.com

ISBN: 978-1-78716-411-6

This book is also available in E-book formats.
Please visit www.tpbooks.com or the major online bookstores.

HEBREW VOCABULARY
for English speakers

T&P Books vocabularies are intended to help you learn, memorize, and review foreign words. The vocabulary contains over 7000 commonly used words arranged thematically.

- Vocabulary contains the most commonly used words
- Recommended as an addition to any language course
- Meets the needs of beginners and advanced learners of foreign languages
- Convenient for daily use, revision sessions, and self-testing activities
- Allows you to assess your vocabulary

Special features of the vocabulary

- Words are organized according to their meaning, not alphabetically
- Words are presented in three columns to facilitate the reviewing and self-testing processes
- Words in groups are divided into small blocks to facilitate the learning process
- The vocabulary offers a convenient and simple transcription of each foreign word

The vocabulary has 198 topics including:

Basic Concepts, Numbers, Colors, Months, Seasons, Units of Measurement, Clothing & Accessories, Food & Nutrition, Restaurant, Family Members, Relatives, Character, Feelings, Emotions, Diseases, City, Town, Sightseeing, Shopping, Money, House, Home, Office, Working in the Office, Import & Export, Marketing, Job Search, Sports, Education, Computer, Internet, Tools, Nature, Countries, Nationalities and more ...

T&P BOOKS' THEME-BASED DICTIONARIES

The Correct System for Memorizing Foreign Words

Acquiring vocabulary is one of the most important elements of learning a foreign language, because words allow us to express our thoughts, ask questions, and provide answers. An inadequate vocabulary can impede communication with a foreigner and make it difficult to understand a book or movie well.

The pace of activity in all spheres of modern life, including the learning of modern languages, has increased. Today, we need to memorize large amounts of information (grammar rules, foreign words, etc.) within a short period. However, this does not need to be difficult. All you need to do is to choose the right training materials, learn a few special techniques, and develop your individual training system.

Having a system is critical to the process of language learning. Many people fail to succeed in this regard; they cannot master a foreign language because they fail to follow a system comprised of selecting materials, organizing lessons, arranging new words to be learned, and so on. The lack of a system causes confusion and eventually, lowers self-confidence.

T&P Books' theme-based dictionaries can be included in the list of elements needed for creating an effective system for learning foreign words. These dictionaries were specially developed for learning purposes and are meant to help students effectively memorize words and expand their vocabulary.

Generally speaking, the process of learning words consists of three main elements:

- Reception (creation or acquisition) of a training material, such as a word list
- Work aimed at memorizing new words
- Work aimed at reviewing the learned words, such as self-testing

All three elements are equally important since they determine the quality of work and the final result. All three processes require certain skills and a well-thought-out approach.

New words are often encountered quite randomly when learning a foreign language and it may be difficult to include them all in a unified list. As a result, these words remain written on scraps of paper, in book margins, textbooks, and so on. In order to systematize such words, we have to create and continually update a "book of new words." A paper notebook, a netbook, or a tablet PC can be used for these purposes.

This "book of new words" will be your personal, unique list of words. However, it will only contain the words that you came across during the learning process. For example, you might have written down the words "Sunday," "Tuesday," and "Friday." However, there are additional words for days of the week, for example, "Saturday," that are missing, and your list of words would be incomplete. Using a theme dictionary, in addition to the "book of new words," is a reasonable solution to this problem.

The theme-based dictionary may serve as the basis for expanding your vocabulary.

It will be your big "book of new words" containing the most frequently used words of a foreign language already included. There are quite a few theme-based dictionaries available, and you should ensure that you make the right choice in order to get the maximum benefit from your purchase.

Therefore, we suggest using theme-based dictionaries from T&P Books Publishing as an aid to learning foreign words. Our books are specially developed for effective use in the sphere of vocabulary systematization, expansion and review.

Theme-based dictionaries are not a magical solution to learning new words. However, they can serve as your main database to aid foreign-language acquisition. Apart from theme dictionaries, you can have copybooks for writing down new words, flash cards, glossaries for various texts, as well as other resources; however, a good theme dictionary will always remain your primary collection of words.

T&P Books' theme-based dictionaries are specialty books that contain the most frequently used words in a language.

The main characteristic of such dictionaries is the division of words into themes. For example, the *City* theme contains the words "street," "crossroads," "square," "fountain," and so on. The *Talking* theme might contain words like "to talk," "to ask," "question," and "answer".

All the words in a theme are divided into smaller units, each comprising 3–5 words. Such an arrangement improves the perception of words and makes the learning process less tiresome. Each unit contains a selection of words with similar meanings or identical roots. This allows you to learn words in small groups and establish other associative links that have a positive effect on memorization.

The words on each page are placed in three columns: a word in your native language, its translation, and its transcription. Such positioning allows for the use of techniques for effective memorization. After closing the translation column, you can flip through and review foreign words, and vice versa. "This is an easy and convenient method of review – one that we recommend you do often."

Our theme-based dictionaries contain transcriptions for all the foreign words. Unfortunately, none of the existing transcriptions are able to convey the exact nuances of foreign pronunciation. That is why we recommend using the transcriptions only as a supplementary learning aid. Correct pronunciation can only be acquired with the help of sound. Therefore our collection includes audio theme-based dictionaries.

The process of learning words using T&P Books' theme-based dictionaries gives you the following advantages:

- You have correctly grouped source information, which predetermines your success at subsequent stages of word memorization
- Availability of words derived from the same root (lazy, lazily, lazybones), allowing you to memorize word units instead of separate words
- Small units of words facilitate the process of establishing associative links needed for consolidation of vocabulary
- You can estimate the number of learned words and hence your level of language knowledge
- The dictionary allows for the creation of an effective and high-quality revision process
- You can revise certain themes several times, modifying the revision methods and techniques
- Audio versions of the dictionaries help you to work out the pronunciation of words and develop your skills of auditory word perception

The T&P Books' theme-based dictionaries are offered in several variants differing in the number of words: 1.500, 3.000, 5.000, 7.000, and 9.000 words. There are also dictionaries containing 15,000 words for some language combinations. Your choice of dictionary will depend on your knowledge level and goals.

We sincerely believe that our dictionaries will become your trusty assistant in learning foreign languages and will allow you to easily acquire the necessary vocabulary.

TABLE OF CONTENTS

PRONUNCIATION GUIDE

Letter's name	Letter	Hebrew example	T&P phonetic alphabet	English example
Alef	א	אריה	[a], [ɑ:]	bath, to pass
	א	אחד	[ɛ], [ɛ:]	habit, bad
	א	מָאָה	[']	glottal stop
Bet	ב	בית	[b]	baby, book
Gimel	ג	גמל	[g]	game, gold
Gimel+geresh	ג'	ג'ונגל	[dʒ]	joke, general
Dalet	ד	דג	[d]	day, doctor
Hei	ה	הר	[h]	home, have
Vav	ו	וסת	[v]	very, river
Zayin	ז	זאב	[z]	zebra, please
Zayin+geresh	ז'	ז'ורנל	[ʒ]	forge, pleasure
Chet	ח	חוט	[x]	as in Scots 'loch'
Tet	ט	טוב	[t]	tourist, trip
Yud	י	יום	[j]	yes, New York
Kaph	ך כ	בריש	[k]	clock, kiss
Lamed	ל	לחם	[l]	lace, people
Mem	ם מ	מלך	[m]	magic, milk
Nun	ן נ	נר	[n]	name, normal
Samech	ס	סוס	[s]	city, boss
Ayin	ע	עין	[a], [ɑ:]	bath, to pass
	ע	תשעים	[']	voiced pharyngeal fricative
Pei	ף פ	פיל	[p]	pencil, private
Tsadi	ץ צ	צעצוע	[ts]	cats, tsetse fly
Tsadi+geresh	צ'י'	צ'ק	[tʃ]	church, French
Qoph	ק	קוף	[k]	clock, kiss
Resh	ר	רכבת	[r]	French (guttural) R
Shin	ש	שלחן, עשרים	[s], [ʃ]	city, machine
Tav	ת	תפוז	[t]	tourist, trip

ABBREVIATIONS
used in the vocabulary

English abbreviations

ab.	-	about
adj	-	adjective
adv	-	adverb
anim.	-	animate
as adj	-	attributive noun used as adjective
e.g.	-	for example
etc.	-	et cetera
fam.	-	familiar
fem.	-	feminine
form.	-	formal
inanim.	-	inanimate
masc.	-	masculine
math	-	mathematics
mil.	-	military
n	-	noun
pl	-	plural
pron.	-	pronoun
sb	-	somebody
sing.	-	singular
sth	-	something
v aux	-	auxiliary verb
vi	-	intransitive verb
vi, vt	-	intransitive, transitive verb
vt	-	transitive verb

Hebrew abbreviations

ז	-	masculine
ז"ר	-	masculine plural
ז , נ	-	masculine, feminine
נ	-	feminine
נ"ר	-	feminine plural

BASIC CONCEPTS

Basic concepts. Part 1

1. Pronouns

I, me	ani	אֲנִי (ז, נ)
you (masc.)	ata	אַתָה (ז)
you (fem.)	at	אַת (נ)
he	hu	הוּא (ז)
she	hi	הִיא (נ)
we	a'naχnu	אֲנַחְנוּ (ז, נ)
you (masc.)	atem	אַתֶם (ז"ר)
you (fem.)	aten	אַתֶן (נ"ר)
you (polite, sing.)	ata, at	אַתָה (ז), אַת (נ)
you (polite, pl)	atem, aten	אַתֶם (ז"ר), אַתֶן (נ"ר)
they (masc.)	hem	הֵם (ז"ר)
they (fem.)	hen	הֵן (נ"ר)

2. Greetings. Salutations. Farewells

Hello! (fam.)	ʃalom!	שָׁלוֹם!
Hello! (form.)	ʃalom!	שָׁלוֹם!
Good morning!	'boker tov!	בּוֹקֶר טוֹב!
Good afternoon!	tsaha'rayim tovim!	צָהֳרַיִים טוֹבִים!
Good evening!	'erev tov!	עֶרֶב טוֹב!
to say hello	lomar ʃalom	לוֹמַר שָׁלוֹם
Hi! (hello)	hai!	הָיי!
greeting (n)	ahlan	אַהְלָן
to greet (vt)	lomar ʃalom	לוֹמַר שָׁלוֹם
How are you? (form.)	ma ʃlomeχ?, ma ʃlomχa?	מַה שְׁלוֹמֵךָ? (נ), מַה שְׁלוֹמְךָ?(ז)
How are you? (fam.)	ma niʃma?	מַה נִשְׁמָע?
What's new?	ma χadaʃ?	מַה חָדָשׁ?
Bye-Bye! Goodbye!	lehitra'ot!	לְהִתְרָאוֹת!
Bye!	bai!	בָּיי!
See you soon!	lehitra'ot bekarov!	לְהִתְרָאוֹת בְּקָרוֹב!
Farewell!	heye ʃalom!	הֱיֵה שָׁלוֹם!
Farewell! (form.)	lehitra'ot!	לְהִתְרָאוֹת!
to say goodbye	lomar lehitra'ot	לוֹמַר לְהִתְרָאוֹת

So long!	bai!	בַּיי!
Thank you!	toda!	תּוֹדָה!
Thank you very much!	toda raba!	תּוֹדָה רַבָּה!
You're welcome	bevakaʃa	בְּבַקָשָׁה
Don't mention it!	al lo davar	עַל לֹא דָבָר
It was nothing	ein haʼad ma	אֵין בְּעַד מָה
Excuse me!	sliχa!	סלִיחָה!
to excuse (forgive)	lis'loaχ	לִסלוֹחַ
to apologize (vi)	lehitnatsel	לְהִתנַצֵל
My apologies	ani mitnatsel,	אֲנִי מִתנַצֵל (ז),
	ani mitna'tselet	אֲנִי מִתנַצֶלֶת (נ)
I'm sorry!	ani mitsta'er,	אֲנִי מִצטַעֵר (ז),
	ani mitsta''eret	אֲנִי מִצטַעֶרֶת (נ)
to forgive (vt)	lis'loaχ	לִסלוֹחַ
It's okay! (that's all right)	lo nora	לֹא נוֹרָא
please (adv)	bevakaʃa	בְּבַקָשָׁה
Don't forget!	al tiʃkaχ!	אַל תִשׁכַּח! (ז)
Certainly!	'betaχ!	בֶּטַח!
Of course not!	'betaχ ʃelo!	בֶּטַח שֶׁלֹא!
Okay! (I agree)	okei!	אוֹקֵיי!
That's enough!	maspik!	מַספִּיק!

3. Cardinal numbers. Part 1

0 zero	'efes	אֶפֶס (ז)
1 one	eχad	אֶחָד (ז)
1 one (fem.)	aχat	אַחַת (נ)
2 two	'ʃtayim	שׁתַיִים (נ)
3 three	ʃaloʃ	שָׁלוֹשׁ (נ)
4 four	arba	אַרבַּע (נ)
5 five	χameʃ	חָמֵשׁ (נ)
6 six	ʃeʃ	שֵׁשׁ (נ)
7 seven	'ʃeva	שֶׁבַע (נ)
8 eight	'ʃmone	שׁמוֹנֶה (נ)
9 nine	'teʃa	תֵשַׁע (נ)
10 ten	'eser	עֶשֶׂר (נ)
11 eleven	aχat-esre	אַחַת-עֶשׂרֵה (נ)
12 twelve	ʃteim esre	שׁתֵים-עֶשׂרֵה (נ)
13 thirteen	ʃloʃ esre	שׁלוֹש-עֶשׂרֵה (נ)
14 fourteen	arba esre	אַרבַּע-עֶשׂרֵה (נ)
15 fifteen	χameʃ esre	חָמֵשׁ-עֶשׂרֵה (נ)
16 sixteen	ʃeʃ esre	שֵׁש-עֶשׂרֵה (נ)
17 seventeen	ʃva esre	שׁבַע-עֶשׂרֵה (נ)
18 eighteen	ʃmone esre	שׁמוֹנֶה-עֶשׂרֵה (נ)

19 nineteen	tʃa esre	תשע־עֶשׂרֵה (נ)
20 twenty	esrim	עֶשׂרִים
21 twenty-one	esrim ve'eχad	עֶשׂרִים וְאֶחָד
22 twenty-two	esrim u'ʃnayim	עֶשׂרִים וּשׁנַיִים
23 twenty-three	esrim uʃloʃa	עֶשׂרִים וּשׁלוֹשָה
30 thirty	ʃloʃim	שׁלוֹשִים
31 thirty-one	ʃloʃim ve'eχad	שׁלוֹשִים וְאֶחָד
32 thirty-two	ʃloʃim u'ʃnayim	שׁלוֹשִים וּשׁנַיִים
33 thirty-three	ʃloʃim uʃloʃa	שׁלוֹשִים וּשׁלוֹשָה
40 forty	arbaʿim	אַרבָּעִים
41 forty-one	arbaʿim ve'eχad	אַרבָּעִים וְאֶחָד
42 forty-two	arbaʿim u'ʃnayim	אַרבָּעִים וּשׁנַיִים
43 forty-three	arbaʿim uʃloʃa	אַרבָּעִים וּשׁלוֹשָה
50 fifty	χamiʃim	חֲמִישִים
51 fifty-one	χamiʃim ve'eχad	חֲמִישִים וְאֶחָד
52 fifty-two	χamiʃim u'ʃnayim	חֲמִישִים וּשׁנַיִים
53 fifty-three	χamiʃim uʃloʃa	חֲמִישִים וּשׁלוֹשָה
60 sixty	ʃiʃim	שִישִים
61 sixty-one	ʃiʃim ve'eχad	שִישִים וְאֶחָד
62 sixty-two	ʃiʃim u'ʃnayim	שִישִים וּשׁנַיִים
63 sixty-three	ʃiʃim uʃloʃa	שִישִים וּשׁלוֹשָה
70 seventy	ʃivʿim	שִבעִים
71 seventy-one	ʃivʿim ve'eχad	שִבעִים וְאֶחָד
72 seventy-two	ʃivʿim u'ʃnayim	שִבעִים וּשׁנַיִים
73 seventy-three	ʃivʿim uʃloʃa	שִבעִים וּשׁלוֹשָה
80 eighty	ʃmonim	שׁמוֹנִים
81 eighty-one	ʃmonim ve'eχad	שׁמוֹנִים וְאֶחָד
82 eighty-two	ʃmonim u'ʃnayim	שׁמוֹנִים וּשׁנַיִים
83 eighty-three	ʃmonim uʃloʃa	שׁמוֹנִים וּשׁלוֹשָה
90 ninety	tiʃim	תִשעִים
91 ninety-one	tiʃim ve'eχad	תִשעִים וְאֶחָד
92 ninety-two	tiʃim u'ʃayim	תִשעִים וּשׁנַיִים
93 ninety-three	tiʃim uʃloʃa	תִשעִים וּשׁלוֹשָה

4. Cardinal numbers. Part 2

100 one hundred	'me'a	מֵאָה (נ)
200 two hundred	ma'tayim	מָאתַיִים
300 three hundred	ʃloʃ me'ot	שׁלוֹש מֵאוֹת (נ)
400 four hundred	arba me'ot	אַרבַּע מֵאוֹת (נ)
500 five hundred	χameʃ me'ot	חָמֵש מֵאוֹת (נ)
600 six hundred	ʃeʃ me'ot	שֵש מֵאוֹת (נ)
700 seven hundred	ʃva me'ot	שׁבַע מֵאוֹת (נ)

| 800 eight hundred | ʃmone me'ot | שְׁמוֹנֶה מֵאוֹת (נ) |
| 900 nine hundred | tʃa me'ot | תְּשַׁע מֵאוֹת (נ) |

1000 one thousand	'elef	אֶלֶף (ז)
2000 two thousand	al'payim	אַלְפַּיִם (ז)
3000 three thousand	'ʃloʃet alafim	שְׁלוֹשֶׁת אֲלָפִים (ז)
10000 ten thousand	a'seret alafim	עֲשֶׂרֶת עֲלָחִים (ז)
one hundred thousand	me'a 'elef	מֵאָה אֶלֶף (ז)
million	milyon	מִילְיוֹן (ז)
billion	milyard	מִילְיַארד (ז)

5. Numbers. Fractions

fraction	'ʃever	שֶׁבֶר (ז)
one half	'xetsi	חֲצִי (ז)
one third	ʃliʃ	שְׁלִיש (ז)
one quarter	'reva	רֶבַע (ז)

one eighth	ʃminit	שְׁמִינִית (נ)
one tenth	asirit	עֲשִׂירִית (נ)
two thirds	ʃnei ʃliʃim	שְׁנֵי שְׁלִישִׁים (ז)
three quarters	'ʃloʃet riv'ei	שְׁלוֹשֶׁת רְבָעֵי

6. Numbers. Basic operations

subtraction	xisur	חִיסוּר (ז)
to subtract (vi, vt)	lexaser	לְחַסֵר
division	xiluk	חִילוּק (ז)
to divide (vt)	lexalek	לְחַלֵק

addition	xibur	חִיבּוּר (ז)
to add up (vt)	lexaber	לְחַבֵּר
to add (vi, vt)	lexaber	לְחַבֵּר
multiplication	'kefel	כֶּפֶל (ז)
to multiply (vt)	lehaxpil	לְהַכְפִּיל

7. Numbers. Miscellaneous

digit, figure	sifra	סִפְרָה (נ)
number	mispar	מִסְפָּר (ז)
numeral	ʃem mispar	שֵׁם מִסְפָּר (ז)
minus sign	'minus	מִינוּס (ז)
plus sign	plus	פְּלוּס (ז)
formula	nusxa	נוֹסְחָה (נ)
calculation	xiʃuv	חִישׁוּב (ז)
to count (vi, vt)	lispor	לִסְפּוֹר

to count up	lexaʃev	לְחַשֵׁב
to compare (vt)	lehaʃvot	לְהַשְׁווֹת
How much?	'kama?	כַּמָה?
How many?	'kama?	כַּמָה?
sum, total	sxum	סכוּם (ז)
result	totsa'a	תּוֹצָאָה (נ)
remainder	ʃe'erit	שְׁאֵרִית (נ)
a few (e.g., ~ years ago)	'kama	כַּמָה
little (I had ~ time)	ktsat	קצָת
few (I have ~ friends)	me'at	מְעַט
a little (~ tired)	me'at	מְעַט
the rest	ʃe'ar	שְׁאָר (ז)
one and a half	exad va'xetsi	אֶחָד וָחֵצִי (ז)
dozen	tresar	תְּרֵיסָר (ז)
in half (adv)	'xetsi 'xetsi	חֵצִי חֵצִי
equally (evenly)	ʃave beʃave	שָׁווֶה בְּשָׁווֶה
half	'xetsi	חֵצִי (ז)
time (three ~s)	'pa'am	פַּעַם (נ)

8. The most important verbs. Part 1

to advise (vt)	leya'ets	לְייַעֵץ
to agree (say yes)	lehaskim	לְהַסכִּים
to answer (vi, vt)	la'anot	לַעֲנוֹת
to apologize (vi)	lehitnatsel	לְהִתנַצֵל
to arrive (vi)	leha'gi'a	לְהַגִיעַ
to ask (~ oneself)	liʃ'ol	לִשְׁאוֹל
to ask (~ sb to do sth)	levakeʃ	לְבַקֵשׁ
to be (vi)	lihyot	לִהיוֹת
to be afraid	lefaxed	לְפַחֵד
to be hungry	lihyot ra'ev	לִהיוֹת רָעֵב
to be interested in …	lehit'anyen be…	לְהִתעַנייֵן בְּ...
to be needed	lehidareʃ	לְהִידָרֵשׁ
to be surprised	lehitpale	לְהִתפַּלֵא
to be thirsty	lihyot tsame	לִהיוֹת צָמֵא
to begin (vt)	lehatxil	לְהַתחִיל
to belong to …	lehiʃtayex	לְהִשְׁתייֵך
to boast (vi)	lehitravrev	לְהִתרַברֵב
to break (split into pieces)	liʃbor	לִשְׁבּוֹר
to call (~ for help)	likro	לִקרוֹא
can (v aux)	yaxol	יָכוֹל
to catch (vt)	litfos	לִתפּוֹס
to change (vt)	leʃanot	לְשַׁנוֹת

to choose (select)	livχor	לִבְחוֹר
to come down (the stairs)	la'redet	לָרֶדֶת
to compare (vt)	lehaʃvot	לְהַשְׁווֹת
to complain (vi, vt)	lehitlonen	לְהִתְלוֹנֵן
to confuse (mix up)	lehitbalbel	לְהִתְבַּלְבֵּל
to continue (vt)	lehamʃiχ	לְהַמְשִׁיךְ
to control (vt)	liʃlot	לִשְׁלוֹט
to cook (dinner)	levaʃel	לְבַשֵׁל
to cost (vt)	la'alot	לַעֲלוֹת
to count (add up)	lispor	לִסְפּוֹר
to count on ...	lismoχ al	לִסְמוֹךְ עַל
to create (vt)	litsor	לִיצוֹר
to cry (weep)	livkot	לִבְכּוֹת

9. The most important verbs. Part 2

to deceive (vi, vt)	leramot	לְרַמוֹת
to decorate (tree, street)	lekaʃet	לְקַשֵׁט
to defend (a country, etc.)	lehagen	לְהָגֵן
to demand (request firmly)	lidroʃ	לִדְרוֹשׁ
to dig (vt)	laχpor	לַחְפּוֹר
to discuss (vt)	ladun	לָדוּן
to do (vt)	la'asot	לַעֲשׂוֹת
to doubt (have doubts)	lefakpek	לְפַקְפֵּק
to drop (let fall)	lehapil	לְהַפִּיל
to enter (room, house, etc.)	lehikanes	לְהִיכָּנֵס
to excuse (forgive)	lis'loaχ	לִסְלוֹחַ
to exist (vi)	lehitkayem	לְהִתְקַיֵּים
to expect (foresee)	laχazot	לַחֲזוֹת
to explain (vt)	lehasbir	לְהַסְבִּיר
to fall (vi)	lipol	לִיפּוֹל
to find (vt)	limtso	לִמְצוֹא
to finish (vt)	lesayem	לְסַיֵּים
to fly (vi)	la'uf	לָעוּף
to follow ... (come after)	la'akov aχarei	לַעֲקוֹב אַחֲרֵי
to forget (vi, vt)	liʃ'koaχ	לִשְׁכּוֹחַ
to forgive (vt)	lis'loaχ	לִסְלוֹחַ
to give (vt)	latet	לָתֵת
to give a hint	lirmoz	לִרְמוֹז
to go (on foot)	la'leχet	לָלֶכֶת
to go for a swim	lehitraχets	לְהִתְרַחֵץ
to go out (for dinner, etc.)	latset	לָצֵאת
to guess (the answer)	lenaχeʃ	לְנַחֵשׁ

to have (vt)	lehaχzik	לְהַחֲזִיק
to have breakfast	le'eχol aruχat 'boker	לֶאֱכוֹל אֲרוּחַת בּוֹקֶר
to have dinner	le'eχol aruχat 'erev	לֶאֱכוֹל אֲרוּחַת עֶרֶב
to have lunch	le'eχol aruχat tsaha'rayim	לֶאֱכוֹל אֲרוּחַת צָהֳרַיים
to hear (vt)	liʃmo'a	לִשְמוֹעַ
to help (vt)	la'azor	לַעֲזוֹר
to hide (vt)	lehastir	לְהַסְתִיר
to hope (vi, vt)	lekavot	לְקווֹת
to hunt (vi, vt)	latsud	לָצוּד
to hurry (vi)	lemaher	לְמַהֵר

10. The most important verbs. Part 3

to inform (vt)	leho'dia	לְהוֹדִיעַ
to insist (vi, vt)	lehit'akeʃ	לְהִתְעַקֵש
to insult (vt)	leha'aliv	לְהַעֲלִיב
to invite (vt)	lehazmin	לְהַזְמִין
to joke (vi)	lehitba'deaχ	לְהִתְבַּדֵחַ
to keep (vt)	liʃmor	לִשְמוֹר
to keep silent	liʃtok	לִשְתוֹק
to kill (vt)	laharog	לָהֲרוֹג
to know (sb)	lehakir et	לְהַכִּיר אֶת
to know (sth)	la'da'at	לָדַעַת
to laugh (vi)	litsχok	לִצחוֹק
to liberate (city, etc.)	leʃaχrer	לְשַחְרֵר
to like (I like …)	limtso χen be'ei'nayim	לִמצוֹא חֵן בְּעֵינַיים
to look for … (search)	leχapes	לְחַפֵּש
to love (sb)	le'ehov	לָאֱהוֹב
to make a mistake	lit'ot	לִטעוֹת
to manage, to run	lenahel	לְנַהֵל
to mean (signify)	lomar	לוֹמַר
to mention (talk about)	lehazkir	לְהַזְכִּיר
to miss (school, etc.)	lehaχsir	לְהַחְסִיר
to notice (see)	lasim lev	לָשִים לֵב
to object (vi, vt)	lehitnaged	לְהִתְנַגֵד
to observe (see)	litspot, lehaʃkif	לצפּוֹת, לְהַשְקִיף
to open (vt)	lif'toaχ	לִפתוֹחַ
to order (meal, etc.)	lehazmin	לְהַזְמִין
to order (mil.)	lifkod	לִפקוֹד
to own (possess)	lihyot 'ba'al ʃel	לִהיוֹת בַּעַל שֶל
to participate (vi)	lehiʃtatef	לְהִשְתַתֵף
to pay (vi, vt)	leʃalem	לְשַלֵם
to permit (vt)	leharʃot	לְהַרְשוֹת
to plan (vt)	letaχnen	לְתַכנֵן

to play (children)	lesayek	לְשַׂחֵק
to pray (vi, vt)	lehitpalel	לְהִתְפַּלֵּל
to prefer (vt)	leha'adif	לְהַעֲדִיף
to promise (vt)	lehav'tiax	לְהַבְטִיחַ
to pronounce (vt)	levate	לְבַטֵּא
to propose (vt)	leha'tsi'a	לְהַצִּיעַ
to punish (vt)	leha'aniʃ	לְהַעֲנִישׁ

11. The most important verbs. Part 4

to read (vi, vt)	likro	לִקְרֹא
to recommend (vt)	lehamlits	לְהַמְלִיץ
to refuse (vi, vt)	lesarev	לְסָרֵב
to regret (be sorry)	lehitsta'er	לְהִצְטַעֵר
to rent (sth from sb)	liskor	לִשְׂכֹּר
to repeat (say again)	laxazor al	לַחֲזֹר עַל
to reserve, to book	lehazmin meroʃ	לְהַזְמִין מֵרֹאשׁ
to run (vi)	laruts	לָרוּץ
to save (rescue)	lehatsil	לְהַצִּיל
to say (~ thank you)	lomar	לוֹמַר
to scold (vt)	linzof	לִנְזֹף
to see (vt)	lir'ot	לִרְאוֹת
to sell (vt)	limkor	לִמְכֹּר
to send (vt)	liʃ'loax	לִשְׁלוֹחַ
to shoot (vi)	lirot	לִירוֹת
to shout (vi)	lits'ok	לִצְעֹק
to show (vt)	lehar'ot	לְהַרְאוֹת
to sign (document)	laxtom	לַחְתֹּם
to sit down (vi)	lehityaʃev	לְהִתְיַשֵּׁב
to smile (vi)	lexayex	לְחַיֵּךְ
to speak (vi, vt)	ledaber	לְדַבֵּר
to steal (money, etc.)	lignov	לִגְנֹב
to stop (for pause, etc.)	la'atsor	לַעֲצֹר
to stop (please ~ calling me)	lehafsik	לְהַפְסִיק
to study (vt)	lilmod	לִלְמֹד
to swim (vi)	lisxot	לִשְׂחוֹת
to take (vt)	la'kaxat	לָקַחַת
to think (vi, vt)	laxʃov	לַחְשֹׁב
to threaten (vt)	le'ayem	לְאַיֵּם
to touch (with hands)	la'ga'at	לָגַעַת
to translate (vt)	letargem	לְתַרְגֵּם
to trust (vt)	liv'toax	לִבְטֹחַ
to try (attempt)	lenasot	לְנַסּוֹת

to turn (e.g., ~ left)	lifnot	לִפְנוֹת
to underestimate (vt)	leham'it be''erex	לְהַמְעִיט בְּעֶרֶךְ
to understand (vt)	lehavin	לְהָבִין
to unite (vt)	le'axed	לְאַחֵד
to wait (vt)	lehamtin	לְהַמְתִּין

to want (wish, desire)	lirtsot	לִרְצוֹת
to warn (vt)	lehazhir	לְהַזְהִיר
to work (vi)	la'avod	לַעֲבוֹד
to write (vt)	lixtov	לִכְתּוֹב
to write down	lirʃom	לִרְשׁוֹם

12. Colors

color	'tseva	צֶבַע (ז)
shade (tint)	gavan	גָּוֶון (ז)
hue	gavan	גָּוֶון (ז)
rainbow	'keʃet	קֶשֶׁת (נ)

white (adj)	lavan	לָבָן
black (adj)	ʃaxor	שָׁחוֹר
gray (adj)	afor	אָפוֹר

green (adj)	yarok	יָרוֹק
yellow (adj)	tsahov	צָהוֹב
red (adj)	adom	אָדוֹם

blue (adj)	kaxol	כָּחוֹל
light blue (adj)	taxol	תְּכֹל
pink (adj)	varod	וָרוֹד
orange (adj)	katom	כָּתוֹם
violet (adj)	segol	סָגוֹל
brown (adj)	xum	חוּם

| golden (adj) | zahov | זָהוֹב |
| silvery (adj) | kasuf | כָּסוּף |

beige (adj)	beʒ	בֶּז'
cream (adj)	be'tseva krem	בְּצֶבַע קְרֶם
turquoise (adj)	turkiz	טוּרְקִיז
cherry red (adj)	bordo	בּוֹרְדוֹ
lilac (adj)	segol	סָגוֹל
crimson (adj)	patol	פָּטוֹל

light (adj)	bahir	בָּהִיר
dark (adj)	kehe	כֵּהֶה
bright, vivid (adj)	bohek	בּוֹהֵק

| colored (pencils) | tsiv'oni | צִבְעוֹנִי |
| color (e.g., ~ film) | tsiv'oni | צִבְעוֹנִי |

black-and-white (adj)	ʃaxor lavan	שָׁחוֹר־לָבָן
plain (one-colored)	xad tsiv'i	חַד־צִבְעִי
multicolored (adj)	sasgoni	סַסְגּוֹנִי

13. Questions

Who?	mi?	מִי?
What?	ma?	מָה?
Where? (at, in)	'eifo?	אֵיפֹה?
Where (to)?	le'an?	לְאָן?
From where?	me''eifo?	מֵאֵיפֹה?
When?	matai?	מָתַי?
Why? (What for?)	'lama?	לָמָה?
Why? (~ are you crying?)	ma'du‘a?	מַדּוּעַ?
What for?	biʃvil ma?	בִּשְׁבִיל מָה?
How? (in what way)	eix, keitsad?	כֵּיצַד? אֵיךְ?
What? (What kind of ...?)	'eize?	אֵיזֶה?
Which?	'eize?	אֵיזֶה?
To whom?	lemi?	לְמִי?
About whom?	al mi?	עַל מִי?
About what?	al ma?	עַל מָה?
With whom?	im mi?	עִם מִי?
How many? How much?	'kama?	כַּמָּה?
Whose?	ʃel mi?	שֶׁל מִי?

14. Function words. Adverbs. Part 1

Where? (at, in)	'eifo?	אֵיפֹה?
here (adv)	po, kan	פֹּה, כָּאן
there (adv)	ʃam	שָׁם
somewhere (to be)	'eifo ʃehu	אֵיפֹה שֶׁהוּא
nowhere (not anywhere)	beʃum makom	בְּשׁוּם מָקוֹם
by (near, beside)	leyad ...	לְיַד ...
by the window	leyad haxalon	לְיַד הַחַלּוֹן
Where (to)?	le'an?	לְאָן?
here (e.g., come ~!)	'hena, lekan	הֵנָה; לְכָאן
there (e.g., to go ~)	leʃam	לְשָׁם
from here (adv)	mikan	מִכָּאן
from there (adv)	miʃam	מִשָּׁם
close (adv)	karov	קָרוֹב
far (adv)	raxok	רָחוֹק

near (e.g., ~ Paris)	leyad	לְיַד
nearby (adv)	karov	קָרוֹב
not far (adv)	lo raxok	לֹא רָחוֹק
left (adj)	smali	שְׂמָאלִי
on the left	mismol	מִשְׂמֹאל
to the left	'smola	שְׂמֹאלָה
right (adj)	yemani	יְמָנִי
on the right	miyamin	מִיָמִין
to the right	ya'mina	יָמִינָה
in front (adv)	mika'dima	מִקָדִימָה
front (as adj)	kidmi	קִדמִי
ahead (the kids ran ~)	ka'dima	קָדִימָה
behind (adv)	me'axor	מֵאָחוֹר
from behind	me'axor	מֵאָחוֹר
back (towards the rear)	a'xora	אֲחוֹרָה
middle	'emtsa	אֶמצַע (ז)
in the middle	ba''emtsa	בָּאֶמצַע
at the side	mehatsad	מֵהַצַד
everywhere (adv)	bexol makom	בְּכָל מָקוֹם
around (in all directions)	misaviv	מִסָבִיב
from inside	mibifnim	מִבִּפנִים
somewhere (to go)	le'an ʃehu	לְאָן שֶהוּא
straight (directly)	yaʃar	יָשָר
back (e.g., come ~)	baxazara	בַּחֲזָרָה
from anywhere	me'ei ʃam	מֵאֵי שָם
from somewhere	me'ei ʃam	מֵאֵי שָם
firstly (adv)	reʃit	רֵאשִית
secondly (adv)	ʃenit	שֵנִית
thirdly (adv)	ʃliʃit	שְלִישִית
suddenly (adv)	pit'om	פִּתאוֹם
at first (in the beginning)	behatslaxa	בַּהַתחָלָה
for the first time	lariʃona	לָרִאשוֹנָה
long before ...	zman rav lifnei ...	... זמַן רַב לִפנֵי
anew (over again)	mexadaʃ	מֵחָדָש
for good (adv)	letamid	לְתָמִיד
never (adv)	af 'pa'am, me'olam	מֵעוֹלָם, אַף פַּעַם
again (adv)	ʃuv	שוב
now (adv)	axʃav, ka'et	עַכשָיו, כָּעֵת
often (adv)	le'itim krovot	לְעִיתִים קרוֹבוֹת
then (adv)	az	אָז
urgently (quickly)	bidxifut	בִּדחִיפוּת

usually (adv)	be'dereχ klal	בְּדֶרֶךְ כְּלָל
by the way, ...	'dereχ 'agav	דֶּרֶךְ אַגָּב
possible (that is ~)	efʃari	אֶפְשָׁרִי
probably (adv)	kanir'e	כַּנִּרְאֶה
maybe (adv)	ulai	אוּלַי
besides ...	χuts mize ...	חוּץ מִזֶּה ...
that's why ...	laχen	לָכֵן
in spite of ...	lamrot ɪɪɪ	לַמְרוֹת ...
thanks to ...	hodot le...	הוֹדוֹת לְ...
what (pron.)	ma	מָה
that (conj.)	ʃe	שֶׁ
something	'maʃehu	מַשֶּׁהוּ
anything (something)	'maʃehu	מַשֶּׁהוּ
nothing	klum	כְּלוּם
who (pron.)	mi	מִי
someone	'miʃehu, 'miʃehi	מִישֶׁהוּ (ז), מִישֶׁהִי (נ)
somebody	'miʃehu, 'miʃehi	מִישֶׁהוּ (ז), מִישֶׁהִי (נ)
nobody	af eχad, af aχat	אַף אֶחָד (ז), אַף אַחַת (נ)
nowhere (a voyage to ~)	leʃum makom	לְשׁוּם מָקוֹם
nobody's	lo ʃayaχ le'af eχad	לֹא שַׁיָּךְ לְאַף אֶחָד
somebody's	ʃel 'miʃehu	שֶׁל מִישֶׁהוּ
so (I'm ~ glad)	kol kaχ	כָּל-כָּךְ
also (as well)	gam	גַּם
too (as well)	gam	גַּם

15. Function words. Adverbs. Part 2

Why?	ma'du'a?	מַדּוּעַ?
for some reason	miʃum ma	מִשּׁוּם-מָה
because ...	miʃum ʃe	מִשּׁוּם שֶׁ
for some purpose	lematara 'kolʃehi	לְמַטָּרָה כָּלְשֶׁהִי
and	ve ...	וְ ...
or	o	אוֹ
but	aval, ulam	אֲבָל, אוּלָם
for (e.g., ~ me)	biʃvil	בִּשְׁבִיל
too (~ many people)	yoter midai	יוֹתֵר מִדַּי
only (exclusively)	rak	רַק
exactly (adv)	bediyuk	בְּדִיּוּק
about (more or less)	be''ereχ	בְּעֵרֶךְ
approximately (adv)	be''ereχ	בְּעֵרֶךְ
approximate (adj)	meʃo'ar	מְשׁוֹעָר
almost (adv)	kim'at	כִּמְעַט
the rest	ʃe'ar	שְׁאָר (ז)

the other (second)	aχer	אַחֵר
other (different)	aχer	אַחֵר
each (adj)	kol	כֹּל
any (no matter which)	kolʃehu	כָּלשֶׁהוּ
many, much (a lot of)	harbe	הַרבֵּה
many people	harbe	הַרבֵּה
all (everyone)	kulam	כּוּלָם
in return for ...	tmurat ...	תמוּרַת ...
in exchange (adv)	bitmura	בִּתמוּרָה
by hand (made)	bayad	בְּיָד
hardly (negative opinion)	safek im	סָפֵק אִם
probably (adv)	karov levadai	קָרוֹב לְוַודַאי
on purpose (intentionally)	'davka	דַווקָא
by accident (adv)	bemikre	בְּמִקרֶה
very (adv)	me'od	מְאוֹד
for example (adv)	lemaʃal	לְמָשָׁל
between	bein	בֵּין
among	be'kerev	בְּקֶרֶב
so much (such a lot)	kol kaχ harbe	כָּל־כָּך הַרבֵּה
especially (adv)	bimyuχad	בְּמְיוּחָד

Basic concepts. Part 2

16. Weekdays

Monday	yom ʃeni	יוֹם שֵׁנִי (ז)
Tuesday	yom ʃliʃi	יוֹם שְׁלִישִׁי (ז)
Wednesday	yom revi'i	יוֹם רְבִיעִי (ז)
Thursday	yom xamiʃi	יוֹם חֲמִישִׁי (ז)
Friday	yom ʃiʃi	יוֹם שִׁישִׁי (ז)
Saturday	ʃabat	שַׁבָּת (נ)
Sunday	yom riʃon	יוֹם רִאשׁוֹן (ז)

today (adv)	hayom	הַיּוֹם
tomorrow (adv)	maxar	מָחָר
the day after tomorrow	maxara'tayim	מָחֳרָתַיִם
yesterday (adv)	etmol	אֶתְמוֹל
the day before yesterday	ʃilʃom	שִׁלְשׁוֹם

day	yom	יוֹם (ז)
working day	yom avoda	יוֹם עֲבוֹדָה (ז)
public holiday	yom xag	יוֹם חַג (ז)
day off	yom menuxa	יוֹם מְנוּחָה (ז)
weekend	sof ʃa'vu'a	סוֹף שָׁבוּעַ

all day long	kol hayom	כָּל הַיּוֹם
the next day (adv)	lamaxarat	לַמָּחֳרָת
two days ago	lifnei yo'mayim	לִפְנֵי יוֹמַיִם
the day before	'erev	עֶרֶב
daily (adj)	yomyomi	יוֹמְיוֹמִי
every day (adv)	midei yom	מִדֵּי יוֹם

week	ʃa'vua	שָׁבוּעַ (ז)
last week (adv)	baʃa'vu'a ʃe'avar	בַּשָּׁבוּעַ שֶׁעָבַר
next week (adv)	baʃa'vu'a haba	בַּשָּׁבוּעַ הַבָּא
weekly (adj)	ʃvu'i	שְׁבוּעִי
every week (adv)	kol ʃa'vu'a	כָּל שָׁבוּעַ
twice a week	pa'a'mayim beʃa'vu'a	פַּעֲמַיִם בְּשָׁבוּעַ
every Tuesday	kol yom ʃliʃi	כָּל יוֹם שְׁלִישִׁי

17. Hours. Day and night

morning	'boker	בּוֹקֶר (ז)
in the morning	ba'boker	בַּבּוֹקֶר
noon, midday	tsaha'rayim	צָהֳרַיִם (ז"ר)

in the afternoon	aχar hatsaha'rayim	אַחַר הַצְהֳרַיִם
evening	'erev	עֶרֶב (ז)
in the evening	ba''erev	בָּעֶרֶב
night	'laila	לַיְלָה (ז)
at night	ba'laila	בַּלַּיְלָה
midnight	χatsot	חֲצוֹת (נ)
second	ʃniya	שְׁנִיָּה (נ)
minute	daka	דַּקָּה (נ)
hour	ʃa'a	שָׁעָה (נ)
half an hour	χatsi ʃa'a	חֲצִי שָׁעָה (נ)
a quarter-hour	'reva ʃa'a	רֶבַע שָׁעָה (ז)
fifteen minutes	χameʃ esre dakot	חָמֵשׁ עֶשְׂרֵה דַּקּוֹת
24 hours	yemama	יְמָמָה (נ)
sunrise	zriχa	זְרִיחָה (נ)
dawn	'ʃaχar	שַׁחַר (ז)
early morning	'ʃaχar	שַׁחַר (ז)
sunset	ʃki'a	שְׁקִיעָה (נ)
early in the morning	mukdam ba'boker	מוקְדָם בַּבּוֹקֶר
this morning	ha'boker	הַבּוֹקֶר
tomorrow morning	maχar ba'boker	מָחָר בַּבּוֹקֶר
this afternoon	hayom aχarei hatzaha'rayim	הַיּוֹם אַחֲרֵי הַצְהֳרַיִם
in the afternoon	aχar hatsaha'rayim	אַחַר הַצְהֳרַיִם
tomorrow afternoon	maχar aχarei hatsaha'rayim	מָחָר אַחֲרֵי הַצְהֳרַיִם
tonight (this evening)	ha''erev	הָעֶרֶב
tomorrow night	maχar ba''erev	מָחָר בָּעֶרֶב
at 3 o'clock sharp	baʃa'a ʃaloʃ bediyuk	בְּשָׁעָה שָׁלוֹשׁ בְּדִיּוּק
about 4 o'clock	bisvivot arba	בִּסְבִיבוֹת אַרְבַּע
by 12 o'clock	ad ʃteim esre	עַד שְׁתֵּים-עֶשְׂרֵה
in 20 minutes	be'od esrim dakot	בְּעוֹד עֶשְׂרִים דַּקּוֹת
in an hour	be'od ʃa'a	בְּעוֹד שָׁעָה
on time (adv)	bazman	בַּזְמַן
a quarter of ...	'reva le...	רֶבַע לְ...
within an hour	toχ ʃa'a	תּוֹךְ שָׁעָה
every 15 minutes	kol 'reva ʃa'a	כָּל רֶבַע שָׁעָה
round the clock	misaviv laʃa'on	מִסָּבִיב לַשָּׁעוֹן

18. Months. Seasons

January	'yanu'ar	יָנוּאָר (ז)
February	'febru'ar	פֶבְּרוּאָר (ז)

March	merts	מֶרְץ (ז)
April	april	אַפְּרִיל (ז)
May	mai	מַאי (ז)
June	'yuni	יוּנִי (ז)
July	'yuli	יוּלִי (ז)
August	'ogust	אוֹגוּסְט (ז)
September	sep'tember	סֶפְּטֶמְבֶּר (ז)
October	ok'tober	אוֹקְטוֹבֶּר (ז)
November	no'vember	נוֹבֶמְבֶּר (ז)
December	de'tsember	דֶצֶמְבֶּר (ז)
spring	aviv	אָבִיב (ז)
in spring	ba'aviv	בָּאָבִיב
spring (as adj)	avivi	אָבִיבִי
summer	'kayits	קַיִץ (ז)
in summer	ba'kayits	בַּקַיִץ
summer (as adj)	ketsi	קֵיצִי
fall	stav	סְתָיו (ז)
in fall	bestav	בְּסְתָיו
fall (as adj)	stavi	סְתָווִי
winter	'xoref	חוֹרֶף (ז)
in winter	ba'xoref	בַּחוֹרֶף
winter (as adj)	xorpi	חוֹרְפִּי
month	'xodeʃ	חוֹדֶשׁ (ז)
this month	ha'xodeʃ	הַחוֹדֶשׁ
next month	ba'xodeʃ haba	בַּחוֹדֶשׁ הַבָּא
last month	ba'xodeʃ ʃe'avar	בַּחוֹדֶשׁ שֶׁעָבַר
a month ago	lifnei 'xodeʃ	לִפְנֵי חוֹדֶשׁ
in a month (a month later)	be'od 'xodeʃ	בְּעוֹד חוֹדֶשׁ
in 2 months (2 months later)	be'od xod'ʃayim	בְּעוֹד חוֹדְשַׁיִים
the whole month	kol ha'xodeʃ	כָּל הַחוֹדֶשׁ
all month long	kol ha'xodeʃ	כָּל הַחוֹדֶשׁ
monthly (~ magazine)	xodʃi	חוֹדְשִׁי
monthly (adv)	xodʃit	חוֹדְשִׁית
every month	kol 'xodeʃ	כָּל חוֹדֶשׁ
twice a month	pa'a'mayim be'xodeʃ	פַּעֲמַיִים בְּחוֹדֶשׁ
year	ʃana	שָׁנָה (נ)
this year	haʃana	הַשָׁנָה
next year	baʃana haba'a	בַּשָׁנָה הַבָּאָה
last year	baʃana ʃe'avra	בַּשָׁנָה שֶׁעָבְרָה
a year ago	lifnei ʃana	לִפְנֵי שָׁנָה
in a year	be'od ʃana	בְּעוֹד שָׁנָה

in two years	be'od ʃna'tayim	בְּעוֹד שְׁנָתַיִים
the whole year	kol haʃana	כָּל הַשָּׁנָה
all year long	kol haʃana	כָּל הַשָּׁנָה

every year	kol ʃana	כָּל שָׁנָה
annual (adj)	ʃnati	שְׁנָתִי
annually (adv)	midei ʃana	מִדֵּי שָׁנָה
4 times a year	arba pa'amim be'χodeʃ	אַרְבַּע פְּעָמִים בְּחוֹדֶשׁ

date (e.g., today's ~)	ta'ariχ	תַּאֲרִיךְ (ז)
date (e.g., ~ of birth)	ta'ariχ	תַּאֲרִיךְ (ז)
calendar	'luaχ ʃana	לוּחַ שָׁנָה (ז)

half a year	χatsi ʃana	חֲצִי שָׁנָה (ז)
six months	ʃiʃa χodaʃim, χatsi ʃana	חֲצִי שָׁנָה, שִׁישָׁה חוֹדָשִׁים
season (summer, etc.)	ona	עוֹנָה (נ)
century	'me'a	מֵאָה (נ)

19. Time. Miscellaneous

time	zman	זְמַן (ז)
moment	'rega	רֶגַע (ז)
instant (n)	'rega	רֶגַע (ז)
instant (adj)	miyadi	מִיָּדִי
lapse (of time)	tkufa	תְּקוּפָה (נ)
life	χayim	חַיִּים (ז"ר)
eternity	'netsaχ	נֶצַח (ז)

epoch	idan	עִידָן (ז)
era	idan	עִידָן (ז)
cycle	maχzor	מַחְזוֹר (ז)
period	tkufa	תְּקוּפָה (נ)
term (short-~)	tkufa	תְּקוּפָה (נ)

the future	atid	עָתִיד (ז)
future (as adj)	haba	הַבָּא
next time	ba'pa'am haba'a	בַּפַּעַם הַבָּאָה
the past	avar	עָבָר (ז)
past (recent)	ʃe'avar	שֶׁעָבַר
last time	ba'pa'am hako'demet	בַּפַּעַם הַקּוֹדֶמֶת

later (adv)	me'uχar yoter	מְאוּחָר יוֹתֵר
after (prep.)	aχarei	אַחֲרֵי
nowadays (adv)	kayom	כַּיּוֹם
now (adv)	aχʃav, ka'et	עַכְשָׁיו, כָּעֵת
immediately (adv)	miyad	מִיָּד
soon (adv)	bekarov	בְּקָרוֹב
in advance (beforehand)	meroʃ	מֵרֹאשׁ
a long time ago	mizman	מִזְּמַן
recently (adv)	lo mizman	לֹא מִזְּמַן

destiny	goral	גּוֹרָל (ז)
memories (childhood ~)	ziχronot	זִיכרוֹנוֹת (ז״ר)
archives	arχiyon	אַרכִיוֹן (ז)
during ...	bezman ʃel ...	בְּזמַן שֶל ...
long, a long time (adv)	zman rav	זמַן רַב
not long (adv)	lo zman rav	לא זמַן רַב
early (in the morning)	mukdam	מוּקדָם
late (not early)	me'uχar	מְאוּחָר
forever (for good)	la'netsaχ	לָנֶצַח
to start (begin)	lehatχil	לְהַתחִיל
to postpone (vt)	lidχot	לִדחוֹת
at the same time	bo zmanit	בּוֹ זמַנִית
permanently (adv)	bikvi'ut	בִּקבִיעוּת
constant (noise, pain)	ka'vu'a	קָבוּעַ
temporary (adj)	zmani	זמַנִי
sometimes (adv)	lif'amim	לִפעָמִים
rarely (adv)	le'itim reχokot	לְעִיתִים רְחוֹקוֹת
often (adv)	le'itim krovot	לְעִיתִים קרוֹבוֹת

20. Opposites

rich (adj)	aʃir	עָשִיר
poor (adj)	ani	עָנִי
ill, sick (adj)	χole	חוֹלֶה
well (not sick)	bari	בָּרִיא
big (adj)	gadol	גָדוֹל
small (adj)	katan	קָטָן
quickly (adv)	maher	מַהֵר
slowly (adv)	le'at	לְאַט
fast (adj)	mahir	מָהִיר
slow (adj)	iti	אִיטִי
glad (adj)	sa'meaχ	שָׂמֵחַ
sad (adj)	atsuv	עָצוּב
together (adv)	be'yaχad	בְּיַחַד
separately (adv)	levad	לְבַד
aloud (to read)	bekol ram	בְּקוֹל רָם
silently (to oneself)	belev, be'ʃeket	בְּלֵב, בְּשֶקֶט
tall (adj)	ga'voha	גָבוֹהַ
low (adj)	namuχ	נָמוּך

deep (adj)	amok	עָמוֹק
shallow (adj)	radud	רָדוּד
yes	ken	כֵּן
no	lo	לֹא
distant (in space)	raχok	רָחוֹק
nearby (adj)	karov	קָרוֹב
far (adv)	raχok	רָחוֹק
nearby (adv)	samuχ	סָמוּך
long (adj)	aroχ	אָרוֹך
short (adj)	katsar	קָצָר
good (kindhearted)	tov lev	טוֹב לֵב
evil (adj)	raʃa	רָשָׁע
married (adj)	nasui	נָשׂוּי
single (adj)	ravak	כַּוָּק
to forbid (vt)	le'esor al	לָאֶסוֹר עַל
to permit (vt)	leharʃot	לְהַרְשׁוֹת
end	sof	סוֹף (ז)
beginning	hatχala	הַתְחָלָה (נ)
left (adj)	smali	שְׂמָאלִי
right (adj)	yemani	יְמָנִי
first (adj)	riʃon	רָאשׁוֹן
last (adj)	aχaron	אַחֲרוֹן
crime	'peʃa	פֶּשַׁע (ז)
punishment	'oneʃ	עוֹנֶשׁ (ז)
to order (vt)	letsavot	לְצַוּוֹת
to obey (vi, vt)	letsayet	לְצַיֵּת
straight (adj)	yaʃar	יָשָׁר
curved (adj)	me'ukal	מְעוּקָל
paradise	gan 'eden	גַּן עֵדֶן (ז)
hell	gehinom	גֵּיהִינוֹם (ז)
to be born	lehivaled	לְהִיוָּלֵד
to die (vi)	lamut	לָמוּת
strong (adj)	χazak	חָזָק
weak (adj)	χalaʃ	חַלָשׁ
old (adj)	zaken	זָקֵן
young (adj)	tsa'ir	צָעִיר

old (adj)	yaʃan	יָשָׁן
new (adj)	χadaʃ	חָדָשׁ
hard (adj)	kaʃe	קָשֶׁה
soft (adj)	raχ	רַךְ
warm (tepid)	χamim	חָמִים
cold (adj)	kar	קַר
fat (adj)	ʃamen	שָׁמֵן
thin (adj)	raze	רָזֶה
narrow (adj)	tsar	צַר
wide (adj)	raχav	רָחָב
good (adj)	tov	טוֹב
bad (adj)	ra	רַע
brave (adj)	amits	אַמִּיץ
cowardly (adj)	paχdani	פַּחְדָּנִי

21. Lines and shapes

square	ri'bu'a	רִיבּוּעַ (ז)
square (as adj)	meruba	מְרוּבָּע
circle	ma'agal, igul	מַעְגָּל, עִיגוּל (ז)
round (adj)	agol	עָגוֹל
triangle	meʃulaʃ	מְשׁוּלָשׁ (ז)
triangular (adj)	meʃulaʃ	מְשׁוּלָשׁ
oval	e'lipsa	אֶלִיפְּסָה (נ)
oval (as adj)	e'lipti	אֶלִיפְּטִי
rectangle	malben	מַלְבֵּן (ז)
rectangular (adj)	malbeni	מַלְבֵּנִי
pyramid	pira'mida	פִּירָמִידָה (נ)
rhombus	me'uyan	מְעוּיָן (ז)
trapezoid	trapez	טְרַפֵּז (ז)
cube	kubiya	קוּבִּיָּה (נ)
prism	minsara	מִנְסָרָה (נ)
circumference	ma'agal	מַעְגָּל (ז)
sphere	sfira	סְפִירָה (נ)
ball (solid sphere)	kadur	כַּדּוּר (ז)
diameter	'koter	קוֹטֶר (ז)
radius	'radyus	רַדְיוּס (ז)
perimeter (circle's ~)	hekef	הֶיקֵף (ז)
center	merkaz	מֶרְכָּז (ז)
horizontal (adj)	ofki	אוֹפְקִי
vertical (adj)	anaχi	אֲנָכִי

parallel (n)	kav makbil	קַו מַקְבִּיל (ז)
parallel (as adj)	makbil	מַקְבִּיל
line	kav	קַו (ז)
stroke	kav	קַו (ז)
straight line	kav yaʃar	קַו יָשָׁר (ז)
curve (curved line)	akuma	עֲקוּמָה (נ)
thin (line, etc.)	dak	דַק
contour (outline)	mit'ar	מִתְאָר (ז)
intersection	xitux	חִיתּוּךְ (ז)
right angle	zavit yaʃara	זָוִית יָשָׁרָה (נ)
segment	mikta	מִקְטָע (ז)
sector	gizra	גִזְרָה (נ)
side (of triangle)	'tsela	צֶלַע (ז)
angle	zavit	זָוִית (נ)

22. Units of measurement

weight	miʃkal	מִשְׁקָל (ז)
length	'orex	אוֹרֶךְ (ז)
width	'roxav	רוֹחַב (ז)
height	'gova	גוֹבַה (ז)
depth	'omek	עוֹמֶק (ז)
volume	'nefax	נֶפַח (ז)
area	'ʃetax	שֶׁטַח (ז)
gram	gram	גרָם (ז)
milligram	miligram	מִילִיגרָם (ז)
kilogram	kilogram	קִילוֹגרָם (ז)
ton	ton	טוֹן (ז)
pound	'pa'und	פָּאוּנד (ז)
ounce	'unkiya	אוּנקָיָה (נ)
meter	'meter	מֶטֶר (ז)
millimeter	mili'meter	מִילִימֶטֶר (ז)
centimeter	senti'meter	סֶנטִימֶטֶר (ז)
kilometer	kilo'meter	קִילוֹמֶטֶר (ז)
mile	mail	מָיִיל (ז)
inch	intʃ	אִינץ' (ז)
foot	'regel	רֶגֶל (נ)
yard	yard	יַרד (ז)
square meter	'meter ra'vu'a	מֶטֶר רָבוּעַ (ז)
hectare	hektar	הֶקטָר (ז)
liter	litr	לִיטר (ז)
degree	ma'ala	מַעֲלָה (נ)
volt	volt	וֹולט (ז)

ampere	amper	אַמְפֵּר (ז)
horsepower	'koaχ sus	כּוֹחַ סוּס (ז)
quantity	kamut	כַּמוּת (נ)
a little bit of ...	ktsat ...	קְצָת ...
half	'χetsi	חֵצִי (ז)
dozen	tresar	תְּרֵיסָר (ז)
piece (item)	yeχida	יְחִידָה (נ)
size	'godel	גּוֹדֶל (ז)
scale (map ~)	kne mida	קְנֵה מִידָה (ז)
minimal (adj)	mini'mali	מִינִימָאלִי
the smallest (adj)	hakatan beyoter	הַקָּטָן בְּיוֹתֵר
medium (adj)	memutsa	מְמוּצָע
maximal (adj)	maksi'mali	מַקְסִימָלִי
the largest (adj)	hagadol beyoter	הַגָּדוֹל בְּיוֹתֵר

23. Containers

canning jar (glass ~)	tsin'tsenet	צִנְצֶנֶת (נ)
can	paχit	פַּחִית (נ)
bucket	dli	דְּלִי (ז)
barrel	χavit	חָבִית (נ)
wash basin (e.g., plastic ~)	gigit	גִּיגִית (נ)
tank (100L water ~)	meiχal	מֵיכָל (ז)
hip flask	meimiya	מֵימִיָה (נ)
jerrycan	'dʒerikan	גֶ'רִיקָן (ז)
tank (e.g., tank car)	meχalit	מֵיכָלִית (נ)
mug	'sefel	סֵפֶל (ז)
cup (of coffee, etc.)	'sefel	סֵפֶל (ז)
saucer	taχtit	תַּחְתִּית (נ)
glass (tumbler)	kos	כּוֹס (נ)
wine glass	ga'viʿa	גָּבִיעַ (ז)
stock pot (soup pot)	sir	סִיר (ז)
bottle (~ of wine)	bakbuk	בַּקְבּוּק (ז)
neck (of the bottle, etc.)	tsavar habakbuk	צַוַואר הַבַּקְבּוּק (ז)
carafe (decanter)	kad	כַּד (ז)
pitcher	kankan	קַנְקַן (ז)
vessel (container)	kli	כְּלִי (ז)
pot (crock, stoneware ~)	sir 'χeres	סִיר חֶרֶס (ז)
vase	agartal	אֲגַרְטָל (ז)
bottle (perfume ~)	tsloχit	צְלוֹחִית (נ)
vial, small bottle	bakbukon	בַּקְבּוּקוֹן (ז)

tube (of toothpaste)	ʃfo'feret	שְׁפוֹפֶרֶת (נ)
sack (bag)	sak	שַׂק (ז)
bag (paper ~, plastic ~)	sakit	שַׂקִּית (נ)
pack (of cigarettes, etc.)	χafisa	חֲפִיסָה (נ)

box (e.g., shoebox)	kufsa	קוּפְסָה (נ)
crate	argaz	אַרְגָּז (ז)
basket	sal	סַל (ז)

24. Materials

material	'χomer	חוֹמֶר (ז)
wood (n)	ets	עֵץ (ז)
wood-, wooden (adj)	me'ets	מֵעֵץ

| glass (n) | zχuχit | זְכוּכִית (נ) |
| glass (as adj) | mizχuχit | מִזְּכוּכִית |

| stone (n) | 'even | אֶבֶן (נ) |
| stone (as adj) | me''even | מֵאֶבֶן |

| plastic (n) | 'plastik | פְּלַסְטִיק (ז) |
| plastic (as adj) | mi'plastik | מִפְּלַסְטִיק |

| rubber (n) | 'gumi | גּוּמִי (ז) |
| rubber (as adj) | mi'gumi | מִגּוּמִי |

| cloth, fabric (n) | bad | בַּד (ז) |
| fabric (as adj) | mibad | מִבַּד |

| paper (n) | neyar | נְיָיר (ז) |
| paper (as adj) | mineyar | מִנְּיָיר |

| cardboard (n) | karton | קַרְטוֹן (ז) |
| cardboard (as adj) | mikarton | מִקַּרְטוֹן |

| polyethylene | 'nailon | נַיְילוֹן (ז) |
| cellophane | tselofan | צֶלוֹפָן (ז) |

| linoleum | li'nole'um | לִינוֹלֶיאוּם (ז) |
| plywood | dikt | דִּיקְט (ז) |

| porcelain (n) | χar'sina | חַרְסִינָה (נ) |
| porcelain (as adj) | meχar'sina | מֵחַרְסִינָה |

| clay (n) | χarsit | חַרְסִית (נ) |
| clay (as adj) | me'χeres | מֵחֶרֶס |

| ceramic (n) | ke'ramika | קֵרָמִיקָה (נ) |
| ceramic (as adj) | ke'rami | קֵרָמִי |

25. Metals

metal (n)	ma'texet	מַתֶּכֶת (נ)
metal (as adj)	mataxti	מַתַּכְתִּי
alloy (n)	sag'soget	סַגְסֹגֶת (נ)
gold (n)	zahav	זָהָב (ז)
gold, golden (adj)	mizahav, zahov	מִזָּהָב, זָהֹב
silver (n)	'kesef	כֶּסֶף (ז)
silver (as adj)	kaspi	כַּסְפִּי
iron (n)	barzel	בַּרְזֶל (ז)
iron-, made of iron (adj)	mibarzel	מִבַּרְזֶל
steel (n)	plada	פְּלָדָה (נ)
steel (as adj)	miplada	מִפְּלָדָה
copper (n)	ne'xoʃet	נְחֹשֶׁת (נ)
copper (as adj)	mine'xoʃet	מִנְחֹשֶׁת
aluminum (n)	alu'minyum	אָלוּמִינְיוּם (ז)
aluminum (as adj)	me'alu'minyum	מֵאָלוּמִינְיוּם
bronze (n)	arad	אָרָד (ז)
bronze (as adj)	me'arad	מֵאָרָד
brass	pliz	פְּלִיז (ז)
nickel	'nikel	נִיקֶל (ז)
platinum	'platina	פְּלָטִינָה (נ)
mercury	kaspit	כַּסְפִּית (נ)
tin	bdil	בְּדִיל (ז)
lead	o'feret	עוֹפֶרֶת (נ)
zinc	avats	אָבָץ (ז)

HUMAN BEING

Human being. The body

26. Humans. Basic concepts

human being	ben adam	בֶּן אָדָם (ז)
man (adult male)	'gever	גֶּבֶר (ז)
woman	iʃa	אִשָּׁה (נ)
child	'yeled	יֶלֶד (ז)
girl	yalda	יַלְדָּה (נ)
boy	'yeled	יֶלֶד (ז)
teenager	'na'ar	נַעַר (ז)
old man	zaken	זָקֵן (ז)
old woman	zkena	זְקֵנָה (נ)

27. Human anatomy

organism (body)	guf ha'adam	גוּף הָאָדָם (ז)
heart	lev	לֵב (ז)
blood	dam	דָּם (ז)
artery	'orek	עוֹרֶק (ז)
vein	vrid	וְרִיד (ז)
brain	'moaχ	מוֹחַ (ז)
nerve	atsav	עָצָב (ז)
nerves	atsabim	עֲצַבִּים (ז"ר)
vertebra	χulya	חוּלְיָה (נ)
spine (backbone)	amud haʃidra	עַמוּד הַשִּׁדְרָה (ז)
stomach (organ)	keiva	קֵיבָה (נ)
intestines, bowels	me''ayim	מֵעַיִים (ז"ר)
intestine (e.g., large ~)	me'i	מְעִי (ז)
liver	kaved	כָּבֵד (ז)
kidney	kilya	כְּלָיָה (נ)
bone	'etsem	עֶצֶם (נ)
skeleton	'ʃeled	שֶׁלֶד (ז)
rib	'tsela	צֵלָע (ז)
skull	gul'golet	גוּלְגּוֹלֶת (נ)
muscle	ʃrir	שְׁרִיר (ז)
biceps	ʃrir du raʃi	שְׁרִיר דּוּ־רָאשִׁי (ז)

triceps	ʃrir tlat raʃi	שְׁרִיר תְּלָת־רָאשִׁי (ז)
tendon	gid	גִּיד (ז)
joint	'perek	פֶּרֶק (ז)
lungs	re'ot	רֵיאוֹת (נ"ר)
genitals	evrei min	אֵבְרֵי מִין (ז"ר)
skin	or	עוֹר (ז)

28. Head

head	roʃ	רֹאשׁ (ז)
face	panim	פָּנִים (ז"ר)
nose	af	אַף (ז)
mouth	pe	פֶּה (ז)
eye	'ayin	עַיִן (נ)
eyes	ei'nayim	עֵינַיִים (נ"ר)
pupil	iʃon	אִישׁוֹן (ז)
eyebrow	gaba	גַּבָּה (נ)
eyelash	ris	רִיס (ז)
eyelid	af'af	עַפְעַף (ז)
tongue	laʃon	לָשׁוֹן (נ)
tooth	ʃen	שֵׁן (נ)
lips	sfa'tayim	שְׂפָתַיִים (נ"ר)
cheekbones	atsamot leχa'yayim	עַצְמוֹת לְחָיַיִם (נ"ר)
gum	χani'χayim	חֲנִיכַיִים (ז"ר)
palate	χeχ	חֵךְ (ז)
nostrils	neχi'rayim	נְחִירַיִים (ז"ר)
chin	santer	סַנְטֵר (ז)
jaw	'leset	לֶסֶת (נ)
cheek	'leχi	לֶחִי (נ)
forehead	'metsaχ	מֵצַח (ז)
temple	raka	רַקָּה (נ)
ear	'ozen	אוֹזֶן (נ)
back of the head	'oref	עוֹרֶף (ז)
neck	tsavar	צַוָּאר (ז)
throat	garon	גָּרוֹן (ז)
hair	se'ar	שֵׂיעָר (ז)
hairstyle	tis'roket	תִּסְרוֹקֶת (נ)
haircut	tis'poret	תִּסְפוֹרֶת (נ)
wig	pe'a	פֵּאָה (נ)
mustache	safam	שָׂפָם (ז)
beard	zakan	זָקָן (ז)
to have (a beard, etc.)	legadel	לְגַדֵּל
braid	tsama	צַמָּה (נ)
sideburns	pe'ot leχa'yayim	פֵּאוֹת לְחָיַיִם (נ"ר)

red-haired (adj)	'dʒindʒi	גִ'ינגִ'י
gray (hair)	kasuf	כָּסוּף
bald (adj)	ke'reaχ	קֵירֵחַ
bald patch	ka'raχat	קָרַחַת (נ)
ponytail	'kuku	קוּקוּ (ז)
bangs	'poni	פּוֹנִי (ז)

29. Human body

hand	kaf yad	כַּף יָד (נ)
arm	yad	יָד (נ)
finger	'etsba	אֶצבַּע (נ)
toe	'bohen	בּוֹהֶן (נ)
thumb	agudal	אֲגוּדָל (ז)
little finger	'zeret	זֶרֶת (נ)
nail	tsi'poren	צִיפּוֹרֶן (נ)
fist	egrof	אֶגרוֹף (ז)
palm	kaf yad	כַּף יָד (נ)
wrist	'ʃoreʃ kaf hayad	שוֹרֶש כַּף הַיָד (ז)
forearm	ama	אַמָה (נ)
elbow	marpek	מַרפֵּק (ז)
shoulder	katef	כָּתֵף (נ)
leg	'regel	רֶגֶל (נ)
foot	kaf 'regel	כַּף רֶגֶל (נ)
knee	'bereχ	בֶּרֶך (נ)
calf (part of leg)	ʃok	שוֹק (נ)
hip	yareχ	יָרֵך (נ)
heel	akev	עָקֵב (ז)
body	guf	גוּף (ז)
stomach	'beten	בֶּטֶן (נ)
chest	χaze	חָזֶה (ז)
breast	ʃad	שַד (ז)
flank	tsad	צַד (ז)
back	gav	גַב (ז)
lower back	mot'nayim	מוֹתנַיִים (ז"ר)
waist	'talya	טַליָה (נ)
navel (belly button)	tabur	טַבּוּר (ז)
buttocks	aχo'rayim	אֲחוֹרַיִים (ז"ר)
bottom	yaʃvan	יַשבָן (ז)
beauty mark	nekudat χen	נְקוּדַת חֵן (נ)
birthmark (café au lait spot)	'ketem leida	כֶּתֶם לֵידָה (ז)
tattoo	ka'a'ku'a	קַעֲקוּעַ (ז)
scar	tsa'leket	צַלֶקֶת (נ)

Clothing & Accessories

30. Outerwear. Coats

clothes	bgadim	בְּגָדִים (ז״ר)
outerwear	levuʃ elyon	לְבוּש עֶלְיוֹן (ז)
winter clothing	bigdei 'xoref	בִּגְדֵי חוֹרֶף (ז״ר)
coat (overcoat)	me'il	מְעִיל (ז)
fur coat	me'il parva	מְעִיל פַּרְוָה (ז)
fur jacket	me'il parva katsar	מְעִיל פַּרְוָה קָצָר (ז)
down coat	me'il pux	מְעִיל פּוּךְ (ז)
jacket (e.g., leather ~)	me'il katsar	מְעִיל קָצָר (ז)
raincoat (trenchcoat, etc.)	me'il 'geʃem	מְעִיל גֶּשֶם (ז)
waterproof (adj)	amid be'mayim	עָמִיד בְּמַיִם

31. Men's & women's clothing

shirt (button shirt)	xultsa	חוּלְצָה (נ)
pants	mixna'sayim	מִכְנָסַיִים (ז״ר)
jeans	mixnesei 'dʒins	מִכְנְסֵי ג׳ינְס (ז״ר)
suit jacket	ʒaket	ז׳קֵט (ז)
suit	xalifa	חֲלִיפָה (נ)
dress (frock)	simla	שִׂמְלָה (נ)
skirt	xatsa'it	חֲצָאִית (נ)
blouse	xultsa	חוּלְצָה (נ)
knitted jacket (cardigan, etc.)	ʒaket 'tsemer	ז׳קֵט צֶמֶר (ז)
jacket (of woman's suit)	ʒaket	ז׳קֵט (ז)
T-shirt	ti ʃert	טִי שֶרְט (ז)
shorts (short trousers)	mixna'sayim ktsarim	מִכְנָסַיִים קְצָרִים (ז״ר)
tracksuit	'trening	טְרֶנִינג (ז)
bathrobe	xaluk raxatsa	חָלוּק רַחְצָה (ז)
pajamas	pi'dʒama	פִּיג׳מָה (נ)
sweater	'sveder	סְוֶודֶר (ז)
pullover	afuda	אֲפוּדָה (נ)
vest	vest	וֶסְט (ז)
tailcoat	frak	פְרָאק (ז)
tuxedo	tuk'sido	טוּקְסִידוֹ (ז)

uniform	madim	מַדִּים (ז״ר)
workwear	bigdei avoda	בִּגְדֵי עֲבוֹדָה (ז״ר)
overalls	sarbal	סַרְבָּל (ז)
coat (e.g., doctor's smock)	χaluk	חָלוּק (ז)

32. Clothing. Underwear

underwear	levanim	לְבָנִים (ז״ר)
boxers, briefs	taχtonim	תַּחְתּוֹנִים (ז״ר)
panties	taχtonim	תַּחְתּוֹנִים (ז״ר)
undershirt (A-shirt)	gufiya	גוּפִיָּה (נ)
socks	gar'bayim	גַּרְבַּיִם (ז״ר)
nightgown	'ktonet 'laila	כּתוֹנֶת לַיְלָה (נ)
bra	χaziya	חֲזִיָּה (נ)
knee highs	birkon	בִּרְכּוֹן (ז)
(knee-high socks)		
pantyhose	garbonim	גַּרְבּוֹנִים (ז״ר)
stockings (thigh highs)	garbei 'nailon	גַּרְבֵּי נַיְלוֹן (ז״ר)
bathing suit	'beged yam	בֶּגֶד יָם (ז)

33. Headwear

hat	'kova	כּוֹבַע (ז)
fedora	'kova 'leved	כּוֹבַע לֶבֶד (ז)
baseball cap	'kova 'beisbol	כּוֹבַע בֵּייסְבּוֹל (ז)
flatcap	'kova mitsχiya	כּוֹבַע מִצְחִיָּה (ז)
beret	baret	בֶּרֶט (ז)
hood	bardas	בַּרְדָּס (ז)
panama hat	'kova 'tembel	כּוֹבַע טֶמְבֶּל (ז)
knit cap (knitted hat)	'kova 'gerev	כּוֹבַע גֶּרֶב (ז)
headscarf	mit'paχat	מִטְפַּחַת (נ)
women's hat	'kova	כּוֹבַע (ז)
hard hat	kasda	קַסְדָּה (נ)
garrison cap	kumta	כּוּמְתָּה (נ)
helmet	kasda	קַסְדָּה (נ)
derby	mig'ba'at me'u'gelet	מִגְבַּעַת מְעוּגֶּלֶת (נ)
top hat	tsi'linder	צִילִינְדֶר (ז)

34. Footwear

footwear	han'ala	הַנְעָלָה (נ)
shoes (men's shoes)	na'a'layim	נַעֲלַיִם (נ״ר)

shoes (women's shoes)	na'a'layim	נַעֲלַיִים (נ״ר)
boots (e.g., cowboy ~)	maga'fayim	מַגָּפַיִים (ז״ר)
slippers	na'alei 'bayit	נַעֲלֵי בַּיִת (נ״ר)
tennis shoes (e.g., Nike ~)	na'alei sport	נַעֲלֵי סְפּוֹרְט (נ״ר)
sneakers (e.g., Converse ~)	na'alei sport	נַעֲלֵי סְפּוֹרְט (נ״ר)
sandals	sandalim	סַנְדָלִים (ז״ר)
cobbler (shoe repairer)	sandlar	סַנְדְלָר (ז)
heel	akev	עָקֵב (ז)
pair (of shoes)	zug	זוּג (ז)
shoestring	sroχ	שְׂרוֹךְ (ז)
to lace (vt)	lisroχ	לִשְׂרוֹךְ
shoehorn	kaf na'a'layim	כַּף נַעֲלַיִים (נ)
shoe polish	miʃχat na'a'layim	מִשְׁחַת נַעֲלַיִים (נ)

35. Textile. Fabrics

cotton (n)	kutna	כּוּתְנָה (נ)
cotton (as adj)	mikutna	מְכּוּתְנָה
flax (n)	piʃtan	פְּשְׁתָן (ז)
flax (as adj)	mipiʃtan	מִפְּשְׁתָן
silk (n)	'meʃi	מֶשִׁי (ז)
silk (as adj)	miʃyi	מֶשִׁיִי
wool (n)	'tsemer	צֶמֶר (ז)
wool (as adj)	tsamri	צַמְרִי
velvet	ktifa	קְטִיפָה (נ)
suede	zamʃ	זַמְש (ז)
corduroy	'korderoi	קוֹרְדָרוֹי (ז)
nylon (n)	'nailon	נַיְילוֹן (ז)
nylon (as adj)	mi'nailon	מֶנַיְילוֹן
polyester (n)	poli''ester	פּוֹלִיאֶסְטֶר (ז)
polyester (as adj)	mipoli''ester	מְפּוֹלִיאֶסְטֶר
leather (n)	or	עוֹר (ז)
leather (as adj)	me'or	מֵעוֹר
fur (n)	parva	פַּרְוָוה (נ)
fur (e.g., ~ coat)	miparva	מִפַּרְוָוה

36. Personal accessories

gloves	kfafot	כְּפָפוֹת (נ״ר)
mittens	kfafot	כְּפָפוֹת (נ״ר)

scarf (muffler)	tsa'if	צָעִיף (ז)
glasses (eyeglasses)	miʃka'fayim	מִשְׁקָפַיִים (ז״ר)
frame (eyeglass ~)	mis'geret	מִסְגֶּרֶת (נ)
umbrella	mitriya	מִטְרִיָּה (נ)
walking stick	makel haliχa	מַקֵּל הֲלִיכָה (ז)
hairbrush	miv'reʃet se'ar	מִבְרֶשֶׁת שֵׂעָר (נ)
fan	menifa	מְנִיפָה (נ)
tie (necktie)	aniva	עֲנִיבָה (נ)
bow tie	anivat parpar	עֲנִיבַת פַּרְפַּר (נ)
suspenders	ktefiyot	כְּתֵפִיּוֹת (נ״ר)
handkerchief	mimχata	מִמְחָטָה (נ)
comb	masrek	מַסְרֵק (ז)
barrette	sikat roʃ	סִיכַּת רֹאשׁ (נ)
hairpin	sikat se'ar	סִיכַּת שֵׂעָר (נ)
buckle	avzam	אַבְזָם (ז)
belt	χagora	חֲגוֹרָה (נ)
shoulder strap	retsu'at katef	רְצוּעַת כָּתֵף (נ)
bag (handbag)	tik	תִּיק (ז)
purse	tik	תִּיק (ז)
backpack	tarmil	תַּרְמִיל (ז)

37. Clothing. Miscellaneous

fashion	ofna	אוֹפְנָה (נ)
in vogue (adj)	ofnati	אוֹפְנָתִי
fashion designer	me'atsev ofna	מְעַצֵּב אוֹפְנָה (ז)
collar	tsavaron	צַוָּארוֹן (ז)
pocket	kis	כִּיס (ז)
pocket (as adj)	ʃel kis	שֶׁל כִּיס
sleeve	ʃarvul	שַׁרְווּל (ז)
hanging loop	mitle	מִתְלֶה (ז)
fly (on trousers)	χanut	חֲנוּת (נ)
zipper (fastener)	roχsan	רוֹכְסָן (ז)
fastener	'keres	קֶרֶס (ז)
button	kaftor	כַּפְתּוֹר (ז)
buttonhole	lula'a	לוּלָאָה (נ)
to come off (ab. button)	lehitaleʃ	לְהִיתָּלֵשׁ
to sew (vi, vt)	litpor	לִתְפּוֹר
to embroider (vi, vt)	lirkom	לִרְקוֹם
embroidery	rikma	רִקְמָה (נ)
sewing needle	'maχat tfira	מַחַט תְּפִירָה (נ)
thread	χut	חוּט (ז)
seam	'tefer	תֶּפֶר (ז)

to get dirty (vi)	lehitlaxlex	לְהִתְלַכְלֵךְ
stain (mark, spot)	'ketem	כֶּתֶם (ז)
to crease, crumple (vt)	lehitkamet	לְהִתְקַמֵּט
to tear, to rip (vt)	lik'ro'a	לִקְרוֹעַ
clothes moth	aʃ	עָשׁ (ז)

38. Personal care. Cosmetics

toothpaste	miʃxat ʃi'nayim	מִשְׁחַת שִׁינַיִים (נ)
toothbrush	miv'reʃet ʃi'nayim	מִבְרֶשֶׁת שִׁינַיִים (נ)
to brush one's teeth	letsax'tseax ʃi'nayim	לְצַחְצֵחַ שִׁינַיִים
razor	'ta'ar	תַּעַר (ז)
shaving cream	'ketsef gi'luax	קֶצֶף גִּילוּחַ (ז)
to shave (vi)	lehitga'leax	לְהִתְגַּלֵּחַ
soap	sabon	סַבּוֹן (ז)
shampoo	ʃampu	שַׁמְפּוּ (ז)
scissors	mispa'rayim	מִסְפָּרַיִים (ז״ר)
nail file	ptsira	פְּצִירָה (נ)
nail clippers	gozez tsipor'nayim	גּוֹזֵז צִיפּוֹרְנַיִים (ז)
tweezers	pin'tseta	פִּינְצֶטָה (נ)
cosmetics	tamrukim	תַּמְרוּקִים (ז״ר)
face mask	masexa	מַסֵּכָה (נ)
manicure	manikur	מָנִיקוּר (ז)
to have a manicure	la'asot manikur	לַעֲשׂוֹת מָנִיקוּר
pedicure	pedikur	פֶּדִיקוּר (ז)
make-up bag	tik ipur	תִּיק אִיפּוּר (ז)
face powder	'pudra	פּוּדְרָה (נ)
powder compact	pudriya	פּוּדְרִיָּיה (נ)
blusher	'somek	סוֹמֶק (ז)
perfume (bottled)	'bosem	בּוֹשֶׂם (ז)
toilet water (lotion)	mei 'bosem	מֵי בּוֹשֶׂם (ז״ר)
lotion	mei panim	מֵי פָּנִים (ז״ר)
cologne	mei 'bosem	מֵי בּוֹשֶׂם (ז״ר)
eyeshadow	tslalit	צְלָלִית (נ)
eyeliner	ai 'lainer	אַי לַיינֶר (ז)
mascara	'maskara	מַסְקָרָה (נ)
lipstick	sfaton	שְׂפָתוֹן (ז)
nail polish, enamel	'laka letsipor'nayim	לַכָּה לְצִיפּוֹרְנַיִים (נ)
hair spray	tarsis lese'ar	תַּרְסִיס לְשֵׂיעָר (ז)
deodorant	de'odo'rant	דֵאוֹדוֹרַנְט (ז)
cream	krem	קְרֶם (ז)
face cream	krem panim	קְרֶם פָּנִים (ז)

hand cream	krem ya'dayim	קְרֶם יָדַיִם (ז)
anti-wrinkle cream	krem 'neged kmatim	קְרֶם נֶגֶד קְמָטִים (ז)
day cream	krem yom	קְרֶם יוֹם (ז)
night cream	krem 'laila	קְרֶם לַיְלָה (ז)
day (as adj)	yomi	יוֹמִי
night (as adj)	leili	לֵילִי
tampon	tampon	טַמְפּוֹן (ז)
toilet paper (toilet roll)	neyar tu'alet	נְיָיר טוּאָלֶט (ז)
hair dryer	meyabeʃ se'ar	מְיַיבֵּשׁ שֵׂיעָר (ז)

39. Jewelry

jewelry	taχʃitim	תַּכְשִׁיטִים (ז״ר)
precious (e.g., ~ stone)	yekar 'ereχ	יְקַר עֵרֶךְ
hallmark stamp	tav tsorfim, bχina	תָּו צוֹרְפִים (ז), בְּחִינָה (נ)
ring	ta'ba'at	טַבַּעַת (נ)
wedding ring	ta'ba'at nisu'in	טַבַּעַת נִישׂוּאִין (נ)
bracelet	tsamid	צָמִיד (ז)
earrings	agilim	עֲגִילִים (ז״ר)
necklace (~ of pearls)	maχ'rozet	מַחְרוֹזֶת (נ)
crown	'keter	כֶּתֶר (ז)
bead necklace	maχ'rozet	מַחְרוֹזֶת (נ)
diamond	yahalom	יַהֲלוֹם (ז)
emerald	ba'reket	בָּרֶקֶת (נ)
ruby	'odem	אוֹדֶם (ז)
sapphire	sapir	סַפִּיר (ז)
pearl	pnina	פְּנִינָה (נ)
amber	inbar	עַנְבָּר (ז)

40. Watches. Clocks

watch (wristwatch)	ʃe'on yad	שְׁעוֹן יָד (ז)
dial	'luaχ ʃa'on	לוּחַ שָׁעוֹן (ז)
hand (of clock, watch)	maχog	מָחוֹג (ז)
metal watch band	tsamid	צָמִיד (ז)
watch strap	retsu'a leʃa'on	רְצוּעָה לְשָׁעוֹן (נ)
battery	solela	סוֹלְלָה (נ)
to be dead (battery)	lehitroken	לְהִתְרוֹקֵן
to change a battery	lehaχlif	לְהַחְלִיף
to run fast	lemaher	לְמַהֵר
to run slow	lefager	לְפַגֵּר
wall clock	ʃe'on kir	שְׁעוֹן קִיר (ז)
hourglass	ʃe'on χol	שְׁעוֹן חוֹל (ז)

sundial	ʃeˈon ˈʃemeʃ	שְׁעוֹן שֶׁמֶשׁ (ז)
alarm clock	ʃaˈon meˈorer	שְׁעוֹן מְעוֹרֵר (ז)
watchmaker	ʃaˈan	שָׁעָן (ז)
to repair (vt)	letaken	לְתַקֵן

Food. Nutricion

41. Food

meat	basar	בָּשָׂר (ז)
chicken	of	עוֹף (ז)
Rock Cornish hen (poussin)	pargit	פַּרְגִּית (נ)
duck	barvaz	בַּרְוָז (ז)
goose	avaz	אֲוָז (ז)
game	'tsayid	צַיִד (ז)
turkey	'hodu	הוֹדוּ (ז)
pork	basar xazir	בְּשַׂר חֲזִיר (ז)
veal	basar 'egel	בְּשַׂר עֵגֶל (ז)
lamb	basar 'keves	בְּשַׂר כֶּבֶשׂ (ז)
beef	bakar	בָּקָר (ז)
rabbit	arnav	אַרְנָב (ז)
sausage (bologna, pepperoni, etc.)	naknik	נַקְנִיק (ז)
vienna sausage (frankfurter)	naknikiya	נַקְנִיקִיָּה (נ)
bacon	'kotel xazir	קוֹטֶל חֲזִיר (ז)
ham	basar xazir me'uʃan	בְּשַׂר חֲזִיר מְעוּשָּׁן (ז)
gammon	'kotel xazir me'uʃan	קוֹטֶל חֲזִיר מְעוּשָּׁן (ז)
pâté	pate	פָּטֶה (ז)
liver	kaved	כָּבֵד (ז)
hamburger (ground beef)	basar taxun	בְּשַׂר טָחוּן (ז)
tongue	laʃon	לָשׁוֹן (נ)
egg	beitsa	בֵּיצָה (נ)
eggs	beitsim	בֵּיצִים (נ"ר)
egg white	xelbon	חֶלְבּוֹן (ז)
egg yolk	xelmon	חֶלְמוֹן (ז)
fish	dag	דָּג (ז)
seafood	perot yam	פֵּירוֹת יָם (ז"ר)
crustaceans	sartana'im	סַרְטָנָאִים (ז"ר)
caviar	kavyar	קָווִיאָר (ז)
crab	sartan yam	סַרְטָן יָם (ז)
shrimp	ʃrimps	שְׁרִימְפְּס (ז"ר)
oyster	tsidpat ma'axal	צִדְפַּת מַאֲכָל (נ)
spiny lobster	'lobster kotsani	לוֹבְּסְטֶר קוֹצָנִי (ז)

octopus	tamnun	תַּמְנוּן (ז)
squid	kala'mari	קָלָמָארִי (ז)
sturgeon	basar haχidkan	בְּשַׂר הֶחִדְקָן (ז)
salmon	'salmon	סַלְמוֹן (ז)
halibut	putit	פּוּטִית (נ)
cod	ʃibut	שִׁיבּוּט (ז)
mackerel	kolyas	קוֹלְיָיס (ז)
tuna	'tuna	טוּנָה (נ)
eel	tslofaχ	צְלוֹפָח (ז)
trout	forel	פּוֹרֶל (ז)
sardine	sardin	סַרְדִין (ז)
pike	ze'ev 'mayim	זְאֵב מַיִם (ז)
herring	ma'liaχ	מָלִיחַ (ז)
bread	'leχem	לֶחֶם (ז)
cheese	gvina	גְבִינָה (נ)
sugar	sukar	סוּכָּר (ז)
salt	'melaχ	מֶלַח (ז)
rice	'orez	אוֹרֶז (ז)
pasta (macaroni)	'pasta	פַּסְטָה (נ)
noodles	irtiyot	אִטְרִיּוֹת (נ"ר)
butter	χem'a	חֶמְאָה (נ)
vegetable oil	'ʃemen tsimχi	שֶׁמֶן צִמְחִי (ז)
sunflower oil	'ʃemen χamaniyot	שֶׁמֶן חַמָנִיּוֹת (ז)
margarine	marga'rina	מַרְגָרִינָה (נ)
olives	zeitim	זֵיתִים (ז"ר)
olive oil	'ʃemen 'zayit	שֶׁמֶן זַיִת (ז)
milk	χalav	חָלָב (ז)
condensed milk	χalav merukaz	חָלָב מְרוּכָּז (ז)
yogurt	'yogurt	יוֹגוּרט (ז)
sour cream	ʃa'menet	שַׁמֶנֶת (נ)
cream (of milk)	ʃa'menet	שַׁמֶנֶת (נ)
mayonnaise	mayonez	מָיוֹנֵז (ז)
buttercream	ka'tsefet χem'a	קַצֶפֶת חֶמְאָה (נ)
cereal grains (wheat, etc.)	grisim	גְרִיסִים (ז"ר)
flour	'kemaχ	קֶמַח (ז)
canned food	ʃimurim	שִׁימוּרִים (ז"ר)
cornflakes	ptitei 'tiras	פְּתִיתֵי תִּירָס (ז"ר)
honey	dvaʃ	דְבַשׁ (ז)
jam	riba	רִיבָּה (נ)
chewing gum	'mastik	מַסְטִיק (ז)

42. Drinks

water	'mayim	מַיִם (ז״ר)
drinking water	mei ʃtiya	מֵי שתִיָּה (ז״ר)
mineral water	'mayim mine'raliyim	מַיִם מִינֶרָלִיִּים (ז״ר)
still (adj)	lo mugaz	לֹא מוּגָז
carbonated (adj)	mugaz	מוּגָז
sparkling (adj)	mugaz	מוּגָז
ice	'keraχ	קֶרַח (ז)
with ice	im 'keraχ	עִם קֶרַח
non-alcoholic (adj)	natul alkohol	נָטוּל אַלכּוֹהוֹל
soft drink	maʃke kal	מַשקֶה קַל (ז)
refreshing drink	maʃke mera'anen	מַשקֶה מְרַעֲנֵן (ז)
lemonade	limo'nada	לִימוֹנָדָה (נ)
liquors	maʃka'ot χarifim	מַשקָאוֹת חֲרִיפִים (ז״ר)
wine	'yayin	יַיִן (ז)
white wine	'yayin lavan	יַיִן לָבָן (ז)
red wine	'yayin adom	יַיִן אָדוֹם (ז)
liqueur	liker	לִיקֶר (ז)
champagne	ʃam'panya	שַמפַּניָה (נ)
vermouth	'vermut	וֶרמוּט (ז)
whiskey	'viski	וִיסקִי (ז)
vodka	'vodka	וֹודקָה (נ)
gin	dʒin	ג׳ין (ז)
cognac	'konyak	קוֹניָאק (ז)
rum	rom	רוֹם (ז)
coffee	kafe	קָפֶּה (ז)
black coffee	kafe ʃaχor	קָפֶּה שָחוֹר (ז)
coffee with milk	kafe hafuχ	קָפֶּה הָפוּך (ז)
cappuccino	kapu'tʃino	קָפּוּצִ׳ינוֹ (ז)
instant coffee	kafe names	קָפֶּה נָמֵס (ז)
milk	χalav	חָלָב (ז)
cocktail	kokteil	קוֹקטֵיל (ז)
milkshake	'milkʃeik	מִילקשֵייק (ז)
juice	mits	מִיץ (ז)
tomato juice	mits agvaniyot	מִיץ עַגבָנִיּוֹת (ז)
orange juice	mits tapuzim	מִיץ תַפּוּזִים (ז)
freshly squeezed juice	mits saχut	מִיץ סָחוּט (ז)
beer	'bira	בִּירָה (נ)
light beer	'bira bahira	בִּירָה בָּהִירָה (נ)
dark beer	'bira keha	בִּירָה כֵּהָה (נ)
tea	te	תֵה (ז)

| black tea | te ʃaχor | תֵה שָׁחוֹר (ז) |
| green tea | te yarok | תֵה יָרוֹק (ז) |

43. Vegetables

| vegetables | yerakot | יְרָקוֹת (ז"ר) |
| greens | 'yerek | יֶרֶק (ז) |

tomato	agvaniya	עַגְבָנִיָה (נ)
cucumber	melafefon	מְלָפְפוֹן (ז)
carrot	'gezer	גֶזֶר (ז)
potato	ta'puaχ adama	תַפוּחַ אֲדָמָה (ז)
onion	batsal	בָּצָל (ז)
garlic	ʃum	שוּם (ז)

cabbage	kruv	כְּרוּב (ז)
cauliflower	kruvit	כְּרוּבִית (נ)
Brussels sprouts	kruv nitsanim	כְּרוּב נִצָנִים (ז)
broccoli	'brokoli	בְּרוֹקוֹלִי (ז)

beetroot	'selek	סֶלֶק (ז)
eggplant	χatsil	חָצִיל (ז)
zucchini	kiʃu	קִישוּא (ז)
pumpkin	'dla'at	דְלַעַת (נ)
turnip	'lefet	לֶפֶת (נ)

parsley	petro'zilya	פֶּטרוֹזִילְיָה (נ)
dill	ʃamir	שָׁמִיר (ז)
lettuce	'χasa	חַסָה (נ)
celery	'seleri	סֶלֶרִי (ז)
asparagus	aspa'ragos	אַסְפָּרָגוֹס (ז)
spinach	'tered	תֶרֶד (ז)

pea	afuna	אָפוּנָה (נ)
beans	pol	פּוֹל (ז)
corn (maize)	'tiras	תִירָס (ז)
kidney bean	ʃu'it	שְׁעוּעִית (נ)

bell pepper	'pilpel	פִּלְפֵּל (ז)
radish	tsnonit	צְנוֹנִית (נ)
artichoke	artiʃok	אַרְטִישוֹק (ז)

44. Fruits. Nuts

fruit	pri	פְּרִי (ז)
apple	ta'puaχ	תַפוּחַ (ז)
pear	agas	אַגָס (ז)
lemon	limon	לִימוֹן (ז)

orange	tapuz	תַּפּוּז (ז)
strawberry (garden ~)	tut sade	תּוּת שָׂדֶה (ז)
mandarin	klemen'tina	קְלֵמֶנְטִינָה (נ)
plum	ʃezif	שְׁזִיף (ז)
peach	afarsek	אֲפַרְסֵק (ז)
apricot	'miʃmeʃ	מִשְׁמֵשׁ (ז)
raspberry	'petel	פֶּטֶל (ז)
pineapple	'ananas	אֲנָנָס (ז)
banana	ba'nana	בַּנָנָה (נ)
watermelon	ava'tiaχ	אֲבַטִּיחַ (ז)
grape	anavim	עֲנָבִים (ז"ר)
sour cherry	duvdevan	דּוּבְדְּבָן (ז)
sweet cherry	gudgedan	גּוּדְגְּדָן (ז)
melon	melon	מֶלוֹן (ז)
grapefruit	eʃkolit	אֶשְׁכּוֹלִית (נ)
avocado	avo'kado	אָבוֹקָדוֹ (ז)
papaya	pa'paya	פַּפָּאיָה (נ)
mango	'mango	מַנְגּוֹ (ז)
pomegranate	rimon	רִימּוֹן (ז)
redcurrant	dumdemanit aduma	דּוּמְדְּמָנִית אֲדוּמָה (נ)
blackcurrant	dumdemanit ʃχora	דּוּמְדְּמָנִית שְׁחוֹרָה (נ)
gooseberry	χazarzar	חֲזַרְזַר (ז)
bilberry	uχmanit	אוּכְמָנִית (נ)
blackberry	'petel ʃaχor	פֶּטֶל שָׁחוֹר (ז)
raisin	tsimukim	צִימּוּקִים (ז"ר)
fig	te'ena	תְּאֵנָה (נ)
date	tamar	תָּמָר (ז)
peanut	botnim	בּוֹטְנִים (ז"ר)
almond	ʃaked	שָׁקֵד (ז)
walnut	egoz 'meleχ	אֱגוֹז מֶלֶךְ (ז)
hazelnut	egoz ilsar	אֱגוֹז אִלְסָר (ז)
coconut	'kokus	קוֹקוּס (ז)
pistachios	'fistuk	פִּיסְטוּק (ז)

45. Bread. Candy

bakers' confectionery (pastry)	mutsrei kondi'torya	מוּצְרֵי קוֹנְדִּיטוֹרְיָה (ז"ר)
bread	'leχem	לֶחֶם (ז)
cookies	ugiya	עוּגִיָּה (נ)
chocolate (n)	'ʃokolad	שׁוֹקוֹלָד (ז)
chocolate (as adj)	mi'ʃokolad	מְשׁוֹקוֹלָד
candy (wrapped)	sukariya	סוּכָּרְיָיה (נ)

cake (e.g., cupcake)	uga	עוּגָה (נ)
cake (e.g., birthday ~)	uga	עוּגָה (נ)
pie (e.g., apple ~)	pai	פַּאי (ז)
filling (for cake, pie)	milui	מִילוּי (ז)
jam (whole fruit jam)	riba	רִיבָּה (נ)
marmalade	marme'lada	מַרְמֶלָדָה (נ)
waffles	'vaflim	וָפְלִים (ז"ר)
ice-cream	'glida	גְלִידָה (נ)
pudding	'puding	פּוּדִינג (ז)

46. Cooked dishes

course, dish	mana	מָנָה (נ)
cuisine	mitbax	מִטְבָּח (ז)
recipe	matkon	מַתְכּוֹן (ז)
portion	mana	מָנָה (נ)
salad	salat	סָלָט (ז)
soup	marak	מָרָק (ז)
clear soup (broth)	marak tsax, tsir	מָרָק צַח, צִיר (ז)
sandwich (bread)	karix	כָּרִיך (ז)
fried eggs	beitsat ain	בֵּיצַת עַיִן (נ)
hamburger (beefburger)	'hamburger	הַמְבּוּרְגֶּר (ז)
beefsteak	umtsa, steik	אוּמְצָה (נ), סְטֵייק (ז)
side dish	to'sefet	תּוֹסֶפֶת (נ)
spaghetti	spa'geti	סְפָּגֶטִי (ז)
mashed potatoes	mexit tapuxei adama	מְחִית תַפּוּחֵי אֲדָמָה (נ)
pizza	'pitsa	פִּיצָה (נ)
porridge (oatmeal, etc.)	daysa	דַייסָה (נ)
omelet	xavita	חֲבִיתָה (נ)
boiled (e.g., ~ beef)	mevuʃal	מְבוּשָל
smoked (adj)	me'uʃan	מְעוּשָן
fried (adj)	metugan	מְטוּגָן
dried (adj)	meyubaʃ	מְיוּבָּש
frozen (adj)	kafu	קָפוּא
pickled (adj)	kavuʃ	כָּבוּש
sweet (sugary)	matok	מָתוֹק
salty (adj)	ma'luax	מָלוּחַ
cold (adj)	kar	קַר
hot (adj)	xam	חַם
bitter (adj)	marir	מָרִיר
tasty (adj)	ta'im	טָעִים
to cook in boiling water	levaʃel be'mayim rotxim	לְבַשֵל בְּמַיִם רוֹתְחִים

to cook (dinner)	levaʃel	לְבַשֵׁל
to fry (vt)	letagen	לְטַגֵן
to heat up (food)	leχamem	לְחַמֵם
to salt (vt)	leham'liaχ	לְהַמְלִים
to pepper (vt)	lefalpel	לְפַלְפֵל
to grate (vt)	lerasek	לְכַסֵק
peel (n)	klipa	קְלִיפָּה (נ)
to peel (vt)	lekalef	לְקַלֵף

47. Spices

salt	'melaχ	מֶלַח (ז)
salty (adj)	ma'luaχ	מָלוּם
to salt (vt)	leham'liaχ	לְהַמְלִים
black pepper	'pilpel ʃaχor	פִּלְפֵּל שָׁחוֹר (ז)
red pepper (milled ~)	'pilpel adom	פִּלְפֵּל אָדוֹם (ז)
mustard	χardal	חַרְדָל (ז)
horseradish	χa'zeret	חֲזֶרֶת (נ)
condiment	'rotev	רוֹטֶב (ז)
spice	tavlin	תַבְלִין (ז)
sauce	'rotev	רוֹטֶב (ז)
vinegar	'χomets	חוֹמֶץ (ז)
anise	kamnon	כַּמְנוֹן (ז)
basil	reχan	כֵּיחָן (ז)
cloves	tsi'poren	צִיפּוֹרֶן (ז)
ginger	'dʒindʒer	גִ'ינְגֵ'ר (ז)
coriander	'kusbara	כּוּסְבָּרָה (נ)
cinnamon	kinamon	קִינָמוֹן (ז)
sesame	'ʃumʃum	שׁוּמְשׁוֹם (ז)
bay leaf	ale dafna	עָלֵה דַפְנָה (ז)
paprika	'paprika	פַּפְּרִיקָה (נ)
caraway	'kimel	קִימֵל (ז)
saffron	ze'afran	זְעַפְרָן (ז)

48. Meals

food	'oχel	אוֹכֶל (ז)
to eat (vi, vt)	le'eχol	לֶאֱכוֹל
breakfast	aruχat 'boker	אֲרוּחַת בּוֹקֶר (נ)
to have breakfast	le'eχol aruχat 'boker	לֶאֱכוֹל אֲרוּחַת בּוֹקֶר
lunch	aruχat tsaha'rayim	אֲרוּחַת צָהֳרַיִם (נ)
to have lunch	le'eχol aruχat tsaha'rayim	לֶאֱכוֹל אֲרוּחַת צָהֳרַיִם

dinner	aruxat 'erev	אֲרוּחַת עֶרֶב (נ)
to have dinner	le'exol aruxat 'erev	לֶאֱכוֹל אֲרוּחַת עֶרֶב
appetite	te'avon	תֵּיאָבוֹן (ז)
Enjoy your meal!	betei'avon!	בְּתֵיאָבוֹן!

to open (~ a bottle)	lif'toax	לִפְתּוֹחַ
to spill (liquid)	li∫pox	לִשְׁפּוֹךְ
to spill out (vi)	lehi∫apex	לְהִישָׁפֵךְ

to boil (vi)	lir'toax	לִרְתּוֹחַ
to boil (vt)	lehar'tiax	לְהַרְתִּיחַ
boiled (~ water)	ra'tuax	רָתוּחַ
to chill, cool down (vt)	lekarer	לְקָרֵר
to chill (vi)	lehitkarer	לְהִתְקָרֵר

| taste, flavor | 'ta'am | טַעַם (ז) |
| aftertaste | 'ta'am levai | טַעַם לְוַואי (ז) |

to slim down (lose weight)	lirzot	לִרְזוֹת
diet	di''eta	דִיאֶטָה (נ)
vitamin	vitamin	וִיטָמִין (ז)
calorie	ka'lorya	קָלוֹרְיָה (נ)
vegetarian (n)	ʦimxoni	צִמְחוֹנִי (ז)
vegetarian (adj)	ʦimxoni	צִמְחוֹנִי

fats (nutrient)	∫umanim	שׁוּמָנִים (ז"ר)
proteins	xelbonim	חֶלְבּוֹנִים (ז"ר)
carbohydrates	paxmema	פַּחְמֵימָה (נ)
slice (of lemon, ham)	prusa	פְּרוּסָה (נ)
piece (of cake, pie)	xatixa	חֲתִיכָה (נ)
crumb (of bread, cake, etc.)	perur	פֵּירוּר (ז)

49. Table setting

spoon	kaf	כַּף (נ)
knife	sakin	סַכִּין (ז, נ)
fork	mazleg	מַזְלֵג (ז)
cup (e.g., coffee ~)	'sefel	סֵפֶל (ז)
plate (dinner ~)	ʦa'laxat	צַלַּחַת (נ)
saucer	taxtit	תַּחְתִּית (נ)
napkin (on table)	mapit	מַפִּית (נ)
toothpick	keisam ∫i'nayim	קֵיסָם שִׁינַיִים (ז)

50. Restaurant

| restaurant | mis'ada | מִסְעָדָה (נ) |
| coffee house | beit kafe | בֵּית קָפֶה (ז) |

pub, bar	bar, pab	בָּר, פָּאבּ (ז)
tearoom	beit te	בֵּית תֵּה (ז)
waiter	meltsar	מֶלְצַר (ז)
waitress	meltsarit	מֶלְצָרִית (נ)
bartender	'barmen	בַּרְמֶן (ז)
menu	tafrit	תַּפְרִיט (ז)
wine list	reʃimat yeynot	רְשִׁימַת יֵינוֹת (נ)
to book a table	lehazmin ʃulχan	לְהַזְמִין שׁוּלְחָן
course, dish	mana	מָנָה (נ)
to order (meal)	lehazmin	לְהַזְמִין
to make an order	lehazmin	לְהַזְמִין
aperitif	maʃke meta'aven	מַשְׁקֶה מְתָאָבֵן (ז)
appetizer	meta'aven	מְתָאָבֵן (ז)
dessert	ki'nuaχ	קִינוּחַ (ז)
check	χeʃbon	חֶשְׁבּוֹן (ז)
to pay the check	leʃalem	לְשַׁלֵם
to give change	latet 'odef	לָתֵת עוֹדֶף
tip	tip	טִיפּ (ז)

Family, relatives and friends

51. Personal information. Forms

name (first name)	ʃem	שֵׁם (ז)
surname (last name)	ʃem miʃpaχa	שֵׁם מִשְׁפָּחָה (ז)
date of birth	ta'ariχ leda	תַּאֲרִיך לֵידָה (ז)
place of birth	mekom leda	מְקוֹם לֵידָה (ז)
nationality	le'om	לְאוֹם (ז)
place of residence	mekom megurim	מְקוֹם מְגוּרִים (ז)
country	medina	מְדִינָה (נ)
profession (occupation)	mik'tso'a	מִקְצוֹעַ (ז)
gender, sex	min	מִין (ז)
height	'gova	גּוֹבַה (ז)
weight	miʃkal	מִשְׁקָל (ז)

52. Family members. Relatives

mother	em	אֵם (נ)
father	av	אָב (ז)
son	ben	בֵּן (ז)
daughter	bat	בַּת (נ)
younger daughter	habat haktana	הַבַּת הַקְּטַנָּה (נ)
younger son	haben hakatan	הַבֵּן הַקָּטָן (ז)
eldest daughter	habat habχora	הַבַּת הַבְּכוֹרָה (נ)
eldest son	haben habχor	הַבֵּן הַבְּכוֹר (ז)
brother	aχ	אָח (ז)
elder brother	aχ gadol	אָח גָּדוֹל (ז)
younger brother	aχ katan	אָח קָטָן (ז)
sister	aχot	אָחוֹת (נ)
elder sister	aχot gdola	אָחוֹת גְּדוֹלָה (נ)
younger sister	aχot ktana	אָחוֹת קְטַנָּה (נ)
cousin (masc.)	ben dod	בֶּן דּוֹד (ז)
cousin (fem.)	bat 'doda	בַּת דּוֹדָה (נ)
mom, mommy	'ima	אִמָּא (נ)
dad, daddy	'aba	אַבָּא (ז)
parents	horim	הוֹרִים (ז"ר)
child	'yeled	יֶלֶד (ז)
children	yeladim	יְלָדִים (ז"ר)

grandmother	'savta	סָבְתָא (נ)
grandfather	'saba	סָבָּא (ז)
grandson	'neχed	נֶכֶד (ז)
granddaughter	neχda	נֶכְדָה (נ)
grandchildren	neχadim	נֶכָדִים (ז״ר)
uncle	dod	דוֹד (ז)
aunt	'doda	דוֹדָה (נ)
nephew	aχyan	אַחְיָין (ז)
niece	aχyanit	אַחְיָינִית (נ)
mother-in-law (wife's mother)	χamot	חָמוֹת (נ)
father-in-law (husband's father)	χam	חָם (ז)
son-in-law (daughter's husband)	χatan	חָתָן (ז)
stepmother	em χoreget	אֵם חוֹרֶגֶת (נ)
stepfather	av χoreg	אָב חוֹרֵג (ז)
infant	tinok	תִּינוֹק (ז)
baby (infant)	tinok	תִּינוֹק (ז)
little boy, kid	pa'ot	פָּעוֹט (ז)
wife	iʃa	אִשָׁה (נ)
husband	'ba'al	בַּעַל (ז)
spouse (husband)	ben zug	בֶּן זוּג (ז)
spouse (wife)	bat zug	בַּת זוּג (נ)
married (masc.)	nasui	נָשׂוּי
married (fem.)	nesu'a	נְשׂוּאָה
single (unmarried)	ravak	רַוָּק
bachelor	ravak	רַוָּק (ז)
divorced (masc.)	garuʃ	גָּרוּשׁ
widow	almana	אַלְמָנָה (נ)
widower	alman	אַלְמָן (ז)
relative	karov miʃpaχa	קָרוֹב מִשְׁפָּחָה (ז)
close relative	karov miʃpaχa	קָרוֹב מִשְׁפָּחָה (ז)
distant relative	karov raχok	קָרוֹב רָחוֹק (ז)
relatives	krovei miʃpaχa	קְרוֹבֵי מִשְׁפָּחָה (ז״ר)
orphan (boy)	yatom	יָתוֹם (ז)
orphan (girl)	yetoma	יְתוֹמָה (נ)
guardian (of a minor)	apo'tropos	אַפּוֹטְרוֹפּוֹס (ז)
to adopt (a boy)	le'amets	לְאַמֵץ
to adopt (a girl)	le'amets	לְאַמֵץ

53. Friends. Coworkers

friend (masc.)	χaver	חָבֵר (ז)
friend (fem.)	χavera	חֲבֵרָה (נ)

friendship	yedidut	יְדִידוּת (נ)
to be friends	lihyot yadidim	לִהְיוֹת יָדִידִים
buddy (masc.)	xaver	חָבֵר (ז)
buddy (fem.)	xavera	חֲבֵרָה (נ)
partner	ʃutaf	שׁוּתָף (ז)
chief (boss)	menahel, roʃ	מְנַהֵל (ז), רֹאשׁ (ז)
superior (n)	memune	מְמוּנֶה (ז)
owner, proprietor	beʻalim	בְּעָלִים (ז)
subordinate (n)	kafuf le	כָּפוּף ל (ז)
colleague	amit	עָמִית (ז)
acquaintance (person)	makar	מַכָּר (ז)
fellow traveler	ben levaya	בֶּן לְוָיָה (ז)
classmate	xaver lekita	חָבֵר לְכִּיתָה (ז)
neighbor (masc.)	ʃaxen	שָׁכֵן (ז)
neighbor (fem.)	ʃxena	שְׁכֵנָה (נ)
neighbors	ʃxenim	שְׁכֵנִים (ז"ר)

54. Man. Woman

woman	iʃa	אִשָּׁה (נ)
girl (young woman)	baxura	בַּחוּרָה (נ)
bride	kala	כַּלָּה (נ)
beautiful (adj)	yafa	יָפָּה
tall (adj)	gvoha	גְּבוֹהָה
slender (adj)	tmira	תְּמִירָה
short (adj)	namux	נָמוּךְ
blonde (n)	blon'dinit	בְּלוֹנְדִינִית (נ)
brunette (n)	bru'netit	בְּרוּנֶטִית (נ)
ladies' (adj)	ʃel naʃim	שֶׁל נָשִׁים
virgin (girl)	betula	בְּתוּלָה (נ)
pregnant (adj)	hara	הָרָה
man (adult male)	'gever	גֶּבֶר (ז)
blond (n)	blon'dini	בְּלוֹנְדִינִי (ז)
brunet (n)	ʃxarxar	שְׁחַרְחַר
tall (adj)	ga'voha	גָּבוֹהַ
short (adj)	namux	נָמוּךְ
rude (rough)	gas	גַּס
stocky (adj)	guts	גּוּץ
robust (adj)	xason	חָסוֹן
strong (adj)	xazak	חָזָק
strength	'koax	כּוֹחַ (ז)

stout, fat (adj)	ʃamen	שָׁמֵן
swarthy (adj)	ʃaχum	שָׁחוּם
slender (well-built)	tamir	תָּמִיר
elegant (adj)	ele'ganti	אֶלֶגַנטִי

55. Age

age	gil	גִיל (ז)
youth (young age)	ne'urim	נְעוּרִים (ז"ר)
young (adj)	tsa'ir	צָעִיר

| younger (adj) | tsa'ir yoter | צָעִיר יוֹתֵר |
| older (adj) | mevugar yoter | מְבוּגָר יוֹתֵר |

young man	baχur	בָּחוּר (ז)
teenager	'naʿar	נַעַר (ז)
guy, fellow	baχur	בָּחוּר (ז)

| old man | zaken | זָקֵן (ז) |
| old woman | zkena | זְקֵנָה (נ) |

adult (adj)	mevugar	מְבוּגָר (ז)
middle-aged (adj)	bagil ha'amida	בָּגִיל הָעֲמִידָה
elderly (adj)	zaken	זָקֵן
old (adj)	zaken	זָקֵן

retirement	'pensya	פֶּנסִיָה (נ)
to retire (from job)	latset legimla'ot	לָצֵאת לְגִימלָאוֹת
retiree	pensyoner	פֶּנסִיוֹנֶר (ז)

56. Children

child	'yeled	יֶלֶד (ז)
children	yeladim	יְלָדִים (ז"ר)
twins	te'omim	תְאוֹמִים (ז"ר)

cradle	arisa	עֲרִיסָה (נ)
rattle	ra'aʃan	רַעֲשָׁן (ז)
diaper	χitul	חִיתוּל (ז)

pacifier	motsets	מוֹצֵץ (ז)
baby carriage	agala	עֲגָלָה (נ)
kindergarten	gan yeladim	גַן יְלָדִים (ז)
babysitter	beibi'siter	בֵּיבִּיסִיטֶר (ז, נ)

childhood	yaldut	יַלדוּת (נ)
doll	buba	בּוּבָּה (נ)
toy	tsa'a'tsu'a	צַעֲצוּעַ (ז)

construction set (toy)	misxak harkava	מִשְׂחַק הַרְכָּבָה (ז)
well-bred (adj)	mexunax	מְחוּנָּךְ
ill-bred (adj)	lo mexunax	לֹא מְחוּנָּךְ
spoiled (adj)	mefunak	מְפוּנָק

to be naughty	lehiʃtovev	לְהִשְׁתּוֹבֵב
mischievous (adj)	ʃovav	שׁוֹבָב
mischievousness	ma'ase 'kundes	מַעֲשֵׂה קוּנְדֵּס (ז)
mischievous child	'yeled ʃovav	יֶלֶד שׁוֹבָב (ז)

| obedient (adj) | tsaytan | צַיְתָן |
| disobedient (adj) | lo memuʃma | לֹא מְמוּשְׁמָע |

docile (adj)	ka'nu'a	כָּנוּעַ
clever (smart)	xaxam	חָכָם
child prodigy	'yeled 'pele	יֶלֶד פֶּלֶא (ז)

57. Married couples. Family life

to kiss (vt)	lenaʃek	לְנַשֵּׁק
to kiss (vi)	lehitnaʃek	לְהִתְנַשֵּׁק
family (n)	miʃpaxa	מִשְׁפָּחָה (נ)
family (as adj)	miʃpaxti	מִשְׁפַּחְתִּי
couple	zug	זוּג (ז)
marriage (state)	nisu'im	נִישׂוּאִים (ז"ר)
hearth (home)	ax, ken	אָח (נ), קֵן (ז)
dynasty	ʃo'ʃelet	שׁוֹשֶׁלֶת (נ)

| date | deit | דֵּייט (ז) |
| kiss | neʃika | נְשִׁיקָה (נ) |

love (for sb)	ahava	אַהֲבָה (נ)
to love (sb)	le'ehov	לֶאֱהוֹב
beloved	ahuv	אָהוּב

tenderness	rox	רֹךְ (ז)
tender (affectionate)	adin, rax	עָדִין, רַךְ
faithfulness	ne'emanut	נֶאֱמָנוּת (נ)
faithful (adj)	masur	מָסוּר
care (attention)	de'aga	דְּאָגָה (נ)
caring (~ father)	do'eg	דּוֹאֵג

newlyweds	zug tsa'ir	זוּג צָעִיר (ז)
honeymoon	ya'reax dvaʃ	יֶרַח דְּבַשׁ (ז)
to get married (ab. woman)	lehitxaten	לְהִתְחַתֵּן
to get married (ab. man)	lehitxaten	לְהִתְחַתֵּן

| wedding | xatuna | חֲתוּנָה (נ) |
| golden wedding | xatunat hazahav | חֲתוּנַת הַזָּהָב (נ) |

anniversary	yom nisu'in	יוֹם נִישׂוּאִין (ז)
lover (masc.)	me'ahev	מְאַהֵב (ז)
mistress (lover)	mea'hevet	מְאַהֶבֶת (נ)
adultery	bgida	בְּגִידָה (נ)
to cheat on ... (commit adultery)	livgod be...	לִבְגוֹד בְּ...
jealous (adj)	kanai	קַנַאי
to be jealous	lekane	לְקַנֵא
divorce	geruʃin	גֵרוּשִׁין (ז"ר)
to divorce (vi)	lehitgareʃ mi...	לְהִתְגָרֵשׁ מ...
to quarrel (vi)	lariv	לָרִיב
to be reconciled (after an argument)	lehitpayes	לְהִתְפַּיֵיס
together (adv)	be'yaxad	בְּיַחַד
sex	min	מִין (ז)
happiness	'oʃer	אוֹשֶׁר (ז)
happy (adj)	me'uʃar	מְאוּשָׁר
misfortune (accident)	ason	אָסוֹן (ז)
unhappy (adj)	umlal	אוּמְלָל

Character. Feelings. Emotions

58. Feelings. Emotions

feeling (emotion)	'regeʃ	רֶגֶשׁ (ז)
feelings	regaʃot	רֶגָשׁוֹת (ז"ר)
to feel (vt)	lehargiʃ	לְהַרְגִּישׁ
hunger	'ra'av	רָעָב (ז)
to be hungry	lihyot ra'ev	לִהְיוֹת רָעֵב
thirst	tsima'on	צָמָאוֹן (ז)
to be thirsty	lihyot tsame	לִהְיוֹת צָמֵא
sleepiness	yaʃ'nuniyut	יַשְׁנוּנִיּוּת (נ)
to feel sleepy	lirtsot liʃon	לִרְצוֹת לִישׁוֹן
tiredness	ayefut	עֲיֵיפוּת (נ)
tired (adj)	ayef	עָיֵף
to get tired	lehit'ayef	לְהִתְעַיֵּיף
mood (humor)	matsav 'ruax	מַצַּב רוּחַ (ז)
boredom	ʃi'amum	שִׁעֲמוּם (ז)
to be bored	lehiʃta'amem	לְהִשְׁתַּעֲמֵם
seclusion	hitbodedut	הִתְבּוֹדְדוּת (נ)
to seclude oneself	lehitboded	לְהִתְבּוֹדֵד
to worry (make anxious)	lehad'ig	לְהַדְאִיג
to be worried	lid'og	לִדְאוֹג
worrying (n)	de'aga	דְּאָגָה (נ)
anxiety	xarada	חֲרָדָה (נ)
preoccupied (adj)	mutrad	מוּטְרָד
to be nervous	lihyot atsbani	לִהְיוֹת עַצְבָּנִי
to panic (vi)	lehibahel	לְהִיבָּהֵל
hope	tikva	תִּקְוָה (נ)
to hope (vi, vt)	lekavot	לְקַווֹת
certainty	vada'ut	וַדָּאוּת (נ)
certain, sure (adj)	vada'i	וַדָּאִי
uncertainty	i vada'ut	אִי וַדָּאוּת (נ)
uncertain (adj)	lo ba'tuax	לֹא בָּטוּחַ
drunk (adj)	ʃikor	שִׁיכּוֹר
sober (adj)	pi'keax	פִּיכֵּחַ
weak (adj)	xalaʃ	חַלָּשׁ
happy (adj)	me'uʃar	מְאוּשָׁר
to scare (vt)	lehafxid	לְהַפְחִיד

| fury (madness) | teruf | טֵירוּף |
| rage (fury) | 'za'am | זַעַם (ז) |

depression	dika'on	דִּיכָּאוֹן (ז)
discomfort (unease)	i noxut	אִי נוֹחוּת (נ)
comfort	noxut	נוֹחוּת (נ)
to regret (be sorry)	lehitsta'er	לְהִצְטַעֵר
regret	xarata	חֲרָטָה (נ)
bad luck	'xoser mazal	חוֹסֶר מַזָּל (ז)
sadness	'etsev	עֶצֶב (ז)

shame (remorse)	buʃa	בּוּשָׁה (נ)
gladness	simxa	שִׂמְחָה (נ)
enthusiasm, zeal	hitlahavut	הִתְלַהֲבוּת (נ)
enthusiast	mitlahev	מִתְלַהֵב
to show enthusiasm	lehitlahev	לְהִתְלַהֵב

59. Character. Personality

character	'ofi	אוֹפִי (ז)
character flaw	pgam be''ofi	פְּגָם בָּאוֹפִי (ז)
mind	'sexel	שֵׂכֶל (ז)
reason	bina	בִּינָה (נ)

conscience	matspun	מַצְפּוּן (ז)
habit (custom)	hergel	הֶרְגֵּל (ז)
ability (talent)	ye'xolet	יְכוֹלֶת (נ)
can (e.g., ~ swim)	la'da'at	לָדַעַת

patient (adj)	savlan	סַבְלָן
impatient (adj)	xasar savlanut	חֲסַר סַבְלָנוּת
curious (inquisitive)	sakran	סַקְרָן
curiosity	sakranut	סַקְרָנוּת (נ)

modesty	tsni'ut	צְנִיעוּת (נ)
modest (adj)	tsa'nu'a	צָנוּעַ
immodest (adj)	lo tsa'nu'a	לֹא צָנוּעַ

laziness	atslut	עַצְלוּת (נ)
lazy (adj)	atsel	עָצֵל
lazy person (masc.)	atslan	עַצְלָן (ז)

cunning (n)	armumiyut	עַרְמוּמִיּוּת (נ)
cunning (as adj)	armumi	עַרְמוּמִי
distrust	'xoser emun	חוֹסֶר אֵמוּן (ז)
distrustful (adj)	xadʃani	חַדְשָׁנִי

generosity	nedivut	נְדִיבוּת (נ)
generous (adj)	nadiv	נָדִיב
talented (adj)	muxʃar	מוּכְשָׁר

talent	kiʃaron	כִּישָׁרוֹן (ז)
courageous (adj)	amits	אַמִּיץ
courage	'omets	אוֹמֶץ (ז)
honest (adj)	yaʃar	יָשָׁר
honesty	'yoʃer	יוֹשֶׁר (ז)

careful (cautious)	zahir	זָהִיר
brave (courageous)	amits	אַמִּיץ
serious (adj)	retsini	רְצִינִי
strict (severe, stern)	χamur	חָמוּר

decisive (adj)	neχrats	נֶחֱרָץ
indecisive (adj)	hasesan	הַסְּסָן
shy, timid (adj)	baiʃan	בַּיְישָׁן
shyness, timidity	baiʃanut	בַּיְישָׁנוּת (נ)

confidence (trust)	emun	אֵמוּן (ז)
to believe (trust)	leha'amin	לְהַאֲמִין
trusting (credulous)	tam	תָם

sincerely (adv)	beχenut	בְּכֵנוּת
sincere (adj)	ken	כֵּן
sincerity	kenut	כֵּנוּת (נ)
open (person)	pa'tuaχ	פָּתוּחַ

calm (adj)	ʃalev	שָׁלֵו
frank (sincere)	glui lev	גְלוּי לֵב
naïve (adj)	na''ivi	נָאִיבִי
absent-minded (adj)	mefuzar	מְפוּזָר
funny (odd)	matsχik	מַצְחִיק

greed	ta'avat 'betsa	תַאֲווֹת בֶּצַע (נ)
greedy (adj)	rodef 'betsa	רוֹדֵף בֶּצַע
stingy (adj)	kamtsan	קַמְצָן
evil (adj)	raʃa	רָשָׁע
stubborn (adj)	akʃan	עַקְשָׁן
unpleasant (adj)	lo na'im	לֹא נָעִים

selfish person (masc.)	ego'ist	אֶגוֹאִיסְט (ז)
selfish (adj)	anoχi	אָנוֹכִי
coward	paχdan	פַּחְדָן (ז)
cowardly (adj)	paχdani	פַּחְדָנִי

60. Sleep. Dreams

to sleep (vi)	liʃon	לִישׁוֹן
sleep, sleeping	ʃena	שֵׁינָה (נ)
dream	χalom	חָלוֹם (ז)
to dream (in sleep)	laχalom	לַחֲלוֹם
sleepy (adj)	radum	רָדוּם

bed	mita	מִיטָה (נ)
mattress	mizran	מִזְרָן (ז)
blanket (comforter)	smiχa	שְׂמִיכָה (נ)
pillow	karit	כָּרִית (נ)
sheet	sadin	סָדִין (ז)

insomnia	nedudei ʃena	נְדוּדֵי שֵׁינָה (ז״ר)
sleepless (adj)	χasar ʃena	חֲסַר שֵׁינָה
sleeping pill	kadur ʃena	כַּדּוּר שֵׁינָה (ז)
to take a sleeping pill	la'kaχat kadur ʃena	לָקַחַת כַּדּוּר שֵׁינָה

to feel sleepy	lirtsot liʃon	לִרְצוֹת לִישׁוֹן
to yawn (vi)	lefahek	לְפַהֵק
to go to bed	la'leχet liʃon	לָלֶכֶת לִישׁוֹן
to make up the bed	leha'tsi'a mita	לְהַצִּיעַ מִיטָה
to fall asleep	leheradem	לְהֵירָדֵם

nightmare	siyut	סִיּוּט (ז)
snore, snoring	neχira	נְחִירָה (נ)
to snore (vi)	linχor	לִנְחוֹר

alarm clock	ʃa'on me'orer	שָׁעוֹן מְעוֹרֵר (ז)
to wake (vt)	leha'ir	לְהָעִיר
to wake up	lehit'orer	לְהִתְעוֹרֵר
to get up (vi)	lakum	לָקוּם
to wash up (wash face)	lehitraχets	לְהִתְרַחֵץ

61. Humour. Laughter. Gladness

humor (wit, fun)	humor	הוּמוֹר (ז)
sense of humor	χuʃ humor	חוּשׁ הוּמוֹר (ז)
to enjoy oneself	lehanot	לֵיהָנוֹת
cheerful (merry)	sa'meaχ	שָׂמֵחַ
merriment (gaiety)	alitsut	עֲלִיצוּת (נ)

smile	χiyuχ	חִיּוּךְ (ז)
to smile (vi)	leχayeχ	לְחַיֵּךְ
to start laughing	lifrots bitsχok	לִפְרוֹץ בְּצַחוֹק
to laugh (vi)	litsχok	לִצְחוֹק
laugh, laughter	tsχok	צַחוֹק (ז)

anecdote	anek'dota	אֲנֶקְדּוֹטָה (נ)
funny (anecdote, etc.)	matsχik	מַצְחִיק
funny (odd)	meʃa'a'ʃe'a	מְשֻׁעֲשֵׁעַ

to joke (vi)	lehitba'deaχ	לְהִתְבַּדֵּחַ
joke (verbal)	bdiχa	בְּדִיחָה (נ)
joy (emotion)	simχa	שִׂמְחָה (נ)
to rejoice (vi)	lis'moaχ	לִשְׂמוֹחַ
joyful (adj)	sa'meaχ	שָׂמֵחַ

62. Discussion, conversation. Part 1

communication	'keʃer	קֶשֶׁר (ז)
to communicate	letakʃer	לְתַקְשֵׁר
conversation	siχa	שִׂיחָה (נ)
dialog	du 'siaχ	דּוּ־שִׂיחַ (ז)
discussion (discourse)	diyun	דִּיּוּן (ז)
dispute (debate)	vi'kuaχ	וִיכּוּחַ (ז)
to dispute	lehitva'keaχ	לְהִתְוַוכֵּחַ
interlocutor	ben 'siaχ	בֶּן שִׂיחַ (ז)
topic (theme)	nose	נוֹשֵׂא (ז)
point of view	nekudat mabat	נְקוּדַת מַבָּט (נ)
opinion (point of view)	de'a	דֵּעָה (נ)
speech (talk)	ne'um	נְאוּם (ז)
discussion (of report, etc.)	diyun	דִּיּוּן (ז)
to discuss (vt)	ladun	לָדוּן
talk (conversation)	siχa	שִׂיחָה (נ)
to talk (to chat)	leso'χeaχ	לְשׂוֹחֵחַ
meeting	pgiʃa	פְּגִישָׁה (נ)
to meet (vi, vt)	lehipageʃ	לְהִיפָּגֵשׁ
proverb	pitgam	פִּתְגָם (ז)
saying	pitgam	פִּתְגָם (ז)
riddle (poser)	χida	חִידָה (נ)
to pose a riddle	laχud χida	לָחוּד חִידָה
password	sisma	סִיסְמָה (נ)
secret	sod	סוֹד (ז)
oath (vow)	ʃvu'a	שְׁבוּעָה (נ)
to swear (an oath)	lehiʃava	לְהִישָׁבַע
promise	havtaχa	הַבְטָחָה (נ)
to promise (vt)	lehav'tiaχ	לְהַבְטִיחַ
advice (counsel)	etsa	עֵצָה (נ)
to advise (vt)	leya'ets	לְיַיעֵץ
to follow one's advice	lif'ol lefi ha'etsa	לִפְעוֹל לְפִי הָעֵצָה
to listen to … (obey)	lehiʃama	לְהִישָׁמַע
news	χadaʃot	חֲדָשׁוֹת (נ"ר)
sensation (news)	sen'satsya	סֶנְסַצְיָה (נ)
information (data)	meida	מֵידָע (ז)
conclusion (decision)	maskana	מַסְקָנָה (נ)
voice	kol	קוֹל (ז)
compliment	maχma'a	מַחְמָאָה (נ)
kind (nice)	adiv	אָדִיב
word	mila	מִילָה (נ)
phrase	miʃpat	מִשְׁפָּט (ז)

answer	tʃuva	תְּשׁוּבָה (נ)
truth	emet	אֱמֶת (נ)
lie	'ʃeker	שֶׁקֶר (ז)
thought	maxʃava	מַחֲשָׁבָה (נ)
idea (inspiration)	ra'ayon	רַעֲיוֹן (ז)
fantasy	fan'tazya	פַנְטָזְיָה (נ)

63. Discussion, conversation. Part 2

respected (adj)	mexubad	מְכוּבָּד
to respect (vt)	lexabed	לְכַבֵּד
respect	kavod	כָּבוֹד (ז)
Dear ... (letter)	hayakar ...	הַיָּקָר ...
to introduce (sb to sb)	la'asot hekerut	לַעֲשׂוֹת הֶיכֵּרוּת
to make acquaintance	lehakir	לְהַכִּיר
intention	kavana	כַּוָּנָה (נ)
to intend (have in mind)	lehitkaven	לְהִתְכַּוֵּון
wish	ixul	אִיחוּל (ז)
to wish (~ good luck)	le'axel	לְאַחֵל
surprise (astonishment)	hafta'a	הַפְתָּעָה (נ)
to surprise (amaze)	lehaf'ti'a	לְהַפְתִּיעַ
to be surprised	lehitpale	לְהִתְפַּלֵּא
to give (vt)	latet	לָתֵת
to take (get hold of)	la'kaxat	לָקַחַת
to give back	lehaxzir	לְהַחֲזִיר
to return (give back)	lehaʃiv	לְהָשִׁיב
to apologize (vi)	lehitnatsel	לְהִתְנַצֵּל
apology	hitnatslut	הִתְנַצְּלוּת (נ)
to forgive (vt)	lis'loax	לִסְלוֹחַ
to talk (speak)	ledaber	לְדַבֵּר
to listen (vi)	lehakʃiv	לְהַקְשִׁיב
to hear out	liʃ'mo'a	לִשְׁמוֹעַ
to understand (vt)	lehavin	לְהָבִין
to show (to display)	lehar'ot	לְהַרְאוֹת
to look at ...	lehistakel	לְהִסְתַּכֵּל
to call (yell for sb)	likro le...	לִקְרוֹא לְ...
to distract (disturb)	lehaf'ri'a	לְהַפְרִיעַ
to disturb (vt)	lehaf'ri'a	לְהַפְרִיעַ
to pass (to hand sth)	limsor	לִמְסוֹר
demand (request)	bakaʃa	בַּקָּשָׁה (נ)
to request (ask)	levakeʃ	לְבַקֵּשׁ
demand (firm request)	driʃa	דְּרִישָׁה (נ)

to demand (request firmly)	lidroʃ	לִדְרוֹשׁ
to tease (call names)	lehitgarot	לְהִתְגָּרוֹת
to mock (make fun of)	lil'og	לִלְעוֹג
mockery, derision	'la'ag	לַעַג (ז)
nickname	kinui	כִּינּוּי (ז)

insinuation	'remez	רֶמֶז (ז)
to insinuate (imply)	lirmoz	לִרְמוֹז
to mean (vt)	lehitkaven le...	לְהִתְכַּוֵּון לְ...

description	te'ur	תֵּיאוּר (ז)
to describe (vt)	leta'er	לְתָאֵר
praise (compliments)	ʃevaχ	שֶׁבַח (ז)
to praise (vt)	leʃa'beaχ	לְשַׁבֵּח

disappointment	aχzava	אַכְזָבָה (נ)
to disappoint (vt)	le'aχzev	לְאַכְזֵב
to be disappointed	lehit'aχzev	לְהִתְאַכְזֵב

supposition	hanaχa	הֲנָחָה (נ)
to suppose (assume)	leʃa'er	לְשַׁעֵר
warning (caution)	azhara	אַזְהָרָה (נ)
to warn (vt)	lehazhir	לְהַזְהִיר

64. Discussion, conversation. Part 3

to talk into (convince)	leʃaχ'ne'a	לְשַׁכְנֵעַ
to calm down (vt)	lehar'gi'a	לְהַרְגִּיעַ

silence (~ is golden)	ʃtika	שְׁתִיקָה (נ)
to be silent (not speaking)	liʃtok	לִשְׁתּוֹק
to whisper (vi, vt)	lilχoʃ	לִלְחוֹשׁ
whisper	leχiʃa	לְחִישָׁה (נ)

frankly, sincerely (adv)	beχenut	בְּכֵנוּת
in my opinion ...	leda'ati ...	לְדַעְתִּי ...

detail (of the story)	prat	פְּרָט (ז)
detailed (adj)	meforat	מְפוֹרָט
in detail (adv)	bimfurat	בְּמְפוֹרָט

hint, clue	'remez	רֶמֶז (ז)
to give a hint	lirmoz	לִרְמוֹז

look (glance)	mabat	מַבָּט (ז)
to have a look	lehabit	לְהַבִּיט
fixed (look)	kafu	קָפוּא
to blink (vi)	lematsmets	לְמַצְמֵץ
to wink (vi)	likrots	לִקְרוֹץ
to nod (in assent)	lehanhen	לְהַנְהֵן

sigh	anaxa	אֲנָחָה (נ)
to sigh (vi)	lehe'anax	לְהֵיאָנֵח
to shudder (vi)	lir'od	לִרְעוֹד
gesture	mexva	מֶחֲוָה (נ)
to touch (one's arm, etc.)	la'ga'at be...	לָגַעַת בְּ...
to seize (e.g., ~ by the arm)	litfos	לִתְפּוֹס
to tap (on the shoulder)	lit'poax	לִטְפּוֹח

Look out!	zehirut!	זְהִירוּת!
Really?	be'emet?	בֶּאֱמֶת?
Are you sure?	ata ba'tuax?	אַתָה בָּטוּחַ?
Good luck!	behatslaxa!	בְּהַצְלָחָה!
I see!	muvan!	מוּבָן!
What a pity!	xaval!	חֲבָל!

<h2>65. Agreement. Refusal</h2>

consent	haskama	הַסְכָּמָה (נ)
to consent (vi)	lehaskim	לְהַסְכִּים
approval	iʃur	אִישוּר (ז)
to approve (vt)	le'aʃer	לְאַשֵר
refusal	siruv	סֵירוּב (ז)
to refuse (vi, vt)	lesarev	לְסָרֵב

Great!	metsuyan!	מְצוּיָן!
All right!	tov!	טוֹב!
Okay! (I agree)	be'seder!	בְּסֵדֶר!

forbidden (adj)	asur	אָסוּר
it's forbidden	asur	אָסוּר
it's impossible	'bilti efʃarl	בִּלְתִי אֶפְשָרִי
incorrect (adj)	ʃagui	שָגוּי

to reject (~ a demand)	lidxot	לִדְחוֹת
to support (cause, idea)	litmox be...	לִתְמוֹך בְּ...
to accept (~ an apology)	lekabel	לְקַבֵּל

to confirm (vt)	le'aʃer	לְאַשֵר
confirmation	iʃur	אִישוּר (ז)
permission	reʃut	רְשוּת (נ)
to permit (vt)	leharʃot	לְהַרְשוֹת
decision	haxlata	הַחְלָטָה (נ)
to say nothing (hold one's tongue)	liʃtok	לִשְתוֹק

condition (term)	tnai	תְנַאי (ז)
excuse (pretext)	teruts	תֵירוּץ (ז)
praise (compliments)	'ʃevax	שֶבַח (ז)
to praise (vt)	leʃa'beax	לְשַבֵּחַ

66. Success. Good luck. Failure

success	hatsala	הַצְלָחָה (נ)
successfully (adv)	behatslaχa	בְּהַצְלָחָה
successful (adj)	mutslaχ	מוּצְלָח
luck (good luck)	mazal	מַזָל (ז)
Good luck!	behatslaχa!	בְּהַצְלָחָה!
lucky (e.g., ~ day)	mutslaχ	מוּצְלָח
lucky (fortunate)	bar mazal	בַּר מַזָל
failure	kiʃalon	כִּישָׁלוֹן (ז)
misfortune	'χoser mazal	חוֹסֶר מַזָל (ז)
bad luck	'χoser mazal	חוֹסֶר מַזָל (ז)
unsuccessful (adj)	lo mutslaχ	לֹא מוּצְלָח
catastrophe	ason	אָסוֹן (ז)
pride	ga'ava	גַאֲוָה (נ)
proud (adj)	ge'e	גֵאֶה
to be proud	lehitga'ot	לְהִתְגָאוֹת
winner	zoχe	זוֹכֶה (ז)
to win (vi)	lena'tseaχ	לְנַצֵחַ
to lose (not win)	lehafsid	לְהַפְסִיד
try	nisayon	נִיסָיוֹן (ז)
to try (vi)	lenasot	לְנַסוֹת
chance (opportunity)	hizdamnut	הִזְדַמְנוּת (נ)

67. Quarrels. Negative emotions

shout (scream)	tse'aka	צְעָקָה (נ)
to shout (vi)	lits'ok	לִצְעוֹק
to start to cry out	lehatχil lits'ok	לְהַתְחִיל לִצְעוֹק
quarrel	riv	רִיב (ז)
to quarrel (vi)	lariv	לָרִיב
fight (squabble)	riv	רִיב (ז)
to make a scene	lariv	לָרִיב
conflict	siχsuχ	סִכְסוּךְ (ז)
misunderstanding	i havana	אִי הֲבָנָה (נ)
insult	elbon	עֶלְבּוֹן (ז)
to insult (vt)	leha'aliv	לְהַעֲלִיב
insulted (adj)	ne'elav	נֶעֱלַב
resentment	tina	טִינָה (נ)
to offend (vt)	lif'go'a	לִפְגוֹעַ
to take offense	lehipaga	לְהִיפָּגַע
indignation	hitmarmerut	הִתְמַרְמְרוּת (נ)
to be indignant	lehitra'em	לְהִתְרַעֵם

| complaint | tluna | תְּלוּנָה (נ) |
| to complain (vi, vt) | lehitlonen | לְהִתְלוֹנֵן |

apology	hitnatslut	הִתְנַצְּלוּת (נ)
to apologize (vi)	lehitnatsel	לְהִתְנַצֵּל
to beg pardon	levakeʃ sliχa	לְבַקֵּשׁ סְלִיחָה

criticism	bi'koret	בִּיקּוֹרֶת (נ)
to criticize (vt)	levaker	לְבַקֵּר
accusation	ha'aʃama	הַאֲשָׁמָה (נ)
to accuse (vt)	leha'aʃim	לְהַאֲשִׁים

revenge	nekama	נְקָמָה (נ)
to avenge (get revenge)	linkom	לִנְקוֹם
to pay back	lehaχzir	לְהַחְזִיר

disdain	zilzul	זִלְזוּל (ז)
to despise (vt)	lezalzel be...	לְזַלְזֵל בְּ...
hatred, hate	sin'a	שִׂנְאָה (נ)
to hate (vt)	lisno	לִשְׂנוֹא

nervous (adj)	atsbani	עַצְבָּנִי
to be nervous	lihyot atsbani	לִהְיוֹת עַצְבָּנִי
angry (mad)	ka'us	כָּעוּס
to make angry	lehargiz	לְהַרְגִּיז

humiliation	haʃpala	הַשְׁפָּלָה (נ)
to humiliate (vt)	lehaʃpil	לְהַשְׁפִּיל
to humiliate oneself	lehaʃpil et atsmo	לְהַשְׁפִּיל אֶת עַצְמוֹ

| shock | 'helem | הֶלֶם (ז) |
| to shock (vt) | leza'a'ze'a | לְזַעְזֵעַ |

| trouble (e.g., serious ~) | tsara | צָרָה (נ) |
| unpleasant (adj) | lo na'im | לֹא נָעִים |

fear (dread)	'paχad	פַּחַד (ז)
terrible (storm, heat)	nora	נוֹרָא
scary (e.g., ~ story)	mafχid	מַפְחִיד
horror	zva'a	זְוָעָה (נ)
awful (crime, news)	ayom	אָיוֹם

to begin to tremble	lehera'ed	לְהֵירָעֵד
to cry (weep)	livkot	לִבְכּוֹת
to start crying	lehatχil livkot	לְהַתְחִיל לִבְכּוֹת
tear	dim'a	דִּמְעָה (נ)

fault	aʃma	אַשְׁמָה (נ)
guilt (feeling)	rigʃei aʃam	רִגְשֵׁי אָשָׁם (ז״ר)
dishonor (disgrace)	χerpa	חֶרְפָּה (נ)
protest	meχa'a	מְחָאָה (נ)
stress	'laχats	לַחַץ (ז)

to disturb (vt)	lehaf'ri'a	לְהַפְרִיעַ
to be furious	lix'os	לִכְעוֹס
mad, angry (adj)	zo'em	זוֹעֵם
to end (~ a relationship)	lesayem	לְסַיֵּם
to swear (at sb)	lekalel	לְקַלֵּל

to scare (become afraid)	lehibahel	לְהִיבָּהֵל
to hit (strike with hand)	lehakot	לְהַכּוֹת
to fight (street fight, etc.)	lehitkotet	לְהִתְקוֹטֵט

to settle (a conflict)	lehasdir	לְהַסְדִּיר
discontented (adj)	lo merutse	לֹא מְרוּצֶה
furious (adj)	metoraf	מְטוֹרָף

| It's not good! | ze lo tov! | זֶה לֹא טוֹב! |
| It's bad! | ze ra! | זֶה רַע! |

Medicine

68. Diseases

sickness	maxala	מַחֲלָה (נ)
to be sick	lihyot xole	לִהְיוֹת חוֹלֶה
health	bri'ut	בְּרִיאוּת (נ)
runny nose (coryza)	na'zelet	נַזֶּלֶת (נ)
tonsillitis	da'leket ʃkedim	דַּלֶּקֶת שְׁקֵדִים (נ)
cold (illness)	hitstanenut	הִצְטַנְּנוּת (נ)
to catch a cold	lehitstanen	לְהִצְטַנֵּן
bronchitis	bron'xitis	בְּרוֹנְכִיטִיס (ז)
pneumonia	da'leket re'ot	דַּלֶּקֶת רֵיאוֹת (נ)
flu, influenza	ʃa'pa'at	שַׁפַּעַת (נ)
nearsighted (adj)	ktsar re'iya	קְצַר רְאִיָּה
farsighted (adj)	rexok re'iya	רְחוֹק־רְאִיָּה
strabismus (crossed eyes)	pzila	פְּזִילָה (נ)
cross-eyed (adj)	pozel	פּוֹזֵל
cataract	katarakt	קָטָרַקְט (ז)
glaucoma	gla'u'koma	גְּלָאוּקוֹמָה (נ)
stroke	ʃavats moxi	שָׁבָץ מוֹחִי (ז)
heart attack	hetkef lev	הֶתְקֵף לֵב (ז)
myocardial infarction	'otem ʃrir halev	אוֹטֶם שְׁרִיר הַלֵּב (ז)
paralysis	ʃituk	שִׁיתּוּק (ז)
to paralyze (vt)	leʃatek	לְשַׁתֵּק
allergy	a'lergya	אָלֶרְגְּיָה (נ)
asthma	'astma, ka'tseret	אַסְתְּמָה, קַצֶּרֶת (נ)
diabetes	su'keret	סוּכֶּרֶת (נ)
toothache	ke'ev ʃi'nayim	כְּאֵב שִׁינַיִים (ז)
caries	a'ʃeʃet	עַשֶּׁשֶׁת (נ)
diarrhea	ʃilʃul	שִׁלְשׁוּל (ז)
constipation	atsirut	עֲצִירוּת (נ)
stomach upset	kilkul keiva	קִלְקוּל קֵיבָה (ז)
food poisoning	har'alat mazon	הַרְעָלַת מָזוֹן (נ)
to get food poisoning	laxatof har'alat mazon	לַחֲטוֹף הַרְעָלַת מָזוֹן
arthritis	da'leket mifrakim	דַּלֶּקֶת מִפְרָקִים (נ)
rickets	ra'kexet	רַכֶּכֶת (נ)
rheumatism	ʃigaron	שִׁיגָּרוֹן (ז)

atherosclerosis	ar'teryo skle'rosis	אַרְטֶרְיוֹ־סְקְלֶרוֹסִיס (ז)
gastritis	da'leket keiva	דַּלֶקֶת קֵיבָה (נ)
appendicitis	da'leket toseftan	דַּלֶקֶת תּוֹסֶפְתָן (נ)
cholecystitis	da'leket kis hamara	דַּלֶקֶת כִּיס הַמָרָה (נ)
ulcer	'ulkus, kiv	אוּלְקוּס, כִּיב (ז)
measles	χa'tsevet	חַצֶבֶת (נ)
rubella (German measles)	a'demet	עַדֶמֶת (נ)
jaundice	tsa'hevet	צַהֶבֶת (נ)
hepatitis	da'leket kaved	דַּלֶקֶת כָּבֵד (נ)
schizophrenia	sχizo'frenya	סְכִיזוֹפְרֶנְיָה (נ)
rabies (hydrophobia)	ka'levet	כַּלֶבֶת (נ)
neurosis	noi'roza	נוֹירוֹזָה (נ)
concussion	za'a'zu'a 'moaχ	זַעֲזוּעַ מוֹחַ (ז)
cancer	sartan	סַרְטָן (ז)
sclerosis	ta'refet	טָרֶשֶׁת (נ)
multiple sclerosis	ta'refet nefotsa	טָרֶשֶׁת נְפוֹצָה (נ)
alcoholism	alkoholizm	אַלְכּוֹהוֹלִיזְם (ז)
alcoholic (n)	alkoholist	אַלְכּוֹהוֹלִיסְט (ז)
syphilis	a'gevet	עַגֶבֶת (נ)
AIDS	eids	אֵיידְס (ז)
tumor	gidul	גִּידוּל (ז)
malignant (adj)	mam'ir	מַמְאִיר
benign (adj)	fapir	שַׁפִּיר
fever	ka'daχat	קַדַּחַת (נ)
malaria	ma'larya	מָלַרְיָה (נ)
gangrene	gan'grena	גַּנְגְּרֶנָה (נ)
seasickness	maχalat yam	מַחֲלַת יָם (נ)
epilepsy	maχalat hanefila	מַחֲלַת הַנְּפִילָה (נ)
epidemic	magefa	מַגֵּפָה (נ)
typhus	'tifus	טִיפוּס (ז)
tuberculosis	fa'χefet	שַׁחֶפֶת (נ)
cholera	ko'lera	כּוֹלֵרָה (נ)
plague (bubonic ~)	davar	דֶּבֶר (ז)

69. Symptoms. Treatments. Part 1

symptom	simptom	סִימְפְּטוֹם (ז)
temperature	χom	חוֹם (ז)
high temperature (fever)	χom ga'voha	חוֹם גָּבוֹהַּ (ז)
pulse	'dofek	דּוֹפֶק (ז)
dizziness (vertigo)	sχar'χoret	סְחַרְחוֹרֶת (נ)
hot (adj)	χam	חַם

| shivering | tsmar'moret | צְמַרמוֹרֶת (נ) |
| pale (e.g., ~ face) | xiver | חִיוֵּר |

cough	ʃi'ul	שִׁיעוּל (ז)
to cough (vi)	lehiʃta'el	לְהִשְׁתַּעֵל
to sneeze (vi)	lehit'ateʃ	לְהִתְעַטֵּשׁ
faint	ilafon	עִילָפוֹן (ז)
to faint (vi)	lehit'alef	לְהִתְעַלֵּף

bruise (hématome)	xabura	חַבּוּרָה (נ)
bump (lump)	blita	בְּלִיטָה (נ)
to bang (bump)	lekabel maka	לְקַבֵּל מַכָּה
contusion (bruise)	maka	מַכָּה (נ)
to get a bruise	lekabel maka	לְקַבֵּל מַכָּה

to limp (vi)	lits'lo'a	לְצְלוֹעַ
dislocation	'neka	נֶקַע (ז)
to dislocate (vt)	lin'ko'a	לִנְקוֹעַ
fracture	'ʃever	שֶׁבֶר (ז)
to have a fracture	liʃbor	לִשְׁבּוֹר

cut (e.g., paper ~)	xatax	חָתָךְ (ז)
to cut oneself	lehixatex	לְהִיחָתֵךְ
bleeding	dimum	דִּימוּם (ז)

| burn (injury) | kviya | כְּוִוייָה (נ) |
| to get burned | laxatof kviya | לַחֲטוֹף כְּווִייָה |

to prick (vt)	lidkor	לִדקוֹר
to prick oneself	lehidaker	לְהִידָקֵר
to injure (vt)	lif'tso'a	לִפצוֹעַ
injury	ptsi'a	פְּצִיעָה (נ)
wound	'petsa	פֶּצַע (ז)
trauma	'tra'uma	טרָאוּמָה (נ)

to be delirious	lahazot	לַהֲזוֹת
to stutter (vi)	legamgem	לְגַמגֵּם
sunstroke	makat 'ʃemeʃ	מַכַּת שֶׁמֶשׁ (נ)

70. Symptoms. Treatments. Part 2

| pain, ache | ke'ev | כְּאֵב (ז) |
| splinter (in foot, etc.) | kots | קוֹץ (ז) |

sweat (perspiration)	ze'a	זֵיעָה (נ)
to sweat (perspire)	leha'zi'a	לְהַזִּיעַ
vomiting	haka'a	הֲקָאָה (נ)
convulsions	pirkusim	פִּירפּוּסִים (ז״ר)
pregnant (adj)	hara	הָרָה
to be born	lehivaled	לְהִיווָלֵד

delivery, labor	leda	לֵידָה (נ)
to deliver (~ a baby)	la'ledet	לָלֶדֶת
abortion	hapala	הַפָּלָה (נ)

breathing, respiration	neʃima	נְשִׁימָה (נ)
in-breath (inhalation)	ʃe'ifa	שְׁאִיפָה (נ)
out-breath (exhalation)	neʃifa	נְשִׁיפָה (נ)
to exhale (breathe out)	linʃof	לִנְשׁוֹף
to inhale (vi)	liʃ'of	לִשְׁאוֹף

disabled person	naxe	נָכֶה (ז)
cripple	naxe	נָכֶה (ז)
drug addict	narkoman	נַרְקוֹמָן (ז)

deaf (adj)	xereʃ	חֵירֵשׁ
mute (adj)	ilem	אִילֵם
deaf mute (adj)	xereʃ-ilem	חֵירֵשׁ־אִילֵם

mad, insane (adj)	meʃuga	מְשׁוּגָע
madman (demented person)	meʃuga	מְשׁוּגָע (ז)
madwoman	meʃu'ga'at	מְשׁוּגַעַת (נ)
to go insane	lehiʃta'ge'a	לְהִשְׁתַּגֵּעַ

gene	gen	גֶּן (ז)
immunity	xasinut	חֲסִינוּת (נ)
hereditary (adj)	toraʃti	תּוֹרַשְׁתִּי
congenital (adj)	mulad	מוּלָד

virus	'virus	וִירוּס (ז)
microbe	xaidak	חַיְידָק (ז)
bacterium	bak'terya	בַּקְטֶרְיָה (נ)
infection	zihum	זִיהוּם (ז)

71. Symptoms. Treatments. Part 3

| hospital | beit xolim | בֵּית חוֹלִים (ז) |
| patient | metupal | מְטוּפָּל (ז) |

diagnosis	avxana	אַבְחָנָה (נ)
cure	ripui	רִיפּוּי (ז)
medical treatment	tipul refu'i	טִיפּוּל רְפוּאִי (ז)
to get treatment	lekabel tipul	לְקַבֵּל טִיפּוּל
to treat (~ a patient)	letapel be...	לְטַפֵּל בְּ...
to nurse (look after)	letapel be...	לְטַפֵּל בְּ...
care (nursing ~)	tipul	טִיפּוּל (ז)

operation, surgery	ni'tuax	נִיתוּחַ (ז)
to bandage (head, limb)	laxboʃ	לַחְבּוֹשׁ
bandaging	xaviʃa	חֲבִישָׁה (נ)

vaccination	χisun	חִיסוּן (ז)
to vaccinate (vt)	leχasen	לְחַסֵן
injection, shot	zrika	זְרִיקָה (נ)
to give an injection	lehazrik	לְהַזְרִיק
attack	hetkef	הֶתְקֵף (ז)
amputation	kti'a	קְטִיעָה (נ)
to amputate (vt)	lik'to'a	לִקְטוֹעַ
coma	tar'demet	תַרְדֶמֶת (נ)
to be in a coma	lihyot betar'demet	לִהְיוֹת בְּתַרְדֶמֶת
intensive care	tipul nimrats	טִיפּוּל נִמְרָץ (ז)
to recover (~ from flu)	lehaχlim	לְהַחְלִים
condition (patient's ~)	matsav	מַצָב (ז)
consciousness	hakara	הַכָּרָה (נ)
memory (faculty)	zikaron	זִיכָּרוֹן (ז)
to pull out (tooth)	la'akor	לַעֲקוֹר
filling	stima	סְתִימָה (נ)
to fill (a tooth)	la'asot stima	לַעֲשׂוֹת סְתִימָה
hypnosis	hip'noza	הִיפְּנוֹזָה (נ)
to hypnotize (vt)	lehapnet	לְהַפְנֵט

72. Doctors

doctor	rofe	רוֹפֵא (ז)
nurse	aχot	אָחוֹת (נ)
personal doctor	rofe iʃi	רוֹפֵא אִישִׁי (ז)
dentist	rofe ʃi'nayim	רוֹפֵא שִׁינַיִים (ז)
eye doctor	rofe ei'nayim	רוֹפֵא עֵינַיִים (ז)
internist	rofe pnimi	רוֹפֵא פְּנִימִי (ז)
surgeon	kirurg	כִּירוּרְג (ז)
psychiatrist	psiχi''ater	פְּסִיכְיָאטֶר (ז)
pediatrician	rofe yeladim	רוֹפֵא יְלָדִים (ז)
psychologist	psiχolog	פְּסִיכוֹלוֹג (ז)
gynecologist	rofe naʃim	רוֹפֵא נָשִׁים (ז)
cardiologist	kardyolog	קַרְדִיוֹלוֹג (ז)

73. Medicine. Drugs. Accessories

medicine, drug	trufa	תְרוּפָה (נ)
remedy	trufa	תְרוּפָה (נ)
to prescribe (vt)	lirʃom	לִרְשׁוֹם
prescription	mirʃam	מִרְשָׁם (ז)
tablet, pill	kadur	כַּדוּר (ז)

ointment	miʃχa	מִשְׁחָה (נ)
ampule	'ampula	אַמְפּוּלָה (נ)
mixture	ta'a'rovet	תַּעֲרוֹבֶת (נ)
syrup	sirop	סִירוֹף (ז)
pill	gluya	גְּלוּיָה (נ)
powder	avka	אַבְקָה (נ)
gauze bandage	taχ'boʃet 'gaza	תַּחְבּוֹשֶׁת גָּאזָה (נ)
cotton wool	'tsemer 'gefen	צֶמֶר גֶּפֶן (ז)
iodine	yod	יוֹד (ז)
Band-Aid	'plaster	פְּלַסְטֶר (ז)
eyedropper	taf'tefet	טַפְטֶפֶת (נ)
thermometer	madχom	מַדְחוֹם (ז)
syringe	mazrek	מַזְרֵק (ז)
wheelchair	kise galgalim	כִּיסֵא גַלְגַּלִים (ז)
crutches	ka'bayim	קַבַּיִים (ז"ר)
painkiller	meʃakeχ ke'evim	מְשַׁכֵּךְ כְּאֵבִים (ז)
laxative	trufa meʃal'ʃelet	תְּרוּפָה מְשַׁלְשֶׁלֶת (נ)
spirits (ethanol)	'kohal	כּוֹהַל (ז)
medicinal herbs	isvei marpe	עִשְׂבֵּי מַרְפֵּא (ז"ר)
herbal (~ tea)	ʃel asavim	שֶׁל עֲשָׂבִים

74. Smoking. Tobacco products

tobacco	'tabak	טַבָּק (ז)
cigarette	si'garya	סִיגַרְיָה (נ)
cigar	sigar	סִיגָר (ז)
pipe	mik'teret	מִקְטֶרֶת (נ)
pack (of cigarettes)	χafisa	חֲפִיסָה (נ)
matches	gafrurim	גַּפְרוּרִים (ז"ר)
matchbox	kufsat gafrurim	קוּפְסַת גַפְרוֹרִים (נ)
lighter	matsit	מַצִּית (ז)
ashtray	ma'afera	מַאֲפֵרָה (נ)
cigarette case	nartik lesi'garyot	נַרְתִּיק לְסִיגַרְיוֹת (ז)
cigarette holder	piya	פִּייָה (נ)
filter (cigarette tip)	'filter	פִילְטֶר (ז)
to smoke (vi, vt)	le'aʃen	לְעַשֵּׁן
to light a cigarette	lehadlik si'garya	לְהַדְלִיק סִיגַרְיָה
smoking	iʃun	עִישּׁוּן (ז)
smoker	me'aʃen	מְעַשֵּׁן (ז)
stub, butt (of cigarette)	bdal si'garya	בְּדַל סִיגַרְיָה (ז)
smoke, fumes	aʃan	עָשָׁן (ז)
ash	'efer	אֵפֶר (ז)

HUMAN HABITAT

City

75. City. Life in the city

city, town	ir	עִיר (נ)
capital city	ir bira	עִיר בִּירָה (נ)
village	kfar	כְּפָר (ז)
city map	mapat ha'ir	מַפַּת הָעִיר (נ)
downtown	merkaz ha'ir	מֶרְכַּז הָעִיר (ז)
suburb	parvar	פַּרְווָר (ז)
suburban (adj)	parvari	פַּרְווָרִי
outskirts	parvar	פַּרְווָר (ז)
environs (suburbs)	svivot	סְבִיבוֹת (נ״ר)
city block	ʃxuna	שְׁכוּנָה (נ)
residential block (area)	ʃxunat megurim	שְׁכוּנַת מְגוּרִים (נ)
traffic	tnu'a	תְנוּעָה (נ)
traffic lights	ramzor	רַמְזוֹר (ז)
public transportation	taxbura tsiburit	תַחְבּוּרָה צִיבּוּרִית (נ)
intersection	'tsomet	צוֹמֶת (ז)
crosswalk	ma'avar xatsaya	מַעֲבַר חֲצָיָה (ז)
pedestrian underpass	ma'avar tat karka'i	מַעֲבָר תַת־קַרְקָעִי (ז)
to cross (~ the street)	laxatsot	לַחֲצוֹת
pedestrian	holex 'regel	הוֹלֵך רֶגֶל (ז)
sidewalk	midraxa	מִדְרָכָה (נ)
bridge	'geʃer	גֶּשֶׁר (ז)
embankment (river walk)	ta'yelet	טַיֶּלֶת (נ)
fountain	mizraka	מִזְרָקָה (נ)
allée (garden walkway)	sdera	שְׂדֵרָה (נ)
park	park	פַּארְק (ז)
boulevard	sdera	שְׂדֵרָה (נ)
square	kikar	כִּיכָּר (נ)
avenue (wide street)	rexov raʃi	רְחוֹב רָאשִׁי (ז)
street	rexov	רְחוֹב (ז)
side street	simta	סִמְטָה (נ)
dead end	mavoi satum	מָבוֹי סָתוּם (ז)
house	'bayit	בַּיִת (ז)
building	binyan	בִּנְיָן (ז)

skyscraper	gored ʃχakim	גּוֹרֵד שְׁחָקִים (ז)
facade	χazit	חָזִית (נ)
roof	gag	גַּג (ז)
window	χalon	חַלּוֹן (ז)
arch	'keʃet	קֶשֶׁת (נ)
column	amud	עַמּוּד (ז)
corner	pina	פִּינָה (נ)
store window	χalon ra'ava	חַלּוֹן רַאֲוָה (ז)
signboard (store sign, etc.)	'ʃelet	שֶׁלֶט (ז)
poster	kraza	כְּרָזָה (נ)
advertising poster	'poster	פּוֹסטֶר (ז)
billboard	'luaχ pirsum	לוּחַ פִּרסוּם (ז)
garbage, trash	'zevel	זֶבֶל (ז)
trashcan (public ~)	paχ aʃpa	פַּח אַשׁפָּה (ז)
to litter (vi)	lelaχleχ	לְלַכלֵך
garbage dump	mizbala	מִזבָּלָה (נ)
phone booth	ta 'telefon	תָא טֶלֶפוֹן (ז)
lamppost	amud panas	עַמּוּד פָּנָס (ז)
bench (park ~)	safsal	סַפסָל (ז)
police officer	ʃoter	שׁוֹטֵר (ז)
police	miʃtara	מִשׁטָרָה (נ)
beggar	kabtsan	קַבּצָן (ז)
homeless (n)	χasar 'bayit	חֲסַר בַּיִת (ז)

76. Urban institutions

store	χanut	חֲנוּת (נ)
drugstore, pharmacy	beit mir'kaχat	בֵּית מִרקַחַת (ז)
eyeglass store	χanut miʃka'fayim	חֲנוּת מִשׁקָפַיִים (נ)
shopping mall	kanyon	קַניוֹן (ז)
supermarket	super'market	סוּפֶּרמַרקֶט (ז)
bakery	ma'afiya	מַאֲפִייָה (נ)
baker	ofe	אוֹפֶה (ז)
pastry shop	χanut mamtakim	חֲנוּת מַמתַקִים (נ)
grocery store	ma'kolet	מַכּוֹלֶת (נ)
butcher shop	itliz	אָטלִיז (ז)
produce store	χanut perot viyerakot	חֲנוּת פֵּירוֹת וִירָקוֹת (נ)
market	ʃuk	שׁוּק (ז)
coffee house	beit kafe	בֵּית קָפֶה (ז)
restaurant	mis'ada	מִסעָדָה (נ)
pub, bar	pab	פָּאבּ (ז)
pizzeria	pi'tseriya	פִּיצֶריָה (נ)
hair salon	mispara	מִספָּרָה (נ)

post office	'do'ar	דּוֹאַר (ז)
dry cleaners	nikui yavef	נִיקּוּי יָבֵשׁ (ז)
photo studio	'studyo letsilum	סטוּדְיוֹ לְצִילּוּם (ז)
shoe store	χanut na'a'layim	חֲנוּת נַעֲלַיִים (נ)
bookstore	χanut sfarim	חֲנוּת סְפָרִים (נ)
sporting goods store	χanut sport	חֲנוּת סְפּוֹרט (נ)
clothes repair shop	χanut tikun bgadim	חֲנוּת תִּיקּוּן בְּגָדִים (נ)
formal wear rental	χanut haskarat bgadim	חֲנוּת הַשׂכָּרַת בְּגָדִים (נ)
video rental store	χanut haʃalat sratim	חֲנוּת הַשׁאָלַת סְרָטִים (נ)
circus	kirkas	קִרקָס (ז)
zoo	gan hayot	גַּן חַיּוֹת (ז)
movie theater	kol'no'a	קוֹלנוֹעַ (ז)
museum	muze'on	מוּזֵיאוֹן (ז)
library	sifriya	סִפְרִייָה (נ)
theater	te'atron	תֵיאַטרוֹן (ז)
opera (opera house)	beit 'opera	בֵּית אוֹפֶּרָה (ז)
nightclub	mo'adon 'laila	מוֹעֲדוֹן לַילָה (ז)
casino	ka'zino	קָזִינוֹ (ז)
mosque	misgad	מִסגָד (ז)
synagogue	beit 'kneset	בֵּית כְּנֶסֶת (ז)
cathedral	kated'rala	קָתֶדרָלָה (נ)
temple	mikdaʃ	מִקְדָשׁ (ז)
church	knesiya	כְּנֵסִייָה (נ)
college	miχlala	מִכלָלָה (נ)
university	uni'versita	אוּנִיבֶרסִיטָה (נ)
school	beit 'sefer	בֵּית סֵפֶר (ז)
prefecture	maχoz	מָחוֹז (ז)
city hall	iriya	עִירִייָה (נ)
hotel	beit malon	בֵּית מָלוֹן (ז)
bank	bank	בַּנק (ז)
embassy	ʃagrirut	שַׁגרִירוּת (נ)
travel agency	soχnut nesi'ot	סוֹכנוּת נְסִיעוֹת (נ)
information office	modi'in	מוֹדִיעִין (ז)
currency exchange	misrad hamarat mat'be'a	מִשׂרָד הֲמָרַת מַטבֵּעַ (ז)
subway	ra'kevet taχtit	רַכֶּבֶת תַחתִּית (נ)
hospital	beit χolim	בֵּית חוֹלִים (ז)
gas station	taχanat 'delek	תַחֲנַת דֶּלֶק (נ)
parking lot	migraʃ χanaya	מִגרַש חֲנָיָה (ז)

77. Urban transportation

bus	'otobus	אוֹטוֹבּוּס (ז)
streetcar	ra'kevet kala	רַכֶּבֶת קַלָּה (נ)
trolley bus	tro'leibus	טרוֹלֵיבּוּס (ז)
route (of bus, etc.)	maslul	מַסלוּל (ז)
number (e.g., bus)	mispar	מִספָּר (ז)
to go by ...	lin'so'a be...	לִנסוֹעַ בְּ...
to get on (~ the bus)	la'alot	לַעֲלוֹת
to get off ...	la'redet mi...	לָרֶדֶת מִ...
stop (e.g., bus ~)	taxana	תַחֲנָה (נ)
next stop	hataxana haba'a	הַתַחֲנָה הַבָּאָה (נ)
terminus	hataxana ha'axrona	הַתַחֲנָה הָאַחרוֹנָה (נ)
schedule	'luax zmanim	לוּחַ זמַנִים (ז)
to wait (vt)	lehamtin	לְהַמתִין
ticket	kartis	כַּרטִיס (ז)
fare	mexir hanesiya	מְחִיר הַנְסִיעָה (ז)
cashier (ticket seller)	kupai	קוּפָּאִי (ז)
ticket inspection	bi'koret kartisim	בִּיקוֹרֶת כַּרטִיסִים (נ)
ticket inspector	mevaker	מְבַקֵר (ז)
to be late (for ...)	le'axer	לְאַחֵר
to miss (~ the train, etc.)	lefasfes	לְפַספֵס
to be in a hurry	lemaher	לְמַהֵר
taxi, cab	monit	מוֹנִית (נ)
taxi driver	nahag monit	נֶהַג מוֹנִית (ז)
by taxi	bemonit	בְּמוֹנִית
taxi stand	taxanat moniyot	תַחֲנַת מוֹנִיוֹת (נ)
to call a taxi	lehazmin monit	לְהַזמִין מוֹנִית
to take a taxi	la'kaxat monit	לָקַחַת מוֹנִית
traffic	tnu'a	תנוּעָה (נ)
traffic jam	pkak	פּקָק (ז)
rush hour	ʃa'ot 'omes	שְׁעוֹת עוֹמֶס (נ"ר)
to park (vi)	laxanot	לַחֲנוֹת
to park (vt)	lehaxnot	לְהַחנוֹת
parking lot	xanaya	חֲנָיָה (נ)
subway	ra'kevet taxtit	רַכֶּבֶת תַחתִית (נ)
station	taxana	תַחֲנָה (נ)
to take the subway	lin'so'a betaxtit	לִנסוֹעַ בְּתַחתִית
train	ra'kevet	רַכֶּבֶת (נ)
train station	taxanat ra'kevet	תַחֲנַת רַכֶּבֶת (נ)

78. Sightseeing

monument	an'darta	אַנְדַרְטָה (נ)
fortress	mivtsar	מִבְצָר (ז)
palace	armon	אַרְמוֹן (ז)
castle	tira	טִירָה (נ)
tower	migdal	מִגְדָל (ז)
mausoleum	ma'uzo'le'um	מָאוֹזוֹלִיאוֹם (ז)
architecture	adriχalut	אַדְרִיכָלוּת (נ)
medieval (adj)	benaimi	בֵּינַיְמִי
ancient (adj)	atik	עַתִיק
national (adj)	le'umi	לְאוּמִי
famous (monument, etc.)	mefursam	מְפוּרְסָם
tourist	tayar	תַיָיר (ז)
guide (person)	madriχ tiyulim	מַדְרִיךְ טִיוּלִים (ז)
excursion, sightseeing tour	tiyul	טִיוּל (ז)
to show (vt)	lehar'ot	לְהַרְאוֹת
to tell (vt)	lesaper	לְסַפֵּר
to find (vt)	limtso	לִמְצוֹא
to get lost (lose one's way)	la'leχet le'ibud	לָלֶכֶת לְאִיבּוּד
map (e.g., subway ~)	mapa	מַפָּה (נ)
map (e.g., city ~)	tarʃim	תַרְשִׁים (ז)
souvenir, gift	maz'keret	מַזְכֶּרֶת (נ)
gift shop	χanut matanot	חֲנוּת מַתָנוֹת (נ)
to take pictures	letsalem	לְצַלֵם
to have one's picture taken	lehitstalem	לְהִצְטַלֵם

79. Shopping

to buy (purchase)	liknot	לִקְנוֹת
purchase	kniya	קְנִיָה (נ)
to go shopping	la'leχet lekniyot	לָלֶכֶת לִקְנִיוֹת
shopping	ariχat kniyot	עֲרִיכַת קְנִיוֹת (נ)
to be open (ab. store)	pa'tuaχ	פָּתוּחַ
to be closed	sagur	סָגוּר
footwear, shoes	na'a'layim	נַעֲלַיִים (נ"ר)
clothes, clothing	bgadim	בְּגָדִים (ז"ר)
cosmetics	tamrukim	תַמְרוּקִים (ז"ר)
food products	mutsrei mazon	מוּצְרֵי מָזוֹן (ז"ר)
gift, present	matana	מַתָנָה (נ)
salesman	moχer	מוֹכֵר (ז)
saleswoman	mo'χeret	מוֹכֶרֶת (נ)

check out, cash desk	kupa	קוּפָּה (נ)
mirror	mar'a	מַרְאָה (נ)
counter (store ~)	duχan	דּוּכָן (ז)
fitting room	'χeder halbaʃa	חֶדֶר הַלְבָּשָה (ז)

to try on	limdod	לִמְדוֹד
to fit (ab. dress, etc.)	lehat'im	לְהַתְאִים
to like (I like ...)	limtso χen be'ei'nayim	לִמְצוֹא חֵן בְּעֵינַיִים

price	meχir	מְחִיר (ז)
price tag	tag meχir	תַג מְחִיר (ז)
to cost (vt)	la'alot	לַעֲלוֹת
How much?	'kama?	כַּמָה?
discount	hanaχa	הֲנָחָה (נ)

inexpensive (adj)	lo yakar	לֹא יָקָר
cheap (adj)	zol	זוֹל
expensive (adj)	yakar	יָקָר
It's expensive	ze yakar	זֶה יָקָר

rental (n)	haskara	הַשְׂכָּרָה (נ)
to rent (~ a tuxedo)	liskor	לִשְׂכּוֹר
credit (trade credit)	aʃrai	אַשְרַאי (ז)
on credit (adv)	be'aʃrai	בְּאַשְרַאי

80. Money

money	'kesef	כֶּסֶף (ז)
currency exchange	hamara	הֲמָרָה (נ)
exchange rate	'ʃa'ar χalifin	שַעַר חֲלִיפִין (ז)
ATM	kaspomat	כַּספּוֹמָט (ז)
coin	mat'be'a	מַטבֵּעַ (ז)

dollar	'dolar	דוֹלָר (ז)
euro	'eiro	אֵירוֹ (ז)

lira	'lira	לִירָה (נ)
Deutschmark	mark germani	מַרק גֶרמָנִי (ז)
franc	frank	פרַנק (ז)
pound sterling	'lira 'sterling	לִירָה שטֶרלִינג (נ)
yen	yen	יֶן (ז)

debt	χov	חוֹב (ז)
debtor	'ba'al χov	בַּעַל חוֹב (ז)
to lend (money)	lehalvot	לְהַלווֹת
to borrow (vi, vt)	lilvot	לִלווֹת

bank	bank	בַּנק (ז)
account	χeʃbon	חֶשבּוֹן (ז)
to deposit (vt)	lehafkid	לְהַפקִיד

to deposit into the account	lehafkid lexeʃbon	לְהַפְקִיד לְחֶשׁבּוֹן
to withdraw (vt)	limʃox mexeʃbon	לִמְשׁוֹךְ מֵחֶשׁבּוֹן
credit card	kartis aʃrai	כַּרְטִיס אַשׁרַאי (ז)
cash	mezuman	מְזוּמָן
check	tʃek	צֵ'ק (ז)
to write a check	lixtov tʃek	לִכְתּוֹב צֵ'ק
checkbook	pinkas 'tʃekim	פִּנקָס צֵ'קִים (ז)
wallet	arnak	אַרנָק (ז)
change purse	arnak lematbe''ot	אַרנָק לְמַטבְּעוֹת (ז)
safe	ka'sefet	כַּסֶפֶת (נ)
heir	yoreʃ	יוֹרֵשׁ (ז)
inheritance	yeruʃa	יְרוּשָׁה (נ)
fortune (wealth)	'oʃer	עוֹשֶׁר (ז)
lease	xoze sxirut	חוֹזֶה שׂכִירוּת (ז)
rent (money)	sxar dira	שׂכַר דִּירָה (ז)
to rent (sth from sb)	liskor	לִשׂכּוֹר
price	mexir	מְחִיר (ז)
cost	alut	עֲלוּת (נ)
sum	sxum	סכוּם (ז)
to spend (vt)	lehotsi	לְהוֹצִיא
expenses	hotsa'ot	הוֹצָאוֹת (נ"ר)
to economize (vi, vt)	laxasox	לַחֲסוֹךְ
economical	xesxoni	חֶסכוֹנִי
to pay (vi, vt)	leʃalem	לְשַׁלֵם
payment	taʃlum	תַּשׁלוּם (ז)
change (give the ~)	'odef	עוֹדֶף (ז)
tax	mas	מַס (ז)
fine	knas	קנָס (ז)
to fine (vt)	liknos	לִקנוֹס

81. Post. Postal service

post office	'do'ar	דּוֹאַר (ז)
mail (letters, etc.)	'do'ar	דּוֹאַר (ז)
mailman	davar	דַּוָּר (ז)
opening hours	ʃa'ot avoda	שְׁעוֹת עֲבוֹדָה (נ"ר)
letter	mixtav	מִכְתָּב (ז)
registered letter	mixtav raʃum	מִכְתָּב רָשׁוּם (ז)
postcard	gluya	גלוּיָה (נ)
telegram	mivrak	מִברָק (ז)
package (parcel)	xavila	חֲבִילָה (נ)

money transfer	ha'avarat ksafim	הַעֲבָרַת כְּסָפִים (נ)
to receive (vt)	lekabel	לְקַבֵּל
to send (vt)	liʃloaχ	לִשְׁלוֹחַ
sending	ʃliχa	שְׁלִיחָה (נ)
address	'ktovet	כְּתוֹבֶת (נ)
ZIP code	mikud	מִיקוּד (ז)
sender	ʃo'leaχ	שׁוֹלֵחַ (ז)
receiver	nim'an	נִמְעָן (ז)
name (first name)	ʃem prati	שֵׁם פְּרָטִי (ז)
surname (last name)	ʃem miʃpaχa	שֵׁם מִשְׁפָּחָה (ז)
postage rate	ta'arif	תַּעֲרִיף (ז)
standard (adj)	ragil	רָגִיל
economical (adj)	χesχoni	חֶסְכוֹנִי
weight	miʃkal	מִשְׁקָל (ז)
to weigh (~ letters)	liʃkol	לִשְׁקוֹל
envelope	ma'atafa	מַעֲטָפָה (נ)
postage stamp	bul 'do'ar	בּוּל דּוֹאַר (ז)
to stamp an envelope	lehadbik bul	לְהַדְבִּיק בּוּל

Dwelling. House. Home

82. House. Dwelling

house	'bayit	בַּיִת (ז)
at home (adv)	ba'bayit	בַּבַּיִת
yard	xatser	חָצֵר (נ)
fence (iron ~)	gader	גָּדֵר (נ)
brick (n)	levena	לְבֵנָה (נ)
brick (as adj)	milevenim	מִלְבֵנִים
stone (n)	'even	אֶבֶן (נ)
stone (as adj)	me''even	מֵאֶבֶן
concrete (n)	beton	בֶּטוֹן (ז)
concrete (as adj)	mibeton	מִבֶּטוֹן
new (new-built)	xadaʃ	חָדָשׁ
old (adj)	jaʃan	יָשָׁן
decrepit (house)	balui	בָּלוּי
modern (adj)	mo'derni	מוֹדֶרְנִי
multistory (adj)	rav komot	רַב־קוֹמוֹת
tall (~ building)	ga'voha	גָּבוֹהַּ
floor, story	'koma	קוֹמָה (נ)
single-story (adj)	xad komati	חַד־קוֹמָתִי
1st floor	komat 'karka	קוֹמַת קַרְקַע (נ)
top floor	hakoma ha'elyona	הַקּוֹמָה הָעֶלְיוֹנָה (נ)
roof	gag	גַּג (ז)
chimney	aruba	אֲרוּבָּה (נ)
roof tiles	'ra'af	רַעַף (ז)
tiled (adj)	mere'afim	מֵרְעָפִים
attic (storage place)	aliyat gag	עֲלִיַּת גַּג (נ)
window	xalon	חַלּוֹן (ז)
glass	zxuxit	זְכוּכִית (נ)
window ledge	'eden xalon	אֶדֶן חַלּוֹן (ז)
shutters	trisim	תְּרִיסִים (ז"ר)
wall	kir	קִיר (ז)
balcony	mir'peset	מִרְפֶּסֶת (נ)
downspout	marzev	מַרְזֵב (ז)
upstairs (to be ~)	le'mala	לְמַעְלָה
to go upstairs	la'alot bemadregot	לַעֲלוֹת בְּמַדְרֵגוֹת
to come down (the stairs)	la'redet bemadregot	לָרֶדֶת בְּמַדְרֵגוֹת
to move (to new premises)	la'avor	לַעֲבוֹר

83. House. Entrance. Lift

entrance	knisa	כְּנִיסָה (נ)
stairs (stairway)	madregot	מַדְרֵגוֹת (נ״ר)
steps	madregot	מַדְרֵגוֹת (נ״ר)
banister	ma'ake	מַעֲקֶה (ז)
lobby (hotel ~)	lobi	לוֹבִּי (ז)
mailbox	teivat 'do'ar	תֵּיבַת דּוֹאַר (נ)
garbage can	pax 'zevel	פַּח זֶבֶל (ז)
trash chute	merik aʃpa	מְרִיק אַשְׁפָּה (ז)
elevator	ma'alit	מַעֲלִית (נ)
freight elevator	ma'alit masa	מַעֲלִית מַשָּׂא (נ)
elevator cage	ta ma'alit	תָּא מַעֲלִית (ז)
to take the elevator	lin'so'a bema'alit	לִנְסוֹעַ בְּמַעֲלִית
apartment	dira	דִּירָה (נ)
residents (~ of a building)	dayarim	דַּיָּרִים (ז״ר)
neighbor (masc.)	ʃaxen	שָׁכֵן (ז)
neighbor (fem.)	ʃxena	שְׁכֵנָה (נ)
neighbors	ʃxenim	שְׁכֵנִים (ז״ר)

84. House. Doors. Locks

door	'delet	דֶּלֶת (נ)
gate (vehicle ~)	'ʃa'ar	שַׁעַר (ז)
handle, doorknob	yadit	יָדִית (נ)
to unlock (unbolt)	lif'toax	לִפְתּוֹחַ
to open (vt)	lif'toax	לִפְתּוֹחַ
to close (vt)	lisgor	לִסְגּוֹר
key	maf'teax	מַפְתֵּחַ (ז)
bunch (of keys)	tsror maftexot	צְרוֹר מַפְתְּחוֹת (ז)
to creak (door, etc.)	laxarok	לַחֲרוֹק
creak	xarika	חֲרִיקָה (נ)
hinge (door ~)	tsir	צִיר (ז)
doormat	ʃtixon	שְׁטִיחוֹן (ז)
door lock	man'ul	מַנְעוּל (ז)
keyhole	xor haman'ul	חוֹר הַמַּנְעוּל (ז)
crossbar (sliding bar)	'briax	בְּרִיחַ (ז)
door latch	'briax	בְּרִיחַ (ז)
padlock	man'ul	מַנְעוּל (ז)
to ring (~ the door bell)	letsaltsel	לְצַלְצֵל
ringing (sound)	tsiltsul	צִלְצוּל (ז)
doorbell	pa'amon	פַּעֲמוֹן (ז)
doorbell button	kaftor	כַּפְתּוֹר (ז)

knock (at the door)	hakaʃa	הַקָשָׁה (נ)
to knock (vi)	lehakiʃ	לְהַקִישׁ
code	kod	קוֹד (ז)
combination lock	man'ul kod	מַנְעוּל קוֹד (ז)
intercom	'interkom	אִינְטֶרְקוֹם (ז)
number (on the door)	mispar	מִסְפָּר (ז)
doorplate	luχit	לוּחִית (נ)
peephole	einit	עֵינִית (נ)

85. Country house

village	kfar	כְּפָר (ז)
vegetable garden	gan yarak	גַן יָרָק (ז)
fence	gader	גָדֵר (נ)
picket fence	gader yetedot	גָדֵר יְתֵדוֹת (נ)
wicket gate	piʃpaʃ	פִּשְׁפָּשׁ (ז)
granary	asam	אָסָם (ז)
root cellar	martef	מַרְתֵּף (ז)
shed (garden ~)	maχsan	מַחְסָן (ז)
well (water)	be'er	בְּאֵר (נ)
stove (wood-fired ~)	aχ	אָח (נ)
to stoke the stove	lehasik et ha'aχ	לְהַסִיק אֶת הָאָח
firewood	atsei hasaka	עֲצֵי הַסָקָה (ז״ר)
log (firewood)	bul ets	בּוּל עֵץ (ז)
veranda	mir'peset mekora	מִרְפֶּסֶת מְקוֹרָה (נ)
deck (terrace)	mir'peset	מִרְפֶּסֶת (נ)
stoop (front steps)	madregot ba'petaχ 'bayit	מַדְרֵגוֹת בַּפֶּתַח בַּיִת (נ״ר)
swing (hanging seat)	nadneda	נַדְנֵדָה (נ)

86. Castle. Palace

castle	tira	טִירָה (נ)
palace	armon	אַרְמוֹן (ז)
fortress	mivtsar	מִבְצָר (ז)
wall (round castle)	χoma	חוֹמָה (נ)
tower	migdal	מִגְדָל (ז)
keep, donjon	migdal merkazi	מִגְדָל מֶרְכָּזִי (ז)
portcullis	ʃa'ar anaχi	שַׁעַר אֲנָכִי (ז)
underground passage	ma'avar tat karka'i	מַעֲבָר תַּת־קַרְקָעִי (ז)
moat	χafir	חָפִיר (ז)
chain	ʃal'ʃelet	שַׁלְשֶׁלֶת (נ)
arrow loop	eʃnav 'yeri	אֶשְׁנַב יֶרִי (ז)

magnificent (adj)	mefo'ar	מְפֹאָר
majestic (adj)	malxuti	מַלְכוּתִי
impregnable (adj)	'bilti xadir	בִּלְתִּי חָדִיר
medieval (adj)	benaimi	בֵּינַיְמִי

87. Apartment

apartment	dira	דִּירָה (נ)
room	'xeder	חֶדֶר (ז)
bedroom	xadar ʃena	חֲדַר שֵׁינָה (ז)
dining room	pinat 'oxel	פִּנַת אֹכֶל (נ)
living room	salon	סָלוֹן (ז)
study (home office)	xadar avoda	חֲדַר עֲבוֹדָה (ז)
entry room	prozdor	פְּרוֹזְדוֹר (ז)
bathroom (room with a bath or shower)	xadar am'batya	חֲדַר אַמְבַּטְיָה (ז)
half bath	ʃerutim	שֵׁירוּתִים (ז״ר)
ceiling	tikra	תִּקְרָה (נ)
floor	ritspa	רִצְפָּה (נ)
corner	pina	פִּינָה (נ)

88. Apartment. Cleaning

to clean (vi, vt)	lenakot	לְנַקּוֹת
to put away (to stow)	lefanot	לְפַנּוֹת
dust	avak	אָבָק (ז)
dusty (adj)	me'ubak	מְאוּבָּק
to dust (vt)	lenakot avak	לְנַקּוֹת אָבָק
vacuum cleaner	ʃo'ev avak	שׁוֹאֵב אָבָק (ז)
to vacuum (vt)	liʃov avak	לִשְׁאוֹב אָבָק
to sweep (vi, vt)	letate	לְטַאטֵא
sweepings	'psolet ti'tu	פְּסֹלֶת טְאטוּא (נ)
order	'seder	סֶדֶר (ז)
disorder, mess	i 'seder	אִי סֶדֶר (ז)
mop	magev im smartut	מַגָּב עִם סְמַרְטוּט (ז)
dust cloth	smartut avak	סְמַרְטוּט אָבָק (ז)
short broom	mat'ate katan	מַטְאֲטֵא קָטָן (ז)
dustpan	ya'e	יָעֶה (ז)

89. Furniture. Interior

| furniture | rehitim | רָהִיטִים (ז״ר) |
| table | ʃulxan | שׁוּלְחָן (ז) |

chair	kise	כִּסֵא (ז)
bed	mita	מִיטָה (נ)
couch, sofa	sapa	סַפָּה (נ)
armchair	kursa	כּוּרסָה (נ)
bookcase	aron sfarim	אֲרוֹן סְפָרִים (ז)
shelf	madaf	מַדָף (ז)
wardrobe	aron bgadim	אֲרוֹן בְּגָדִים (ז)
coat rack (wall-mounted ~)	mitle	מִתלֶה (ז)
coat stand	mitle	מִתלֶה (ז)
bureau, dresser	ʃida	שִׁידָה (נ)
coffee table	ʃulχan itonim	שׁוּלחָן עִיתוֹנִים (ז)
mirror	mar'a	מַראָה (נ)
carpet	ʃa'tiaχ	שָׁטִיחַ (ז)
rug, small carpet	ʃa'tiaχ	שָׁטִיחַ (ז)
fireplace	aχ	אָח (נ)
candle	ner	נֵר (ז)
candlestick	pamot	פָּמוֹט (ז)
drapes	vilonot	וִילוֹנוֹת (ז״ר)
wallpaper	tapet	טַפֶּט (ז)
blinds (jalousie)	trisim	תרִיסִים (ז״ר)
table lamp	menorat ʃulχan	מְנוֹרַת שׁוּלחָן (נ)
wall lamp (sconce)	menorat kir	מְנוֹרַת קִיר (נ)
floor lamp	menora o'medet	מְנוֹרָה עוֹמֶדֶת (נ)
chandelier	niv'reʃet	נִברֶשֶׁת (נ)
leg (of chair, table)	'regel	רֶגֶל (נ)
armrest	miʃ'enet yad	מִשׁעֶנֶת יָד (נ)
back (backrest)	miʃ'enet	מִשׁעֶנֶת (נ)
drawer	megera	מְגֵירָה (נ)

90. Bedding

bedclothes	matsa'im	מַצָעִים (ז״ר)
pillow	karit	כָּרִית (נ)
pillowcase	tsipit	צִיפִּית (נ)
duvet, comforter	smiχa	שׂמִיכָה (נ)
sheet	sadin	סָדִין (ז)
bedspread	kisui mita	כִּיסוּי מִיטָה (ז)

91. Kitchen

kitchen	mitbaχ	מִטבָּח (ז)
gas	gaz	גָז (ז)

gas stove (range)	tanur gaz	תַּנּוּר גָּז (ז)
electric stove	tanur χaʃmali	תַּנּוּר חַשְׁמַלִּי (ז)
oven	tanur afiya	תַּנּוּר אֲפִיָּה (ז)
microwave oven	mikrogal	מִיקְרוֹגַל (ז)

refrigerator	mekarer	מְקָרֵר (ז)
freezer	makpi	מַקְפִּיא (ז)
dishwasher	mo'diaχ kelim	מֵדִיחַ כֵּלִים (ז)

meat grinder	matχenat basar	מַטְחֵנַת בָּשָׂר (נ)
juicer	masχeta	מַסְחֵטָה (נ)
toaster	'toster	טוֹסְטֶר (ז)
mixer	'mikser	מִיקְסֶר (ז)

coffee machine	meχonat kafe	מְכוֹנַת קָפֶה (נ)
coffee pot	findʒan	פִינְגָ'אן (ז)
coffee grinder	matχenat kafe	מַטְחֵנַת קָפֶה (נ)

kettle	kumkum	קוּמְקוּם (ז)
teapot	kumkum	קוּמְקוּם (ז)
lid	miχse	מִכְסֶה (ז)
tea strainer	mis'nenet te	מְסַנֶּנֶת תֵה (נ)

spoon	kaf	כַּף (נ)
teaspoon	kapit	כַּפִּית (נ)
soup spoon	kaf	כַּף (נ)
fork	mazleg	מַזְלֵג (ז)
knife	sakin	סַכִּין (ז, נ)

tableware (dishes)	kelim	כֵּלִים (ז"ר)
plate (dinner ~)	tsa'laχat	צַלַּחַת (נ)
saucer	taχtit	תַּחְתִּית (נ)

shot glass	kosit	כּוֹסִית (נ)
glass (tumbler)	kos	כּוֹס (נ)
cup	'sefel	סֵפֶל (ז)

sugar bowl	mis'keret	מִסְכֶּרֶת (נ)
salt shaker	milχiya	מִלְחִיָּה (נ)
pepper shaker	pilpeliya	פִּלְפְּלִיָּה (נ)
butter dish	maχame'a	מַחֲמָאָה (ז)

| stock pot (soup pot) | sir | סִיר (ז) |
| frying pan (skillet) | maχvat | מַחֲבַת (נ) |

ladle	tarvad	תַּרְוָד (ז)
colander	mis'nenet	מְסַנֶּנֶת (נ)
tray (serving ~)	magaʃ	מַגָּשׁ (ז)

bottle	bakbuk	בַּקְבּוּק (ז)
jar (glass)	tsin'tsenet	צִנְצֶנֶת (נ)
can	paχit	פַּחִית (נ)

bottle opener	potχan bakbukim	פּוֹתְחָן בַּקְבּוּקִים (ז)
can opener	potχan kufsa'ot	פּוֹתְחָן קוּפְסָאוֹת (ז)
corkscrew	maχlets	מַחְלֵץ (ז)
filter	'filter	פִילְטֶר (ז)
to filter (vt)	lesanen	לְסַנֵן
trash, garbage (food waste, etc.)	'zevel	זֶבֶל (ז)
trash can (kitchen ~)	paχ 'zevel	פַּח זֶבֶל (ז)

92. Bathroom

bathroom	χadar am'batya	חֲדַר אַמְבַּטְיָה (ז)
water	'mayim	מַיִם (ז"ר)
faucet	'berez	בֶּרֶז (ז)
hot water	'mayim χamim	מַיִם חָמִים (ז"ר)
cold water	'mayim karim	מַיִם קָרִים (ז"ר)
toothpaste	miʃχat ʃi'nayim	מִשְׁחַת שִׁינַיִים (נ)
to brush one's teeth	letsaχ'tseaχ ʃi'nayim	לְצַחְצֵחַ שִׁינַיִים
toothbrush	miv'reʃet ʃi'nayim	מִבְרֶשֶׁת שִׁינַיִים (נ)
to shave (vi)	lehitga'leaχ	לְהִתְגַלֵחַ
shaving foam	'ketsef gi'luaχ	קֶצֶף גִילוּחַ (ז)
razor	'ta'ar	תַעַר (ז)
to wash (one's hands, etc.)	liʃtof	לִשְׁטוֹף
to take a bath	lehitraχets	לְהִתְרַחֵץ
shower	mik'laχat	מִקְלַחַת (נ)
to take a shower	lehitka'leaχ	לְהִתְקַלֵחַ
bathtub	am'batya	אַמְבַּטְיָה (נ)
toilet (toilet bowl)	asla	אַסְלָה (נ)
sink (washbasin)	kiyor	כִּיוֹר (ז)
soap	sabon	סַבּוֹן (ז)
soap dish	saboniya	סַבּוֹנִיָה (נ)
sponge	sfog 'lifa	סְפוֹג לִיפָה (ז)
shampoo	ʃampu	שַׁמְפּוּ (ז)
towel	ma'gevet	מַגֶבֶת (נ)
bathrobe	χaluk raχatsa	חָלוּק רַחְצָה (ז)
laundry (process)	kvisa	כְּבִיסָה (נ)
washing machine	meχonat kvisa	מְכוֹנַת כְּבִיסָה (נ)
to do the laundry	leχabes	לְכַבֵּס
laundry detergent	avkat kvisa	אַבְקַת כְּבִיסָה (נ)

93. Household appliances

TV set	tele'vizya	טֶלֶוִיזְיָה (נ)
tape recorder	teip	טֵייפּ (ז)
VCR (video recorder)	maxʃir 'vide'o	מַכְשִׁיר וִידֵאוֹ (ז)
radio	'radyo	רַדְיוֹ (ז)
player (CD, MP3, etc.)	nagan	נַגָּן (ז)
video projector	makren	מַקְרֵן (ז)
home movie theater	kol'no'a beiti	קוֹלְנוֹעַ בֵּיתִי (ז)
DVD player	nagan dividi	נַגָּן DVD (ז)
amplifier	magber	מַגְבֵּר (ז)
video game console	maxʃir plei'steiʃen	מַכְשִׁיר פְּלֵייסְטֵיישֶׁן (ז)
video camera	matslemat 'vide'o	מַצְלֵמַת וִידֵאוֹ (נ)
camera (photo)	matslema	מַצְלֵמָה (נ)
digital camera	matslema digi'talit	מַצְלֵמָה דִיגִיטָלִית (נ)
vacuum cleaner	ʃo'ev avak	שׁוֹאֵב אָבָק (ז)
iron (e.g., steam ~)	maghets	מַגְהֵץ (ז)
ironing board	'kereʃ gihuts	קֶרֶשׁ גִּיהוּץ (ז)
telephone	'telefon	טֶלֶפוֹן (ז)
cell phone	'telefon nayad	טֶלֶפוֹן נַיָּד (ז)
typewriter	mexonat ktiva	מְכוֹנַת כְּתִיבָה (נ)
sewing machine	mexonat tfira	מְכוֹנַת תְּפִירָה (נ)
microphone	mikrofon	מִיקְרוֹפוֹן (ז)
headphones	ozniyot	אוֹזְנִיּוֹת (נ"ר)
remote control (TV)	'ʃelet	שֶׁלֶט (ז)
CD, compact disc	taklitor	תַּקְלִיטוֹר (ז)
cassette, tape	ka'letet	קַלֶטֶת (נ)
vinyl record	taklit	תַּקְלִיט (ז)

94. Repairs. Renovation

renovations	ʃiputs	שִׁיפּוּץ (ז)
to renovate (vt)	leʃapets	לְשַׁפֵּץ
to repair, to fix (vt)	letaken	לְתַקֵּן
to put in order	lesader	לְסַדֵּר
to redo (do again)	la'asot mexadaʃ	לַעֲשׂוֹת מֵחָדָשׁ
paint	'tseva	צֶבַע (ז)
to paint (~ a wall)	lits'bo'a	לִצְבּוֹעַ
house painter	tsaba'i	צַבָּעִי (ז)
paintbrush	mikxol	מִכְחוֹל (ז)
whitewash	sid	סִיד (ז)
to whitewash (vt)	lesayed	לְסַיֵּד

wallpaper	tapet	טַפֶּט (ז)
to wallpaper (vt)	lehadbik ta'petim	לְהַדְבִּיק טַפֶּטִים
varnish	'laka	לַכָּה (נ)
to varnish (vt)	lim'roax 'laka	לִמְרוֹחַ לַכָּה

95. Plumbing

water	'mayim	מַיִם (נ״ר)
hot water	'mayim xamim	מַיִם חָמִים (נ״ר)
cold water	'mayim karim	מַיִם קָרִים (נ״ר)
faucet	'berez	בֶּרֶז (ז)

drop (of water)	tipa	טִיפָּה (נ)
to drip (vi)	letaftef	לְטַפְטֵף
to leak (ab. pipe)	lidlof	לִדְלוֹף
leak (pipe ~)	dlifa	דְּלִיפָה (נ)
puddle	ʃlulit	שְׁלוּלִית (נ)

pipe	tsinor	צִינוֹר (ז)
valve (e.g., ball ~)	'berez	בֶּרֶז (ז)
to be clogged up	lehisatem	לְהִיסָתֵם

tools	klei avoda	כְּלֵי עֲבוֹדָה (ז״ר)
adjustable wrench	maf'teax mitkavnen	מַפְתֵּחַ מִתְכַּוֵּנֵן (ז)
to unscrew (lid, filter, etc.)	lif'toax	לִפְתּוֹחַ
to screw (tighten)	lehavrig	לְהַבְרִיג

to unclog (vt)	lif'toax et hastima	לִפְתּוֹחַ אֶת הַסְּתִימָה
plumber	ʃravrav	שְׁרַבְרָב (ז)
basement	martef	מַרְתֵּף (ז)
sewerage (system)	biyuv	בִּיּוּב (ז)

96. Fire. Conflagration

fire (accident)	srefa	שְׂרֵיפָה (נ)
flame	lehava	לֶהָבָה (נ)
spark	nitsots	נִיצוֹץ (ז)
smoke (from fire)	aʃan	עָשָׁן (ז)
torch (flaming stick)	lapid	לַפִּיד (ז)
campfire	medura	מְדוּרָה (נ)

gas, gasoline	'delek	דֶּלֶק (ז)
kerosene (type of fuel)	kerosin	קֵרוֹסִין (ז)
flammable (adj)	dalik	דָּלִיק
explosive (adj)	nafits	נָפִיץ
NO SMOKING	asur le'aʃen!	אָסוּר לְעַשֵׁן!
safety	betixut	בְּטִיחוּת (נ)
danger	sakana	סַכָּנָה (נ)

dangerous (adj)	mesukan	מְסוּכָּן
to catch fire	lehidalek	לְהִידָלֵק
explosion	pitsuts	פִּיצוּץ (ז)
to set fire	lehatsit	לְהַצִּית
arsonist	matsit	מַצִּית (ז)
arson	hatsata	הַצָּתָה (נ)
to blaze (vi)	livʾor	לִבְעוֹר
to burn (be on fire)	laʾalot beʾeʃ	לַעֲלוֹת בְּאֵש
to burn down	lehisaref	לְהִישָׂרֵף
to call the fire department	lehazmin meχabei eʃ	לְהַזְמִין מְכַבֵּי אֵש
firefighter, fireman	kabai	כַּבַּאי (ז)
fire truck	'reχev kibui	רֶכֶב כִּיבּוּי (ז)
fire department	meχabei eʃ	מְכַבֵּי אֵש (ז"ר)
fire truck ladder	sulam kaba'im	סוּלָם כַּבָּאִים (ז)
fire hose	zarnuk	זַרְנוּק (ז)
fire extinguisher	mataf	מַטָף (ז)
helmet	kasda	קַסְדָה (נ)
siren	tsofar	צוֹפָר (ז)
to cry (for help)	lits'ok	לִצְעוֹק
to call for help	likro le'ezra	לִקְרוֹא לְעֶזְרָה
rescuer	matsil	מַצִּיל (ז)
to rescue (vt)	lehatsil	לְהַצִּיל
to arrive (vi)	leha'gi'a	לְהַגִּיעַ
to extinguish (vt)	leχabot	לְכַבּוֹת
water	'mayim	מַיִם (ז"ר)
sand	χol	חוֹל (ז)
ruins (destruction)	χoravot	חוֹרְבוֹת (נ"ר)
to collapse (building, etc.)	likros	לִקְרוֹס
to fall down (vi)	likros	לִקְרוֹס
to cave in (ceiling, floor)	lehitmotet	לְהִתְמוֹטֵט
piece of debris	pisat χoravot	פִּיסַת חוֹרְבוֹת (נ)
ash	'efer	אֵפֶר (ז)
to suffocate (die)	lehiχanek	לְהֵיחָנֵק
to be killed (perish)	lehihareg	לְהֵיהָרֵג

HUMAN ACTIVITIES

Job. Business. Part 1

97. Banking

bank	bank	בַּנק (ז)
branch (of bank, etc.)	snif	סָנִיף (ז)
bank clerk, consultant	yo'ets	יוֹעֵץ (ז)
manager (director)	menahel	מְנַהֵל (ז)
bank account	xeʃbon	חֶשׁבּוֹן (ז)
account number	mispar xeʃbon	מִספַּר חֶשׁבּוֹן (ז)
checking account	xeʃbon over vaʃav	חֶשׁבּוֹן עוֹבֵר וָשָׁב (ז)
savings account	xeʃbon xisaxon	חֶשׁבּוֹן חִסָכוֹן (ז)
to open an account	lif'toax xeʃbon	לִפתוֹחַ חֶשׁבּוֹן
to close the account	lisgor xeʃbon	לִסגוֹר חֶשׁבּוֹן
to deposit into the account	lehafkid lexeʃbon	לְהַפקִיד לְחֶשׁבּוֹן
to withdraw (vt)	limʃox mexeʃbon	לִמשוֹך מֵחֶשׁבּוֹן
deposit	pikadon	פִּיקָדוֹן (ז)
to make a deposit	lehafkid	לְהַפקִיד
wire transfer	ha'avara banka'it	הַעֲבָרָה בַּנקָאִית (נ)
to wire, to transfer	leha'avir 'kesef	לְהַעֲבִיר כֶּסֶף
sum	sxum	סכוּם (ז)
How much?	'kama?	כַּמָה?
signature	xatima	חֲתִימָה (נ)
to sign (vt)	laxtom	לַחתוֹם
credit card	kartis aʃrai	כַּרטִיס אַשׁרַאי (ז)
code (PIN code)	kod	קוֹד (ז)
credit card number	mispar kartis aʃrai	מִספַּר כַּרטִיס אַשׁרַאי (ז)
ATM	kaspomat	כַּספּוֹמָט (ז)
check	tʃek	צֵ'ק (ז)
to write a check	lixtov tʃek	לִכתוֹב צֵ'ק
checkbook	pinkas 'tʃekim	פִּנקַס צֵ'קִים (ז)
loan (bank ~)	halva'a	הַלוָואָה (נ)
to apply for a loan	levakeʃ halva'a	לְבַקֵשׁ הַלוָואָה
to get a loan	lekabel halva'a	לְקַבֵּל הַלוָואָה

| to give a loan | lehalvot | לְהַלְוֹוֹת |
| guarantee | arvut | עַרְבוּת (נ) |

98. Telephone. Phone conversation

telephone	'telefon	טֶלֶפוֹן (ז)
cell phone	'telefon nayad	טֶלֶפוֹן נַיָּיד (ז)
answering machine	meʃivon	מְשִׁיבוֹן (ז)

| to call (by phone) | letsaltsel | לְצַלְצֵל |
| phone call | siχat 'telefon | שִׂיחַת טֶלֶפוֹן (נ) |

to dial a number	leχayeg mispar	לְחַיֵּיג מִסְפָּר
Hello!	'halo!	הָלוֹ!
to ask (vt)	liʃol	לִשְׁאוֹל
to answer (vi, vt)	la'anot	לַעֲנוֹת

to hear (vt)	liʃmo'a	לִשְׁמוֹעַ
well (adv)	tov	טוֹב
not well (adv)	lo tov	לֹא טוֹב
noises (interference)	hafra'ot	הַפְרָעוֹת (נ"ר)

receiver	ʃfo'feret	שְׁפוֹפֶרֶת (נ)
to pick up (~ the phone)	leharim ʃfo'feret	לְהָרִים שְׁפוֹפֶרֶת
to hang up (~ the phone)	leha'niaχ ʃfo'feret	לְהָנִיחַ שְׁפוֹפֶרֶת

busy (engaged)	tafus	תָּפוּס
to ring (ab. phone)	letsaltsel	לְצַלְצֵל
telephone book	'sefer tele'fonim	סֵפֶר טֶלֶפוֹנִים (ז)

local (adj)	mekomi	מְקוֹמִי
local call	siχa mekomit	שִׂיחָה מְקוֹמִית (נ)
long distance (~ call)	bein ironi	בֵּין עִירוֹנִי
long-distance call	siχa bein ironit	שִׂיחָה בֵּין עִירוֹנִית (נ)
international (adj)	benle'umi	בֵּינְלְאוּמִי
international call	siχa benle'umit	שִׂיחָה בֵּינְלְאוּמִית (נ)

99. Cell phone

cell phone	'telefon nayad	טֶלֶפוֹן נַיָּיד (ז)
display	masaχ	מָסָךְ (ז)
button	kaftor	כַּפְתּוֹר (ז)
SIM card	kartis sim	כַּרְטִיס סִים (ז)

battery	solela	סוֹלְלָה (נ)
to be dead (battery)	lehitroken	לְהִתְרוֹקֵן
charger	mit'an	מִטְעָן (ז)
menu	tafrit	תַּפְרִיט (ז)

settings	hagdarot	הַגְדָרוֹת (נ״ר)
tune (melody)	mangina	מַנְגִּינָה (נ)
to select (vt)	livχor	לִבְחוֹר
calculator	maxʃevon	מַחְשְׁבוֹן (ז)
voice mail	ta koli	תָּא קוֹלִי (ז)
alarm clock	ʃaʿon meʿorer	שְׁעוֹן מְעוֹרֵר (ז)
contacts	anʃei 'keʃer	אַנְשֵׁי קֶשֶׁר (ז״ר)
SMS (text message)	misron	מִסְרוֹן (ז)
subscriber	manui	מָנוּי (ז)

100. Stationery

ballpoint pen	et kaduri	עֵט כַּדוּרִי (ז)
fountain pen	et no've'a	עֵט נוֹבֵעַ (ז)
pencil	iparon	עִיפָּרוֹן (ז)
highlighter	'marker	מַרְקֵר (ז)
felt-tip pen	tuʃ	טוּשׁ (ז)
notepad	pinkas	פִּנְקָס (ז)
agenda (diary)	yoman	יוֹמָן (ז)
ruler	sargel	סַרְגֵּל (ז)
calculator	maxʃevon	מַחְשְׁבוֹן (ז)
eraser	'maχak	מַחַק (ז)
thumbtack	'naʿats	נַעַץ (ז)
paper clip	mehadek	מְהַדֵק (ז)
glue	'devek	דֶבֶק (ז)
stapler	ʃadχan	שַׁדְכָן (ז)
hole punch	menakev	מְנַקֵב (ז)
pencil sharpener	maχded	מַחְדֵד (ז)

Job. Business. Part 2

101. Mass Media

newspaper	iton	עִיתוֹן (ז)
magazine	ʒurnal	ז'וּרְנָל (ז)
press (printed media)	itonut	עִיתוֹנוּת (נ)
radio	'radyo	רָדִיוֹ (ז)
radio station	taχanat 'radyo	תַּחֲנַת רָדִיוֹ (נ)
television	tele'vizya	טֶלֶוִויזְיָה (נ)
presenter, host	manχe	מַנְחֶה (ז)
newscaster	karyan	קַרְיָן (ז)
commentator	parʃan	פַּרְשָׁן (ז)
journalist	itonai	עִיתוֹנַאי (ז)
correspondent (reporter)	katav	כַּתָּב (ז)
press photographer	tsalam itonut	צַלָּם עִיתוֹנוּת (ז)
reporter	katav	כַּתָּב (ז)
editor	oreχ	עוֹרֵךְ (ז)
editor-in-chief	oreχ raʃi	עוֹרֵךְ רָאשִׁי (ז)
to subscribe (to ...)	lehasdir manui	לְהַסְדִּיר מָנוּי
subscription	minui	מָנוּי (ז)
subscriber	manui	מָנוּי (ז)
to read (vi, vt)	likro	לִקְרוֹא
reader	kore	קוֹרֵא (ז)
circulation (of newspaper)	tfutsa	תְּפוּצָה (נ)
monthly (adj)	χodʃi	חוֹדְשִׁי
weekly (adj)	ʃvu'i	שְׁבוּעִי
issue (edition)	gilayon	גִּילָיוֹן (ז)
new (~ issue)	tari	טָרִי
headline	ko'teret	כּוֹתֶרֶת (נ)
short article	katava ktsara	כַּתָּבָה קְצָרָה (נ)
column (regular article)	tur	טוּר (ז)
article	ma'amar	מַאֲמָר (ז)
page	amud	עַמוּד (ז)
reportage, report	katava	כַּתָּבָה (נ)
event (happening)	ei'ru'a	אֵירוּעַ (ז)
sensation (news)	sen'satsya	סֶנְסַצְיָה (נ)
scandal	ʃa'aruriya	שַׁעֲרוּרִיָּה (נ)
scandalous (adj)	meviʃ	מֵבִישׁ

great (~ scandal)	gadol	גָּדוֹל
show (e.g., cooking ~)	toxnit	תּוֹכְנִית (נ)
interview	ra'ayon	רֵאָיוֹן (ז)
live broadcast	ʃidur xai	שִׁידוּר חַי (ז)
channel	aruts	עָרוּץ (ז)

102. Agriculture

agriculture	xakla'ut	חַקְלָאוּת (נ)
peasant (masc.)	ikar	אִיכָּר (ז)
peasant (fem.)	xakla'ut	חַקְלָאִית (נ)
farmer	xavai	חַוַואי (ז)
tractor (farm ~)	'traktor	טְרַקְטוֹר (ז)
combine, harvester	kombain	קוֹמְבַּיין (ז)
plow	maxreʃa	מַחְרֵשָׁה (נ)
to plow (vi, vt)	laxaroʃ	לַחֲרוֹשׁ
plowland	sade xaruʃ	שָׂדֶה חָרוּשׁ (ז)
furrow (in field)	'telem	תֶּלֶם (ז)
to sow (vi, vt)	liz'ro'a	לִזְרוֹעַ
seeder	mazre'a	מַזְרֵעָה (נ)
sowing (process)	zri'a	זְרִיעָה (נ)
scythe	xermeʃ	חֶרְמֵשׁ (ז)
to mow, to scythe	liktsor	לִקְצוֹר
spade (tool)	et	אֵת (ז)
to till (vt)	leta'teax	לְתַתֵּחַ
hoe	ma'ader	מַעְדֵּר (ז)
to hoe, to weed	lenakeʃ	לְנַכֵּשׁ
weed (plant)	'esev ʃote	עֵשֶׂב שׁוֹטֶה (ז)
watering can	maʃpex	מַשְׁפֵּךְ (ז)
to water (plants)	lehaʃkot	לְהַשְׁקוֹת
watering (act)	haʃkaya	הַשְׁקָיָה (נ)
pitchfork	kilʃon	קִלְשׁוֹן (ז)
rake	magrefa	מַגְרֵפָה (נ)
fertilizer	'deʃen	דֶּשֶׁן (ז)
to fertilize (vt)	ledaʃen	לְדַשֵּׁן
manure (fertilizer)	'zevel	זֶבֶל (ז)
field	sade	שָׂדֶה (ז)
meadow	axu	אָחוּ (ז)
vegetable garden	gan yarak	גַּן יָרָק (ז)
orchard (e.g., apple ~)	bustan	בּוּסְתָּן (ז)

to graze (vt)	lir'ot	לִרְעוֹת
herder (herdsman)	ro'e tson	רוֹעֵה צֹאן (ז)
pasture	mir'e	מִרְעֶה (ז)
cattle breeding	gidul bakar	גִידוּל בָּקָר (ז)
sheep farming	gidul kvasim	גִידוּל כְּבָשִׂים (ז)
plantation	mata	מַטָע (ז)
row (garden bed ~s)	aruga	עֲרוּגָה (נ)
hothouse	xamama	חֲמָמָה (נ)
drought (lack of rain)	ba'tsoret	בַּצוֹרֶת (נ)
dry (~ summer)	yaveʃ	יָבֵשׁ
grain	tvu'a	תְבוּאָה (נ)
cereal crops	gidulei dagan	גִידוּלֵי דָגָן (ז"ר)
to harvest, to gather	liktof	לִקְטוֹף
miller (person)	toxen	טוֹחֵן (ז)
mill (e.g., gristmill)	taxanat 'kemax	טַחֲנַת קֶמַח (נ)
to grind (grain)	litxon	לִטְחוֹן
flour	'kemax	קֶמַח (ז)
straw	kaʃ	קַשׁ (ז)

103. Building. Building process

construction site	atar bniya	אֲתַר בְּנִיָה (ז)
to build (vt)	livnot	לִבְנוֹת
construction worker	banai	בַּנַאי (ז)
project	proyekt	פְּרוֹיֶיקְט (ז)
architect	adrixal	אַדְרִיכָל (ז)
worker	po'el	פּוֹעֵל (ז)
foundation (of a building)	yesodot	יְסוֹדוֹת (ז"ר)
roof	gag	גַג (ז)
foundation pile	amud yesod	עַמוּד יְסוֹד (ז)
wall	kir	קִיר (ז)
reinforcing bars	mot xizuk	מוֹט חִיזוּק (ז)
scaffolding	pigumim	פִּיגוּמִים (ז"ר)
concrete	beton	בֶּטוֹן (ז)
granite	granit	גְרָנִיט (ז)
stone	'even	אֶבֶן (נ)
brick	levena	לְבֵנָה (נ)
sand	xol	חוֹל (ז)
cement	'melet	מֶלֶט (ז)
plaster (for walls)	'tiax	טִיחַ (ז)

to plaster (vt)	leta'yeaχ	לְטַיֵּחַ
paint	'tseva	צֶבַע (ז)
to paint (~ a wall)	lits'bo'a	לִצְבֹּעַ
barrel	χavit	חָבִית (נ)
crane	aguran	עֲגוּרָן (ז)
to lift, to hoist (vt)	lehanif	לְהָנִיף
to lower (vt)	lehorid	לְהוֹרִיד
bulldozer	daχpor	דַּחְפּוֹר (ז)
excavator	maχper	מַחְפֵּר (ז)
scoop, bucket	ʃa'ov	שְׁאוֹב (ז)
to dig (excavate)	laχpor	לַחְפֹּר
hard hat	kasda	קַסְדָה (נ)

Professions and occupations

104. Job search. Dismissal

job	avoda	עֲבוֹדָה (נ)
staff (work force)	'segel	סֶגֶל (ז)
personnel	'segel	סֶגֶל (ז)

career	kar'yera	קָרְיֶירָה (נ)
prospects (chances)	effaruyot	אֶפְשָׁרוּיוֹת (נ״ר)
skills (mastery)	meyumanut	מְיוּמָנוּת (נ)

selection (screening)	sinun	סִינוּן (ז)
employment agency	soxnut 'koax adam	סוֹכְנוּת כּוֹחַ אָדָם (נ)
résumé	korot xayim	קוֹרוֹת חַיִּים (נ״ר)
job interview	ra'ayon avoda	רַאֲיוֹן עֲבוֹדָה (ז)
vacancy, opening	misra pnuya	מִשְׂרָה פְּנוּיָה (נ)

salary, pay	mas'koret	מַשְׂכּוֹרֶת (נ)
fixed salary	mas'koret kvu'a	מַשְׂכּוֹרֶת קְבוּעָה (נ)
pay, compensation	taflum	תַשְׁלוֹם (ז)

position (job)	tafkid	תַפְקִיד (ז)
duty (of employee)	xova	חוֹבָה (נ)
range of duties	txum axrayut	תְחוּם אַחְרָיוּת (ז)
busy (I'm ~)	asuk	עָסוּק

| to fire (dismiss) | lefater | לְפַטֵּר |
| dismissal | pitur | פִּיטוּר (ז) |

unemployment	avtala	אַבְטָלָה (נ)
unemployed (n)	muvtal	מוּבְטָל (ז)
retirement	'pensya	פֶּנְסְיָה (נ)
to retire (from job)	latset legimla'ot	לָצֵאת לְגִימְלָאוֹת

105. Business people

director	menahel	מְנַהֵל (ז)
manager (director)	menahel	מְנַהֵל (ז)
boss	bos	בּוֹס (ז)

superior	memune	מְמוּנֶה (ז)
superiors	memunim	מְמוּנִים (ז״ר)
president	nasi	נָשִׂיא (ז)

chairman	yoʃev roʃ	יוֹשֵׁב רֹאשׁ (ז)
deputy (substitute)	sgan	סְגָן (ז)
assistant	ozer	עוֹזֵר (ז)
secretary	mazkir	מַזְכִּיר (ז)
personal assistant	mazkir iʃi	מַזְכִּיר אִישִׁי (ז)

businessman	iʃ asakim	אִישׁ עֲסָקִים (ז)
entrepreneur	yazam	יַזָּם (ז)
founder	meyased	מְיַסֵּד (ז)
to found (vt)	leyased	לְיַסֵּד

incorporator	mexonen	מְכוֹנֵן (ז)
partner	ʃutaf	שׁוּתָף (ז)
stockholder	'ba'al menayot	בַּעַל מְנָיוֹת (ז)

millionaire	milyoner	מִילְיוֹנֵר (ז)
billionaire	milyarder	מִילְיַארְדֶּר (ז)
owner, proprietor	be'alim	בְּעָלִים (ז)
landowner	'ba'al adamot	בַּעַל אֲדָמוֹת (ז)

client	la'koax	לָקוֹחַ (ז)
regular client	la'koax ka'vu'a	לָקוֹחַ קָבוּעַ (ז)
buyer (customer)	kone	קוֹנֶה (ז)
visitor	mevaker	מְבַקֵּר (ז)

professional (n)	miktso'an	מִקְצוֹעָן (ז)
expert	mumxe	מוּמְחֶה (ז)
specialist	mumxe	מוּמְחֶה (ז)

| banker | bankai | בַּנְקַאי (ז) |
| broker | soxen | סוֹכֵן (ז) |

cashier, teller	kupai	קוּפַּאי (ז)
accountant	menahel xeʃbonot	מְנָהֵל חֶשְׁבּוֹנוֹת (ז)
security guard	ʃomer	שׁוֹמֵר (ז)

investor	maʃki'a	מַשְׁקִיעַ (ז)
debtor	'ba'al xov	בַּעַל חוֹב (ז)
creditor	malve	מַלְוֶה (ז)
borrower	love	לוֹוֶה (ז)

| importer | yevu'an | יְבוּאָן (ז) |
| exporter | yetsu'an | יְצוּאָן (ז) |

manufacturer	yatsran	יַצְרָן (ז)
distributor	mefits	מֵפִיץ (ז)
middleman	metavex	מְתַוֵּךְ (ז)

consultant	yo'ets	יוֹעֵץ (ז)
sales representative	natsig mexirot	נְצִיג מְכִירוֹת (ז)
agent	soxen	סוֹכֵן (ז)
insurance agent	soxen bi'tuax	סוֹכֵן בִּיטוּחַ (ז)

106. Service professions

cook	tabax	טַבָּח (ז)
chef (kitchen chef)	ʃef	שֶף (ז)
baker	ofe	אוֹפֶה (ז)
bartender	barmen	בַּרמֶן (ז)
waiter	meltsar	מֶלצָר (ז)
waitress	meltsarit	מֶלצָרִית (נ)
lawyer, attorney	orex din	עוֹרֵך דִין (ז)
lawyer (legal expert)	orex din	עוֹרֵך דִין (ז)
notary	notaryon	נוֹטַריוֹן (ז)
electrician	xaʃmalai	חַשמַלַאי (ז)
plumber	ʃravrav	שֲרַבּרַב (ז)
carpenter	nagar	נַגָר (ז)
masseur	ma'ase	מְעַסֶה (ז)
masseuse	masa'ʒistit	מַסָז'יסטִית (נ)
doctor	rofe	רוֹפֵא (ז)
taxi driver	nahag monit	נֶהַג מוֹנִית (ז)
driver	nahag	נֶהָג (ז)
delivery man	ʃa'liax	שָלִיחַ (ז)
chambermaid	xadranit	חַדרָנִית (נ)
security guard	ʃomer	שוֹמֵר (ז)
flight attendant (fem.)	da'yelet	דַייֶלֶת (נ)
schoolteacher	more	מוֹרֶה (ז)
librarian	safran	סַפרָן (ז)
translator	metargem	מְתַרגֵם (ז)
interpreter	meturgeman	מְתוּרגְמָן (ז)
guide	madrix tiyulim	מַדרִיך טִיוּלִים (ז)
hairdresser	sapar	סַפָּר (ז)
mailman	davar	דַוָור (ז)
salesman (store staff)	moxer	מוֹכֵר (ז)
gardener	ganan	גַנָן (ז)
domestic servant	meʃaret	מְשָרֵת (ז)
maid (female servant)	meʃa'retet	מְשָרֶתֶת (נ)
cleaner (cleaning lady)	menaka	מְנַקָה (נ)

107. Military professions and ranks

| private | turai | טוּרַאי (ז) |
| sergeant | samal | סַמָל (ז) |

lieutenant	'segen	סֶגֶן (ז)
captain	'seren	סֶרֶן (ז)
major	rav 'seren	רַב־סֶרֶן (ז)
colonel	aluf miʃne	אַלוּף מִשְׁנֶה (ז)
general	aluf	אַלוּף (ז)
marshal	'marʃal	מַרְשָׁל (ז)
admiral	admiral	אַדְמִירָל (ז)
military (n)	iʃ tsava	אִישׁ צָבָא (ז)
soldier	χayal	חַיָּל (ז)
officer	katsin	קָצִין (ז)
commander	mefaked	מְפַקֵּד (ז)
border guard	ʃomer gvul	שׁוֹמֵר גְּבוּל (ז)
radio operator	alχutai	אַלְחוּטַאי (ז)
scout (searcher)	iʃ modi'in kravi	אִישׁ מוֹדִיעִין קְרָבִי (ז)
pioneer (sapper)	χablan	חַבְּלָן (ז)
marksman	tsalaf	צַלָּף (ז)
navigator	navat	נַוָּט (ז)

108. Officials. Priests

king	'meleχ	מֶלֶךְ (ז)
queen	malka	מַלְכָּה (נ)
prince	nasiχ	נָסִיךְ (ז)
princess	nesiχa	נְסִיכָה (נ)
czar	tsar	צָאר (ז)
czarina	tsa'rina	צָארִינָה (נ)
president	nasi	נָשִׂיא (ז)
Secretary (minister)	sar	שַׂר (ז)
prime minister	roʃ memʃala	רֹאשׁ מֶמְשָׁלָה (ז)
senator	se'nator	סֶנָאטוֹר (ז)
diplomat	diplomat	דִּיפְּלוֹמָט (ז)
consul	'konsul	קוֹנְסוּל (ז)
ambassador	ʃagrir	שַׁגְרִיר (ז)
counsilor (diplomatic officer)	yo'ets	יוֹעֵץ (ז)
official, functionary (civil servant)	pakid	פָּקִיד (ז)
prefect	prefekt	פְּרֶפֶקְט (ז)
mayor	roʃ ha'ir	רֹאשׁ הָעִיר (ז)
judge	ʃofet	שׁוֹפֵט (ז)
prosecutor (e.g., district attorney)	to've'a	תּוֹבֵעַ (ז)

missionary	misyoner	מִיסיוֹנֶר (ז)
monk	nazir	נָזִיר (ז)
abbot	roʃ minzar ka'toli	רֹאש מִנזָר קָתוֹלִי (ז)
rabbi	rav	רַב (ז)
vizier	vazir	וָזִיר (ז)
shah	ʃaχ	שָׁאח (ז)
sheikh	ʃeiχ	שֵׁיח (ז)

109. Agricultural professions

beekeeper	kavran	כַּוורָן (ז)
herder, shepherd	ro'e tson	רוֹעֵה צֹאן (ז)
agronomist	agronom	אַגרוֹנוֹם (ז)
cattle breeder	megadel bakar	מְגַדֵל בָּקָר (ז)
veterinarian	veterinar	וֶטֶרִינָר (ז)
farmer	χavai	חַוואי (ז)
winemaker	yeinan	יֵינָן (ז)
zoologist	zo'olog	זוֹאוֹלוֹג (ז)
cowboy	'ka'uboi	קָאוּבּוֹי (ז)

110. Art professions

actor	saχkan	שַׂחקָן (ז)
actress	saχkanit	שַׂחקָנִית (נ)
singer (masc.)	zamar	זַמָר (ז)
singer (fem.)	za'meret	זַמֶרֶת (נ)
dancer (masc.)	rakdan	רַקדָן (ז)
dancer (fem.)	rakdanit	רַקדָנִית (נ)
performer (masc.)	saχkan	שַׂחקָן (ז)
performer (fem.)	saχkanit	שַׂחקָנִית (נ)
musician	muzikai	מוּזִיקַאי (ז)
pianist	psantran	פּסַנתְרָן (ז)
guitar player	nagan gi'tara	נַגָן גִיטָרָה (ז)
conductor (orchestra ~)	mena'tseaχ	מְנַצֵח (ז)
composer	malχin	מַלחִין (ז)
impresario	amargan	אָמַרגָן (ז)
film director	bamai	בַּמַאי (ז)
producer	mefik	מֵפִיק (ז)
scriptwriter	tasritai	תַסרִיטַאי (ז)
critic	mevaker	מְבַקֵר (ז)

writer	sofer	סוֹפֵר (ז)
poet	meʃorer	מְשׁוֹרֵר (ז)
sculptor	pasal	פַּסָל (ז)
artist (painter)	tsayar	צַייָר (ז)

juggler	lahatutan	לַהֲטוּטָן (ז)
clown	leitsan	לֵיצָן (ז)
acrobat	akrobat	אַקרוֹבָּט (ז)
magician	kosem	קוֹסֵם (ז)

111. Various professions

doctor	rofe	רוֹפֵא (ז)
nurse	aχot	אָחוֹת (נ)
psychiatrist	psiχi''ater	פּסִיכִיאָטֶר (ז)
dentist	rofe ʃi'nayim	רוֹפֵא שִׁינַיִים (ז)
surgeon	kirurg	כִּירוּרג (ז)

astronaut	astro'na'ut	אַסטרוֹנָאוּט (ז)
astronomer	astronom	אַסטרוֹנוֹם (ז)
pilot	tayas	טַייָס (ז)

driver (of taxi, etc.)	nahag	נַהָג (ז)
engineer (train driver)	nahag ra'kevet	נַהָג רַכֶּבֶת (ז)
mechanic	meχonai	מְכוֹנַאי (ז)

miner	kore	כּוֹרֶה (ז)
worker	po'el	פּוֹעֵל (ז)
locksmith	misgad	מַסגֵד (ז)
joiner (carpenter)	nagar	נַגָר (ז)
turner (lathe machine operator)	χarat	חָרָט (ז)
construction worker	banai	בַּנַאי (ז)
welder	rataχ	רַתָּך (ז)

professor (title)	pro'fesor	פּרוֹפֶסוֹר (ז)
architect	adriχal	אַדרִיכָל (ז)
historian	historyon	הִיסטוֹריוֹן (ז)
scientist	mad'an	מַדעָן (ז)
physicist	fizikai	פִיזִיקַאי (ז)
chemist (scientist)	χimai	כִימַאי (ז)

archeologist	arχe'olog	אַרכֵיאוֹלוֹג (ז)
geologist	ge'olog	גֵיאוֹלוֹג (ז)
researcher (scientist)	χoker	חוֹקֵר (ז)

babysitter	ʃmartaf	שׁמַרטַף (ז)
teacher, educator	more, meχaneχ	מוֹרֶה, מְחַנֵך (ז)
editor	oreχ	עוֹרֵך (ז)
editor-in-chief	oreχ raʃi	עוֹרֵך רָאשִׁי (ז)

correspondent	katav	כַּתָּב (ז)
typist (fem.)	kaldanit	קַלְדָנִית (נ)
designer	me'atsev	מְעַצֵב (ז)
computer expert	mumxe maxfevim	מוּמחֶה מַחשָׁבִים (ז)
programmer	metaxnet	מְתַכנֵת (ז)
engineer (designer)	mehandes	מְהַנדֵס (ז)
sailor	yamai	יַמַאי (ז)
seaman	malax	מַלָח (ז)
rescuer	matsil	מַצִיל (ז)
fireman	kabai	כַּבַּאי (ז)
police officer	foter	שׁוֹטֵר (ז)
watchman	fomer	שׁוֹמֵר (ז)
detective	balaf	בַּלָש (ז)
customs officer	pakid 'mexes	פְּקִיד מֶכֶס (ז)
bodyguard	fomer rof	שׁוֹמֵר רֹאש (ז)
prison guard	soher	סוֹהֵר (ז)
inspector	mefa'keax	מְפַקֵחַ (ז)
sportsman	sportai	ספּוֹרטַאי (ז)
trainer, coach	me'amen	מְאַמֵן (ז)
butcher	katsav	קַצָב (ז)
cobbler (shoe repairer)	sandlar	סַנדלָר (ז)
merchant	soxer	סוֹחֵר (ז)
loader (person)	sabal	סַבָּל (ז)
fashion designer	me'atsev ofna	מְעַצֵב אוֹפנָה (ז)
model (fem.)	dugmanit	דוּגמָנִית (נ)

112. Occupations. Social status

schoolboy	talmid	תַלמִיד (ז)
student (college ~)	student	סטוּדֶנט (ז)
philosopher	filosof	פִּילוֹסוֹף (ז)
economist	kalkelan	כַּלכְּלָן (ז)
inventor	mamtsi	מַמצִיא (ז)
unemployed (n)	muvtal	מוּבטָל (ז)
retiree	pensyoner	פֶּנסיוֹנֵר (ז)
spy, secret agent	meragel	מְרַגֵל (ז)
prisoner	asir	אָסִיר (ז)
striker	fovet	שׁוֹבֵת (ז)
bureaucrat	birokrat	בִּירוֹקרָט (ז)
traveler (globetrotter)	metayel	מְטַיֵל (ז)
gay, homosexual (n)	'lesbit, 'homo	לֶסבִּית (נ), הוֹמוֹ (ז)

hacker	'haker	הָאקֶר (ז)
hippie	'hipi	הִיפִּי (ז)
bandit	ʃoded	שׁוֹדֵד (ז)
hit man, killer	ro'tseaχ saχir	רוֹצֵחַ שָׂכִיר (ז)
drug addict	narkoman	נַרקוֹמָן (ז)
drug dealer	soχer samim	סוֹחֵר סַמִּים (ז)
prostitute (fem.)	zona	זוֹנָה (נ)
pimp	sarsur	סַרסוּר (ז)
sorcerer	meχaʃef	מְכַשֵּׁף (ז)
sorceress (evil ~)	maχʃefa	מְכַשֵּׁפָה (נ)
pirate	ʃoded yam	שׁוֹדֵד יָם (ז)
slave	ʃifχa, 'eved	שִׁפחָה (נ), עֶבֶד (ז)
samurai	samurai	סָמוּרַאי (ז)
savage (primitive)	'pere adam	פֶּרֶא אָדָם (ז)

114

Sports

113. Kinds of sports. Sportspersons

sportsman	sportai	ספּוֹרטָאי (ז)
kind of sports	anaf sport	עָנָף ספּוֹרט (ז)
basketball	kadursal	כַּדוּרסַל (ז)
basketball player	kadursalan	כַּדוּרסַלָן (ז)
baseball	'beisbol	בֵּייסבּוֹל (ז)
baseball player	saχkan 'beisbol	שַׂחקָן בֵּייסבּוֹל (ז)
soccer	kadu'regel	כַּדוּרֶגֶל (ז)
soccer player	kaduraglan	כַּדוּרגלָן (ז)
goalkeeper	ʃo'er	שׁוֹעֵר (ז)
hockey	'hoki	הוֹקִי (ז)
hockey player	saχkan 'hoki	שַׂחקָן הוֹקִי (ז)
volleyball	kadur'af	כַּדוּרעָף (ז)
volleyball player	saχkan kadur'af	שַׂחקָן כַּדוּרעָף (ז)
boxing	igruf	אִיגרוּף (ז)
boxer	mit'agref	מִתאַגרֵף (ז)
wrestling	he'avkut	הֵיאָבקוּת (נ)
wrestler	mit'abek	מִתאַבֵּק (ז)
karate	karate	קָרָטֶה (ז)
karate fighter	karatist	קָרָטִיסט (ז)
judo	'dʒudo	ג'וּדוֹ (ז)
judo athlete	dʒudai	ג'וּדָאי (ז)
tennis	'tenis	טֶנִיס (ז)
tennis player	tenisai	טֶנִיסָאי (ז)
swimming	sχiya	שׂחִייָה (נ)
swimmer	saχyan	שַׂחייָן (ז)
fencing	'sayif	סָיִף (ז)
fencer	sayaf	סַיָיף (ז)
chess	'ʃaχmat	שַׁחמָט (ז)
chess player	ʃaχmetai	שַׁחמְטָאי (ז)

alpinism	tipus harim	טִיפּוּס הָרִים (ז)
alpinist	metapes harim	מְטַפֵּס הָרִים (ז)
running	ritsa	רִיצָה (נ)
runner	atsan	אָצָן (ז)
athletics	at'letika kala	אַתלֶטִיקָה קַלָה (נ)
athlete	atlet	אַתלֵט (ז)
horseback riding	reχiva al sus	רְכִיבָה עַל סוּס (נ)
horse rider	paraʃ	פָּרָשׁ (ז)
figure skating	haχlaka omanutit	הַחלָקָה אוֹמָנוּתִית (נ)
figure skater (masc.)	maχlik amanuti	מַחלִיק אָמָנוּתִי (ז)
figure skater (fem.)	maχlika amanutit	מַחלִיקָה אָמָנוּתִית (נ)
powerlifting	haramat miʃkolot	הֲרָמַת מִשׁקוֹלוֹת (נ)
powerlifter	miʃkolan	מִשׁקוֹלָן (ז)
car racing	merots meχoniyot	מֵירוֹץ מְכוֹנִיוֹת (ז)
racing driver	nahag merotsim	נֶהַג מֵרוֹצִים (ז)
cycling	reχiva al ofa'nayim	רְכִיבָה עַל אוֹפַנַיִים (נ)
cyclist	roχev ofa'nayim	רוֹכֵב אוֹפַנַיִים (ז)
broad jump	kfitsa la'roχav	קפִיצָה לָרוֹחַק (נ)
pole vault	kfitsa bemot	קפִיצָה בְּמוֹט (נ)
jumper	kofets	קוֹפֵץ (ז)

114. Kinds of sports. Miscellaneous

football	'futbol	פוּטבּוֹל (ז)
badminton	notsit	נוֹצִית (נ)
biathlon	bi'atlon	בִּיאַתלוֹן (ז)
billiards	bilyard	בִּילִיאַרד (ז)
bobsled	miz'χelet	מִזחֶלֶת (נ)
bodybuilding	pi'tuaχ guf	פִּיתוּחַ גוּף (ז)
water polo	polo 'mayim	פוֹלוֹ מַיִם (ז)
handball	kadur yad	כַּדוּר־יָד (ז)
golf	golf	גוֹלף (ז)
rowing, crew	χatira	חֲתִירָה (נ)
scuba diving	tslila	צלִילָה (נ)
cross-country skiing	ski bemiʃor	סקִי בַּמִישׁוֹר (ז)
table tennis (ping-pong)	'tenis ʃulχan	טֶנִיס שׁוּלחָן (ז)
sailing	'ʃayit	שַׁיִט (ז)
rally racing	'rali	רָאלִי (ז)
rugby	'rogbi	רוֹגבִּי (ז)

| snowboarding | gliʃat 'ʃeleg | גְּלִישַׁת שֶׁלֶג (נ) |
| archery | kaʃatut | קַשָּׁתוּת (נ) |

115. Gym

darbell	miʃ'kolet	מִשְׁקוֹלֶת (נ)
dumbbells	miʃkolot	מִשְׁקוֹלוֹת (נ״ר)
training machine	maxʃir 'koʃer	מַכְשִׁיר כּוֹשֶׁר (ז)
exercise bicycle	ofanei 'koʃer	אוֹפַנֵּי כּוֹשֶׁר (ז״ר)
treadmill	halixon	הֲלִיכוֹן (ז)
horizontal bar	'metax	מָתָח (ז)
parallel bars	makbilim	מַקְבִּילִים (ז״ר)
vault (vaulting horse)	sus	סוּס (ז)
mat (exercise ~)	mizron	מִזְרוֹן (ז)
jump rope	dalgit	דַּלְגִּית (נ)
aerobics	ei'robika	אֵירוֹבִּיקָה (נ)
yoga	'yoga	יוֹגָה (נ)

116. Sports. Miscellaneous

Olympic Games	hamisxakim ha'o'limpiyim	הַמִּשְׂחָקִים הָאוֹלִימְפִּיִּים (ז״ר)
winner	mena'tseax	מְנַצֵּחַ (ז)
to be winning	lena'tseax	לְנַצֵּחַ
to win (vi)	lena'tseax	לְנַצֵּחַ
leader	manhig	מַנְהִיג (ז)
to lead (vi)	lehovil	לְהוֹבִיל
first place	makom riʃon	מָקוֹם רִאשׁוֹן (ז)
second place	makom ʃeni	מָקוֹם שֵׁנִי (ז)
third place	makom ʃliʃi	מָקוֹם שְׁלִישִׁי (ז)
medal	me'dalya	מֶדַלְיָה (נ)
trophy	pras	פְּרָס (ז)
prize cup (trophy)	ga'vi'a nitsaxon	גָּבִיעַ נִיצָּחוֹן (ז)
prize (in game)	pras	פְּרָס (ז)
main prize	pras riʃon	פְּרָס רִאשׁוֹן (ז)
record	si	שִׂיא (ז)
to set a record	lik'bo'a si	לִקְבּוֹעַ שִׂיא
final	gmar	גְּמָר (ז)
final (adj)	ʃel hagmar	שֶׁל הַגְּמָר
champion	aluf	אַלּוּף (ז)
championship	alifut	אַלִּיפוּת (נ)

stadium	itstadyon	אִצְטַדְיוֹן (ז)
stand (bleachers)	bama	בָּמָה (נ)
fan, supporter	ohed	אוֹהֵד (ז)
opponent, rival	yariv	יָרִיב (ז)
start (start line)	kav zinuk	קַו זִינוּק (ז)
finish line	kav hagmar	קַו הַגְמָר (ז)
defeat	tvusa	תְּבוּסָה (נ)
to lose (not win)	lehafsid	לְהַפְסִיד
referee	ʃofet	שׁוֹפֵט (ז)
jury (judges)	xaver ʃoftim	חֶבֶר שׁוֹפְטִים (ז)
score	totsa'a	תּוֹצָאָה (נ)
tie	'teku	תֵּיקוּ (ז)
to tie (vi)	lesayem be'teku	לְסַיֵּים בְּתֵיקוּ
point	nekuda	נְקוּדָה (נ)
result (final score)	totsa'a	תּוֹצָאָה (נ)
period	sivuv	סִיבוּב (ז)
half-time	hafsaka	הַפְסָקָה (נ)
doping	sam	סַם (ז)
to penalize (vt)	leha'aniʃ	לְהַעֲנִישׁ
to disqualify (vt)	lefsol	לִפְסוֹל
apparatus	maxʃir	מַכְשִׁיר (ז)
javelin	kidon	כִּידוֹן (ז)
shot (metal ball)	kadur barzel	כַּדוּר בַּרְזֶל (ז)
ball (snooker, etc.)	kadur	כַּדוּר (ז)
aim (target)	matara	מַטָּרָה (נ)
target	matara	מַטָּרָה (נ)
to shoot (vi)	lirot	לִירוֹת
accurate (~ shot)	meduyak	מְדוּיָק
trainer, coach	me'amen	מְאַמֵּן (ז)
to train (sb)	le'amen	לְאַמֵּן
to train (vi)	lehit'amen	לְהִתְאַמֵּן
training	imun	אִימוּן (ז)
gym	'xeder 'koʃer	חֶדַר כּוֹשֶׁר (ז)
exercise (physical)	imun	אִימוּן (ז)
warm-up (athlete ~)	ximum	חִימוּם (ז)

Education

117. School

school	beit 'sefer	בֵּית סֵפֶר (ז)
principal (headmaster)	menahel beit 'sefer	מְנַהֵל בֵּית סֵפֶר (ז)
pupil (boy)	talmid	תַּלְמִיד (ז)
pupil (girl)	talmida	תַּלְמִידָה (נ)
schoolboy	talmid	תַּלְמִיד (ז)
schoolgirl	talmida	תַּלְמִידָה (נ)
to teach (sb)	lelamed	לְלַמֵּד
to learn (language, etc.)	lilmod	לִלְמוֹד
to learn by heart	lilmod be'al pe	לִלְמוֹד בְּעַל פֶּה
to learn (~ to count, etc.)	lilmod	לִלְמוֹד
to be in school	lilmod	לִלְמוֹד
to go to school	la'leχet le'beit 'sefer	לָלֶכֶת לְבֵית סֵפֶר
alphabet	alefbeit	אָלֶפְבֵּית (ז)
subject (at school)	mik'tso'a	מִקְצוֹעַ (ז)
classroom	kita	כִּיתָה (נ)
lesson	ʃi'ur	שִׁיעוּר (ז)
recess	hafsaka	הַפְסָקָה (נ)
school bell	pa'amon	פַּעֲמוֹן (ז)
school desk	ʃulχan limudim	שׁוּלְחַן לִימוּדִים (ז)
chalkboard	'luaχ	לוּחַ (ז)
grade	tsiyun	צִיּוּן (ז)
good grade	tsiyun tov	צִיּוּן טוֹב (ז)
bad grade	tsiyun ga'ru'a	צִיּוּן גָּרוּעַ (ז)
to give a grade	latet tsiyun	לָתֵת צִיּוּן
mistake, error	ta'ut	טָעוּת (נ)
to make mistakes	la'asot ta'uyot	לַעֲשׂוֹת טָעוּיוֹת
to correct (an error)	letaken	לְתַקֵּן
cheat sheet	ʃlif	שְׁלִיף (ז)
homework	ʃi'urei 'bayit	שִׁיעוּרֵי בַּיִת (ז"ר)
exercise (in education)	targil	תַּרְגִּיל (ז)
to be present	lihyot no'χeaχ	לִהְיוֹת נוֹכֵחַ
to be absent	lehe'ader	לְהֵיעָדֵר
to miss school	lehaχsir	לְהַחְסִיר

to punish (vt)	leha'aniʃ	לְהַעֲנִיש
punishment	'oneʃ	עוֹנֶש (ז)
conduct (behavior)	hitnahagut	הִתְנַהֲגוּת (נ)

report card	yoman beit 'sefer	יוֹמַן בֵּית סֵפֶר (ז)
pencil	iparon	עִיפָּרוֹן (ז)
eraser	'maχak	מַחַק (ז)
chalk	gir	גִיר (ז)
pencil case	kalmar	קַלְמָר (ז)

schoolbag	yalkut	יַלְקוּט (ז)
pen	et	עֵט (ז)
school notebook	maχ'beret	מַחְבֶּרֶת (נ)
textbook	'sefer limud	סֵפֶר לִימוּד (ז)
compasses	meχuga	מְחוּגָה (נ)

| to make technical drawings | lesartet | לְשַׂרְטֵט |
| technical drawing | sirtut | שִׂרְטוּט (ז) |

poem	ʃir	שִׁיר (ז)
by heart (adv)	be'al pe	בְּעַל פֶּה
to learn by heart	lilmod be'al pe	לִלְמוֹד בְּעַל פֶּה

school vacation	χufʃa	חוּפְשָׁה (נ)
to be on vacation	lihyot beχufʃa	לִהְיוֹת בְּחוּפְשָׁה
to spend one's vacation	leha'avir 'χofeʃ	לְהַעֲבִיר חוֹפֶש

test (written math ~)	mivχan	מִבְחָן (ז)
essay (composition)	χibur	חִיבּוּר (ז)
dictation	haχtava	הַכְתָּבָה (נ)
exam (examination)	bχina	בְּחִינָה (נ)
to take an exam	lehibaχen	לְהִיבָּחֵן
experiment (e.g., chemistry ~)	nisui	נִיסוּי (ז)

118. College. University

academy	aka'demya	אֲקָדֶמְיָה (נ)
university	uni'versita	אוּנִיבֶּרְסִיטָה (נ)
faculty (e.g., ~ of Medicine)	fa'kulta	פָקוּלְטָה (נ)

student (masc.)	student	סְטוּדֶנְט (ז)
student (fem.)	stu'dentit	סְטוּדֶנְטִית (נ)
lecturer (teacher)	martse	מַרְצֶה (ז)

lecture hall, room	ulam hartsa'ot	אוּלָם הַרְצָאוֹת (ז)
graduate	boger	בּוֹגֵר (ז)
diploma	di'ploma	דִיפְלוֹמָה (נ)

dissertation	diser'tatsya	דִיסֶרְטַצְיָה (נ)
study (report)	meχkar	מֶחְקָר (ז)
laboratory	ma'abada	מַעֲבָּדָה (נ)
lecture	hartsa'a	הַרְצָאָה (נ)
coursemate	χaver lelimudim	חָבֵר לְלִימוּדִים (ז)
scholarship	milga	מִלְגָה (נ)
academic degree	'to'ar aka'demɪ	תּוֹאַר אָקָדֶמִי (ז)

119. Sciences. Disciplines

mathematics	mate'matika	מָתֶמָטִיקָה (נ)
algebra	'algebra	אַלְגֶבְּרָה (נ)
geometry	ge'o'metriya	גֵיאוֹמֶטְרִיָה (נ)
astronomy	astro'nomya	אַסְטְרוֹנוֹמְיָה (נ)
biology	bio'logya	בִּיוֹלוֹגְיָה (נ)
geography	ge'o'grafya	גֵיאוֹגְרַפְיָה (נ)
geology	ge'o'logya	גֵיאוֹלוֹגְיָה (נ)
history	his'torya	הִיסְטוֹרְיָה (נ)
medicine	refu'a	רְפוּאָה (נ)
pedagogy	χinuχ	חִינוּךְ (ז)
law	miʃpatim	מִשְׁפָּטִים (ז"ר)
physics	'fizika	פִיזִיקָה (נ)
chemistry	'χimya	כִימְיָה (נ)
philosophy	filo'sofya	פִילוֹסוֹפְיָה (נ)
psychology	psiχo'logya	פְּסִיכוֹלוֹגְיָה (נ)

120. Writing system. Orthography

grammar	dikduk	דִקְדוּק (ז)
vocabulary	otsar milim	אוֹצַר מִילִים (ז)
phonetics	torat ha'hege	תּוֹרַת הַהֶגֶה (נ)
noun	ʃem 'etsem	שֵׁם עֶצֶם (ז)
adjective	ʃem 'to'ar	שֵׁם תּוֹאַר (ז)
verb	po'el	פּוֹעַל (ז)
adverb	'to'ar 'po'al	תּוֹאַר פּוֹעַל (ז)
pronoun	ʃem guf	שֵׁם גוּף (ז)
interjection	milat kri'a	מִילַת קְרִיאָה (נ)
preposition	milat 'yaχas	מִילַת יַחַס (נ)
root	'ʃoreʃ	שׁוֹרֶשׁ (ז)
ending	si'yomet	סִיוֹמֶת (נ)
prefix	tχilit	תְחִילִית (נ)

syllable	havara	הֲבָרָה (נ)
suffix	si'yomet	סִיוֹמֶת (נ)
stress mark	'ta'am	טַעַם (ז)
apostrophe	'gere∫	גֶּרֶשׁ (ז)
period, dot	nekuda	נְקוּדָה (נ)
comma	psik	פְּסִיק (ז)
semicolon	nekuda ufsik	נְקוּדָה וּפְסִיק (נ)
colon	nekudo'tayim	נְקוּדוֹתַיִים (נ״ר)
ellipsis	∫alo∫ nekudot	שָׁלוֹשׁ נְקוּדוֹת (נ״ר)
question mark	siman ∫e'ela	סִימָן שְׁאֵלָה (ז)
exclamation point	siman kri'a	סִימָן קְרִיאָה (ז)
quotation marks	merχa'ot	מֵרְכָאוֹת (נ״ר)
in quotation marks	bemerχa'ot	בְּמֵרְכָאוֹת
parenthesis	sog'rayim	סוֹגְרַיִים (נ״ר)
in parenthesis	besog'rayim	בְּסוֹגְרַיִים
hyphen	makaf	מַקָּף (ז)
dash	kav mafrid	קַו מַפְרִיד (ז)
space (between words)	'revaχ	רֶוַח (ז)
letter	ot	אוֹת (נ)
capital letter	ot gdola	אוֹת גְדוֹלָה (נ)
vowel (n)	tnu'a	תְנוּעָה (נ)
consonant (n)	it̪sur	עִיצוּר (ז)
sentence	mi∫pat	מִשְׁפָּט (ז)
subject	nose	נוֹשֵׂא (ז)
predicate	nasu	נָשׂוּא (ז)
line	∫ura	שׁוּרָה (נ)
on a new line	be∫ura χada∫a	בְּשׁוּרָה חֲדָשָׁה
paragraph	piska	פִּסְקָה (נ)
word	mila	מִילָה (נ)
group of words	t̪siruf milim	צֵירוּף מִילִים (ז)
expression	bitui	בִּיטוּי (ז)
synonym	mila nir'defet	מִילָה נִרְדֶּפֶת (נ)
antonym	'hefeχ	הֵפֶךְ (ז)
rule	klal	כְּלָל (ז)
exception	yot̪se min haklal	יוֹצֵא מִן הַכְּלָל (ז)
correct (adj)	naχon	נָכוֹן
conjugation	hataya	הַטָּיָה (נ)
declension	hataya	הַטָּיָה (נ)
nominal case	yaχasa	יַחָסָה (נ)
question	∫e'ela	שְׁאֵלָה (נ)

| to underline (vt) | lehadgiʃ | לְהַדגִיש |
| dotted line | kav nakud | קַו נָקוֹד (ז) |

121. Foreign languages

language	safa	שָׂפָה (נ)
foreign (adj)	zar	זָר
foreign language	safa zara	שָׂפָה זָרָה (נ)
to study (vt)	lilmod	לִלמוֹד
to learn (language, etc.)	lilmod	לִלמוֹד

to read (vi, vt)	likro	לִקרוֹא
to speak (vi, vt)	ledaber	לְדַבֵּר
to understand (vt)	lehavin	לְהָבִין
to write (vt)	liχtov	לִכתוֹב

fast (adv)	maher	מַהֵר
slowly (adv)	le'at	לְאַט
fluently (adv)	χofʃi	חוֹפשִי

rules	klalim	כּלָלִים (ז"ר)
grammar	dikduk	דְקדוק (ז)
vocabulary	otsar milim	אוֹצָר מִילִים (ז)
phonetics	torat ha'hege	תוֹרַת הַהָגָה (נ)

textbook	'sefer limud	סֵפֶר לִימוֹד (ז)
dictionary	milon	מִילוֹן (ז)
teach-yourself book	'sefer lelimud atsmi	סֵפֶר לְלִימוֹד עַצמִי (ז)
phrasebook	siχon	שִיחוֹן (ז)

cassette, tape	ka'letet	קַלֶטֶת (נ)
videotape	ka'letet 'vide'o	קַלֶטֶת וִידֵיאוֹ (נ)
CD, compact disc	taklitor	תַקלִיטוֹר (ז)
DVD	di vi di	דִי. וִי. דִי. (ז)

alphabet	alefbeit	אָלֶפבֵּית (ז)
to spell (vt)	le'ayet	לְאַיֵית
pronunciation	hagiya	הָגִיָיה (נ)

accent	mivta	מִבטָא (ז)
with an accent	im mivta	עִם מִבטָא
without an accent	bli mivta	בּלִי מִבטָא

| word | mila | מִילָה (נ) |
| meaning | maʃma'ut | מַשמָעוֹת (נ) |

course (e.g., a French ~)	kurs	קוֹרס (ז)
to sign up	leheraʃem lekurs	לְהֵירָשֵם לְקוֹרס
teacher	more	מוֹרֶה (ז)
translation (process)	tirgum	תִרגוֹם (ז)

translation (text, etc.)	tirgum	תַּרְגּוּם (ז)
translator	metargem	מְתַרְגֵּם (ז)
interpreter	meturgeman	מְתוּרְגְּמָן (ז)
polyglot	poliglot	פּוֹלִיגְלוֹט (ז)
memory	zikaron	זִיכָּרוֹן (ז)

122. Fairy tale characters

Santa Claus	'santa 'kla'us	סַנְטָה קְלָאוּס (ז)
Cinderella	sinde'rela	סִינְדְּרֶלָה
mermaid	bat yam, betulat hayam	בַּת יָם, בְּתוּלַת הַיָּם (נ)
Neptune	neptun	נֶפְטוּן (ז)
magician, wizard	kosem	קוֹסֵם (ז)
fairy	'feya	פֵיָה (נ)
magic (adj)	kasum	קָסוּם
magic wand	ʃarvit 'kesem	שַׁרְבִיט קֶסֶם (ז)
fairy tale	agada	אַגָּדָה (נ)
miracle	nes	נֵס (ז)
dwarf	gamad	גַּמָּד (ז)
to turn into ...	lahafoχ le...	לַהֲפוֹךְ לְ...
ghost	'ruaχ refa''im	רוּחַ רְפָאִים (נ)
phantom	'ruaχ refa''im	רוּחַ רְפָאִים (נ)
monster	mif'letset	מִפְלֶצֶת (נ)
dragon	drakon	דְּרָקוֹן (ז)
giant	anak	עֲנָק (ז)

123. Zodiac Signs

Aries	tale	טָלֶה (ז)
Taurus	ʃor	שׁוֹר (ז)
Gemini	te'omim	תְּאוֹמִים (ז"ר)
Cancer	sartan	סַרְטָן (ז)
Leo	arye	אַרְיֵה (ז)
Virgo	betula	בְּתוּלָה (נ)
Libra	moz'nayim	מֹאזְנַיִים (ז"ר)
Scorpio	akrav	עַקְרָב (ז)
Sagittarius	kaʃat	קַשָּׁת (ז)
Capricorn	gdi	גְּדִי (ז)
Aquarius	dli	דְּלִי (ז)
Pisces	dagim	דָּגִים (ז"ר)
character	'ofi	אוֹפִי (ז)
character traits	tχunot 'ofi	תְּכוּנוֹת אוֹפִי (נ"ר)

behavior	hitnahagut	הִתְנַהֲגוּת (נ)
to tell fortunes	lenabe et ha'atid	לְנַבֵּא אֶת הָעָתִיד
fortune-teller	ma'gedet atidot	מַגֶּדֶת עֲתִידוֹת (נ)
horoscope	horoskop	הוֹרוֹסְקוֹפ (ז)

Arts

124. Theater

theater	te'atron	תֵּיאַטרוֹן (ז)
opera	'opera	אוֹפֶּרָה (נ)
operetta	ope'reta	אוֹפֶּרֶטָה (נ)
ballet	balet	בָּלֶט (ז)
theater poster	kraza	כְּרָזָה (נ)
troupe	lahaka	לַהֲקָה (נ)
(theatrical company)		
tour	masa hofa'ot	מַסָע הוֹפָעוֹת (ז)
to be on tour	latset lemasa hofa'ot	לָצֵאת לְמַסָע הוֹפָעוֹת
to rehearse (vi, vt)	la'aroχ χazara	לַעֲרוֹך חֲזָרָה
rehearsal	χazara	חֲזָרָה (נ)
repertoire	repertu'ar	רֶפֶּרטוּאָר (ז)
performance	hofa'a	הוֹפָעָה (נ)
theatrical show	hatsaga	הַצָּגָה (נ)
play	maχaze	מַחֲזֶה (ז)
ticket	kartis	כַּרטִיס (ז)
box office (ticket booth)	kupa	קוּפָּה (נ)
lobby, foyer	'lobi	לוֹבִּי (ז)
coat check (cloakroom)	meltaχa	מֶלתָּחָה (נ)
coat check tag	mispar meltaχa	מִספָּר מֶלתָּחָה (ז)
binoculars	miʃkefet	מִשׁקֶפֶת (נ)
usher	sadran	סַדרָן (ז)
orchestra seats	parter	פַּרטֶר (ז)
balcony	mir'peset	מִרפֶּסֶת (נ)
dress circle	ya'tsi'a	יָצִיעַ (ז)
box	ta	תָּא (ז)
row	ʃura	שׁוּרָה (נ)
seat	moʃav	מוֹשָׁב (ז)
audience	'kahal	קָהָל (ז)
spectator	tsofe	צוֹפֶה (ז)
to clap (vi, vt)	limχo ka'payim	לִמחוֹא כַּפַּיִים
applause	meχi'ot ka'payim	מְחִיאוֹת כַּפַּיִים (נ״ר)
ovation	tʃu'ot	תְשׁוּאוֹת (נ״ר)
stage	bama	בָּמָה (נ)
curtain	masaχ	מָסָך (ז)
scenery	taf'ura	תַפאוּרָה (נ)

backstage	klayim	קְלָעִים
scene (e.g., the last ~)	'stsena	סְצֶינָה (נ)
act	ma'araχa	מַעֲרָכָה (נ)
intermission	hafsaka	הַפְסָקָה (נ)

125. Cinema

actor	saχkan	שַׂחְקָן (ז)
actress	saχkanit	שַׂחְקָנִית (נ)
movies (industry)	kol'no'a	קוֹלְנוֹעַ (ז)
movie	'seret	סֶרֶט (ז)
episode	epi'zoda	אֶפִּיזוֹדָה (נ)
detective movie	'seret balaʃi	סֶרֶט בַּלָשִׁי (ז)
action movie	ma'arvon	מַעַרבוֹן (ז)
adventure movie	'seret harpatka'ot	סֶרֶט הַרְפַּתקָאוֹת (ז)
science fiction movie	'seret mada bidyoni	סֶרֶט מַדָע בִּדיוֹנִי (ז)
horror movie	'seret eima	סֶרֶט אֵימָה (ז)
comedy movie	ko'medya	קוֹמֶדיָה (נ)
melodrama	melo'drama	מֶלוֹדרָמָה (נ)
drama	'drama	דרָמָה (נ)
fictional movie	'seret alilati	סֶרֶט עֲלִילָתִי (ז)
documentary	'seret ti'udi	סֶרֶט תִיעוּדִי (ז)
cartoon	'seret ani'matsya	סֶרֶט אֲנִימַציָה (ז)
silent movies	sratim ilmim	סרָטִים אִילמִים (ז"ר)
role (part)	tafkid	תַפְקִיד (ז)
leading role	tafkid raʃi	תַפְקִיד רָאשִׁי (ז)
to play (vi, vt)	lesaχek	לְשַׂחֵק
movie star	koχav kol'no'a	כּוֹכָב קוֹלְנוֹעַ (ז)
well-known (adj)	mefursam	מְפוּרסָם
famous (adj)	mefursam	מְפוּרסָם
popular (adj)	popu'lari	פּוֹפּוּלָרִי
script (screenplay)	tasrit	תַסְרִיט (ז)
scriptwriter	tasritai	תַסרִיטַאי (ז)
movie director	bamai	בָּמַאי (ז)
producer	mefik	מֵפִיק (ז)
assistant	ozer	עוֹזֵר (ז)
cameraman	tsalam	צַלָם (ז)
stuntman	pa'alulan	פַּעֲלוּלָן (ז)
double (stuntman)	saχkan maχlif	שַׂחְקָן מַחֲלִיף (ז)
to shoot a movie	letsalem 'seret	לְצַלֵם סֶרֶט
audition, screen test	mivdak	מִבְדָק (ז)
shooting	hasrata	הַסרָטָה (נ)

movie crew	'tsevet ha'seret	צֶוֶות הַסֶּרֶט (ז)
movie set	atar hatsilum	אֲתַר הַצִּילוּם (ז)
camera	matslema	מַצְלֵמָה (נ)
movie theater	beit kol'no'a	בֵּית קוֹלְנוֹעַ (ז)
screen (e.g., big ~)	masax	מָסָךְ (ז)
to show a movie	lehar'ot 'seret	לְהַרְאוֹת סֶרֶט
soundtrack	paskol	פַּסְקוֹל (ז)
special effects	e'fektim meyuxadim	אֶפֶקְטִים מְיוּחָדִים (ז"ר)
subtitles	ktuviyot	כְּתוּבִיּוֹת (נ"ר)
credits	ktuviyot	כְּתוּבִיּוֹת (נ"ר)
translation	tirgum	תִּרְגּוּם (ז)

126. Painting

art	amanut	אָמָנוּת (נ)
fine arts	omanuyot yafot	אוֹמָנוּיוֹת יָפוֹת (נ"ר)
art gallery	ga'lerya le'amanut	גַּלֶרְיָה לְאָמָנוּת (נ)
art exhibition	ta'aruxat amanut	תַּעֲרוּכַת אָמָנוּת (נ)
painting (art)	tsiyur	צִיּוּר (ז)
graphic art	'grafika	גְרָפִיקָה (נ)
abstract art	amanut muf'fetet	אָמָנוּת מוּפְשֶׁטֶת (נ)
impressionism	impresyonizm	אִימְפְּרֶסְיוֹנִיזְם (ז)
picture (painting)	tmuna	תְּמוּנָה (נ)
drawing	tsiyur	צִיּוּר (ז)
poster	'poster	פּוֹסְטֶר (ז)
illustration (picture)	iyur	אִיּוּר (ז)
miniature	minya'tura	מִינְיָאטוּרָה (נ)
copy (of painting, etc.)	he'etek	הֶעְתֵּק (ז)
reproduction	fi'atuk	שִׁיעָתוּק (ז)
mosaic	psefas	פְּסֵיפָס (ז)
stained glass window	vitraʒ	וִיטְרָאז' (ז)
fresco	fresko	פְרֶסְקוֹ (ז)
engraving	taxrit	תַחְרִיט (ז)
bust (sculpture)	pro'toma	פְּרוֹטוֹמָה (נ)
sculpture	'pesel	פֶּסֶל (ז)
statue	'pesel	פֶּסֶל (ז)
plaster of Paris	'geves	גֶבֶס (ז)
plaster (as adj)	mi'geves	מְגֻבָּס
portrait	dyukan	דְּיוֹקָן (ז)
self-portrait	dyukan atsmi	דְּיוֹקָן עַצְמִי (ז)
landscape painting	tsiyur nof	צִיּוּר נוֹף (ז)
still life	'teva domem	טֶבַע דּוֹמֵם (ז)

| caricature | karika'tura | קָרִיקָטוּרָה (נ) |
| sketch | tarʃim | תַרשִים (ז) |

paint	'tseva	צֶבַע (ז)
watercolor paint	'tseva 'mayim	צֶבַע מַיִם (ז)
oil (paint)	'ʃemen	שֶמֶן (ז)
pencil	iparon	עִיפָּרוֹן (ז)
India ink	tuʃ	טוּש (ז)
charcoal	peχam	פֶּחָם (ז)

| to draw (vi, vt) | letsayer | לְצַיֵיר |
| to paint (vi, vt) | letsayer | לְצַיֵיר |

to pose (vi)	ledagmen	לְדַגמֵן
artist's model (masc.)	dugman eirom	דוּגמָן עֵירוֹם (ז)
artist's model (fem.)	dugmanit erom	דוּגמָנִית עֵירוֹם (נ)

artist (painter)	tsayar	צַייָר (ז)
work of art	yetsirat amanut	יְצִירַת אָמָנוּת (נ)
masterpiece	yetsirat mofet	יְצִירַת מוֹפֵת (נ)
studio (artist's workroom)	'studyo	סטוּדיוֹ (ז)

canvas (cloth)	bad piʃtan	בַּד פִּשתָן (ז)
easel	kan tsiyur	כַּן צִיוּר (ז)
palette	'plata	פָּלֶטָה (נ)

frame (picture ~, etc.)	mis'geret	מִסגֶרֶת (נ)
restoration	ʃiχzur	שִחזוּר (ז)
to restore (vt)	leʃaχzer	לְשַחזֵר

127. Literature & Poetry

literature	sifrut	סִפרוּת (נ)
author (writer)	sofer	סוֹפֵר (ז)
pseudonym	ʃem badui	שֵם בָּדוּי (ז)

book	'sefer	סֵפֶר (ז)
volume	'kereχ	כֶּרֶך (ז)
table of contents	'toχen inyanim	תוֹכֶן עִניָינִים (ז)
page	amud	עַמוּד (ז)
main character	hagibor haraʃi	הַגִיבּוֹר הָרָאשִי (ז)
autograph	χatima	חֲתִימָה (נ)

short story	sipur katsar	סִיפּוּר קָצָר (ז)
story (novella)	sipur	סִיפּוּר (ז)
novel	roman	רוֹמָן (ז)
work (writing)	χibur	חִיבּוּר (ז)
fable	maʃal	מָשָל (ז)
detective novel	roman balaʃi	רוֹמָן בַּלָשִי (ז)
poem (verse)	ʃir	שִיר (ז)

poetry	ʃira	שִׁירָה (נ)
poem (epic, ballad)	po''ema	פּוֹאֶמָה (נ)
poet	meʃorer	מְשׁוֹרֵר (ז)

fiction	sifrut yafa	סִפְרוּת יָפָה (נ)
science fiction	mada bidyoni	מַדָע בִּדְיוֹנִי (ז)
adventures	harpatka'ot	הַרְפַּתְקָאוֹת (נ"ר)
educational literature	sifrut limudit	סִפְרוּת לִימוּדִית (נ)
children's literature	sifrut yeladim	סִפְרוּת יְלָדִים (נ)

128. Circus

circus	kirkas	קִרְקָס (ז)
traveling circus	kirkas nayad	קִרְקָס נַיָּד (ז)
program	toχnit	תּוֹכְנִית (נ)
performance	hofa'a	הוֹפָעָה (נ)

| act (circus ~) | hofa'a | הוֹפָעָה (נ) |
| circus ring | zira | זִירָה (נ) |

| pantomime (act) | panto'mima | פַּנְטוֹמִימָה (נ) |
| clown | leitsan | לֵיצָן (ז) |

acrobat	akrobat	אַקְרוֹבָּט (ז)
acrobatics	akro'batika	אַקְרוֹבָּטִיקָה (נ)
gymnast	mit'amel	מִתְעַמֵּל (ז)
gymnastics	hit'amlut	הִתְעַמְּלוּת (נ)
somersault	'salta	סַלְטָה (נ)

athlete (strongman)	atlet	אַתְלֵט (ז)
tamer (e.g., lion ~)	me'alef	מְאַלֵּף (ז)
rider (circus horse ~)	roχev	רוֹכֵב (ז)
assistant	ozer	עוֹזֵר (ז)

stunt	pa'alul	פַּעֲלוּל (ז)
magic trick	'kesem	קֶסֶם (ז)
conjurer, magician	kosem	קוֹסֵם (ז)

juggler	lahatutan	לַהֲטוּטָן (ז)
to juggle (vi, vt)	lelahtet	לְלַהֲטֵט
animal trainer	me'alef hayot	מְאַלֵּף חַיּוֹת (ז)
animal training	iluf χayot	אִילּוּף חַיּוֹת (ז)
to train (animals)	le'alef	לְאַלֵּף

129. Music. Pop music

| music | 'muzika | מוּזִיקָה (נ) |
| musician | muzikai | מוּזִיקַאי (ז) |

musical instrument	kli negina	כְּלִי נְגִינָה (ז)
to play ...	lenagen be...	לְנַגֵן בְּ...
guitar	gi'tara	גִיטָרָה (נ)
violin	kinor	כִּינוֹר (ז)
cello	'tfelo	צֶ'לוֹ (ז)
double bass	kontrabas	קוֹנטרַבֶּס (ז)
harp	'nevel	נֵבֶל (ז)
piano	psanter	פְּסַנתֵר (ז)
grand piano	psanter kanaf	פְּסַנתֵר כָּנָף (ז)
organ	ugav	עוּגָב (ז)
wind instruments	klei neʃifa	כְּלֵי נְשִיפָה (ז"ר)
oboe	abuv	אַבּוּב (ז)
saxophone	saksofon	סַקסוֹפוֹן (ז)
clarinet	klarinet	קלָרִינֶט (ז)
flute	χalil	חָלִיל (ז)
trumpet	χatsotsra	חֲצוֹצרָה (נ)
accordion	akordyon	אָקוֹרדִיוֹן (ז)
drum	tof	תוֹף (ז)
duo	'du'o	דוּאוֹ (ז)
trio	ʃliʃiya	שלִישִייָה (נ)
quartet	revi'iya	רְבִיעִייָה (נ)
choir	makhela	מַקהֵלָה (נ)
orchestra	tiz'moret	תִזמוֹרֶת (נ)
pop music	'muzikat pop	מוּזִיקַת פּוֹפ (נ)
rock music	'muzikat rok	מוּזִיקַת רוֹק (נ)
rock group	lehakat rok	לַהֲקַת רוֹק (נ)
jazz	dʒez	גָ'ז (ז)
idol	koχav	כּוֹכָב (ז)
admirer, fan	ohed	אוֹהֵד (ז)
concert	kontsert	קוֹנצֶרט (ז)
symphony	si'fonya	סִימפוֹנִיָה (נ)
composition	yetsira	יְצִירָה (נ)
to compose (write)	leχaber	לְחַבֵּר
singing (n)	ʃira	שִירָה (נ)
song	ʃir	שִיר (ז)
tune (melody)	mangina	מַנגִינָה (נ)
rhythm	'ketsev	קֶצֶב (ז)
blues	bluz	בּלוּז (ז)
sheet music	tavim	תָוִים (ז"ר)
baton	ʃarvit ni'tsuaχ	שַרבִיט נִיצוּחַ (ז)
bow	'keʃet	קֶשֶת (נ)
string	meitar	מֵיתָר (ז)
case (e.g., guitar ~)	nartik	נַרתִיק (ז)

Rest. Entertainment. Travel

130. Trip. Travel

tourism, travel	tayarut	תַּיָּרוּת (נ)
tourist	tayar	תַּיָּר (ז)
trip, voyage	tiyul	טִיּוּל (ז)
adventure	harpatka	הַרְפַּתְקָה (נ)
trip, journey	nesiʿa	נְסִיעָה (נ)
vacation	χuffa	חוּפְשָׁה (נ)
to be on vacation	lihyot beχuffa	לִהְיוֹת בְּחוּפְשָׁה
rest	menuχa	מְנוּחָה (נ)
train	ra'kevet	רַכֶּבֶת (נ)
by train	bera'kevet	בְּרַכֶּבֶת
airplane	matos	מָטוֹס (ז)
by airplane	bematos	בְּמָטוֹס
by car	bemeχonit	בִּמְכוֹנִית
by ship	be'oniya	בְּאוֹנִיָּה
luggage	mit'an	מִטְעָן (ז)
suitcase	mizvada	מִזְוָדָה (נ)
luggage cart	eglat mit'an	עֶגְלַת מִטְעָן (נ)
passport	darkon	דַּרְכּוֹן (ז)
visa	'viza, aʃra	וִיזָה, אַשְׁרָה (נ)
ticket	kartis	כַּרְטִיס (ז)
air ticket	kartis tisa	כַּרְטִיס טִיסָה (ז)
guidebook	madriχ	מַדְרִיךְ (ז)
map (tourist ~)	mapa	מַפָּה (נ)
area (rural ~)	ezor	אֵזוֹר (ז)
place, site	makom	מָקוֹם (ז)
exotica (n)	ek'zotika	אֶקְזוֹטִיקָה (נ)
exotic (adj)	ek'zoti	אֶקְזוֹטִי
amazing (adj)	nifla	נִפְלָא
group	kvuʦa	קְבוּצָה (נ)
excursion, sightseeing tour	tiyul	טִיּוּל (ז)
guide (person)	madriχ tiyulim	מַדְרִיךְ טִיּוּלִים (ז)

131. Hotel

hotel	malon	מָלוֹן (ז)
motel	motel	מוֹטֶל (ז)
three-star (~ hotel)	ʃloʃa koχavim	שְׁלוֹשָׁה כּוֹכָבִים
five-star	χamiʃa koχavim	חֲמִישָׁה כּוֹכָבִים
to stay (in a hotel, etc.)	lehit'aχsen	לְהִתְאַכְסֵן
room	'χeder	חֶדֶר (ז)
single room	'χeder yaχid	חֶדֶר יָחִיד (ז)
double room	'χeder zugi	חֶדֶר זוּגִי (ז)
to book a room	lehazmin 'χeder	לְהַזְמִין חֶדֶר
half board	χatsi pensiyon	חֲצִי פֶּנְסִיוֹן (ז)
full board	pensyon male	פֶּנְסִיוֹן מָלֵא (ז)
with bath	im am'batya	עִם אַמְבַּטְיָה
with shower	im mik'laχat	עִם מִקְלַחַת
satellite television	tele'vizya bekvalim	טֶלֶוִיזְיָה בְּכְבָלִים (נ)
air-conditioner	mazgan	מַזְגָן (ז)
towel	ma'gevet	מַגֶּבֶת (נ)
key	maf'teaχ	מַפְתֵּחַ (ז)
administrator	amarkal	אֲמַרְכָּל (ז)
chambermaid	χadranit	חַדְרָנִית (נ)
porter, bellboy	sabal	סַבָּל (ז)
doorman	pakid kabala	פְּקִיד קַבָּלָה (ז)
restaurant	mis'ada	מִסְעָדָה (נ)
pub, bar	bar	בַּר (ז)
breakfast	aruχat 'boker	אֲרוּחַת בּוֹקֶר (נ)
dinner	aruχat 'erev	אֲרוּחַת עֶרֶב (נ)
buffet	miznon	מִזְנוֹן (ז)
lobby	'lobi	לוֹבִּי (ז)
elevator	ma'alit	מַעֲלִית (נ)
DO NOT DISTURB	lo lehaf'ri'a	לֹא לְהַפְרִיעַ
NO SMOKING	asur le'aʃen!	אָסוּר לְעַשֵׁן!

132. Books. Reading

book	'sefer	סֵפֶר (ז)
author	sofer	סוֹפֵר (ז)
writer	sofer	סוֹפֵר (ז)
to write (~ a book)	liχtov	לִכְתּוֹב
reader	kore	קוֹרֵא (ז)
to read (vi, vt)	likro	לִקְרוֹא

reading (activity)	kri'a	קְרִיאָה (נ)
silently (to oneself)	belev, be'ʃeket	בְּלֵב, בְּשֶׁקֶט
aloud (adv)	bekol ram	בְּקוֹל רָם
to publish (vt)	lehotsi la'or	לְהוֹצִיא לָאוֹר
publishing (process)	hotsa'a la'or	הוֹצָאָה לָאוֹר (נ)
publisher	motsi le'or	מוֹצִיא לָאוֹר (ז)
publishing house	hotsa'a la'or	הוֹצָאָה לָאוֹר (נ)
to come out (be released)	latset le'or	לָצֵאת לָאוֹר
release (of a book)	hafatsa	הָפָצָה (נ)
print run	tfutsa	תפוּצָה (נ)
bookstore	χanut sfarim	חָנוּת סְפָרִים (נ)
library	sifriya	סִפְרִיָיה (נ)
story (novella)	sipur	סִיפוּר (ז)
short story	sipur katsar	סִיפוּר קָצָר (ז)
novel	roman	רוֹמָן (ז)
detective novel	roman balaʃi	רוֹמָן בַּלָשִׁי (ז)
memoirs	ziχronot	זִיכרוֹנוֹת (ז"ר)
legend	agada	אַגָדָה (נ)
myth	'mitos	מִיתוֹס (ז)
poetry, poems	ʃirim	שִׁירִים (ז"ר)
autobiography	otobio'grafya	אוֹטוֹבִּיוֹגרַפיָה (נ)
selected works	mivχar ktavim	מִבחָר כּתָבִים (ז)
science fiction	mada bidyoni	מַדָע בִּדיוֹנִי (ז)
title	kotar	כּוֹתָר (ז)
introduction	mavo	מָבוֹא (ז)
title page	amud ha'ʃa'ar	עָמוד הַשַׁעַר (ז)
chapter	'perek	פֶּרֶק (ז)
extract	'keta	קֶטַע (ז)
episode	epi'zoda	אָפִּיזוֹדָה (נ)
plot (storyline)	alila	עָלִילָה (נ)
contents	'toχen	תוֹכֶן (ז)
table of contents	'toχen inyanim	תוֹכֶן עִניָינִים (ז)
main character	hagibor haraʃi	הַגִיבּוֹר הָרָאשִׁי (ז)
volume	'kereχ	כֶּרֶך (ז)
cover	kriχa	כּרִיכָה (נ)
binding	kriχa	כּרִיכָה (נ)
bookmark	simaniya	סִימָנִיָיה (נ)
page	amud	עָמוד (ז)
to page through	ledafdef	לְדַפדֵף
margins	ʃu'layim	שׁוּלַיִים (ז"ר)
annotation (marginal note, etc.)	he'ara	הָעָרָה (נ)

footnote	he'arat ʃu'layim	הֶעָרַת שׁוּלַיִים (נ)
text	tekst	טֶקְסְט (ז)
type, font	gufan	גוּפָן (ז)
misprint, typo	ta'ut dfus	טָעוּת דְפוּס (נ)

translation	tirgum	תַרְגוּם (ז)
to translate (vt)	letargem	לְתַרְגֵם
original (n)	makor	מָקוֹר (ז)

famous (adj)	mefursam	מְפוּרְסָם
unknown (not famous)	lo ya'du'a	לֹא יָדוּעַ
interesting (adj)	me'anyen	מְעַנְיֵין
bestseller	rav 'meχer	רַב־מֶכֶר (ז)

dictionary	milon	מִילוֹן (ז)
textbook	'sefer limud	סֵפֶר לִימוּד (ז)
encyclopedia	entsiklo'pedya	אֶנְצִיקְלוֹפֶּדְיָה (נ)

133. Hunting. Fishing

hunting	'tsayid	צַיִד (ז)
to hunt (vi, vt)	latsud	לָצוּד
hunter	tsayad	צַייָד (ז)

to shoot (vi)	lirot	לִירוֹת
rifle	rove	רוֹבֶה (ז)
bullet (shell)	kadur	כַּדוּר (ז)
shot (lead balls)	kaduriyot	כַּדוּרִיוֹת (נ"ר)

steel trap	mal'kodet	מַלְכּוֹדֶת (נ)
snare (for birds, etc.)	mal'kodet	מַלְכּוֹדֶת (נ)
to fall into the steel trap	lehilaχed bemal'kodet	לְהִילָכֵד בְּמַלְכּוֹדֶת
to lay a steel trap	leha'niaχ mal'kodet	לְהָנִיחַ מַלְכּוֹדֶת

poacher	tsayad lelo reʃut	צַייָד לְלֹא רְשׁוּת (ז)
game (in hunting)	χayot bar	חַיּוֹת בָּר (נ"ר)
hound dog	'kelev 'tsayid	כֶּלֶב צַיִד (ז)
safari	sa'fari	סָפָארִי (ז)
mounted animal	puχlats	פּוּחְלָץ (ז)

fisherman, angler	dayag	דַייָג (ז)
fishing (angling)	'dayig	דַיִג (ז)
to fish (vi)	ladug	לָדוּג

fishing rod	χaka	חַכָּה (נ)
fishing line	χut haχaka	חוּט הַחַכָּה (ז)
hook	'keres	קֶרֶס (ז)
float, bobber	matsof	מָצוֹף (ז)
bait	pitayon	פִּיתָיוֹן (ז)
to cast a line	lizrok et haχaka	לִזְרוֹק אֶת הַחַכָּה

to bite (ab. fish)	liv'lo'a pitayon	לִבְלוֹעַ פִּיתָיוֹן
catch (of fish)	ʃlal 'dayig	שְׁלָל דַיָג (ז)
ice-hole	mivka 'keraχ	מִבְקַע קֶרַח (ז)
fishing net	'reʃet dayagim	רֶשֶׁת דַיָגִים (נ)
boat	sira	סִירָה (נ)
to net (to fish with a net)	ladug be'reʃet	לָדוּג בְּרֶשֶׁת
to cast[throw] the net	lizrok 'reʃet	לִזְרוֹק רֶשֶׁת
to haul the net in	ligror 'reʃet	לִגְרוֹר רֶשֶׁת
to fall into the net	lehilaχed be'reʃet	לְהִילָכֵד בְּרֶשֶׁת
whaler (person)	tsayad livyatanim	צַיָד לִוְויָתָנִים (ז)
whaleboat	sfinat tseid livyetanim	סְפִינַת צֵיד לִוְויָתָנִית (נ)
harpoon	tsiltsal	צִלְצָל (ז)

134. Games. Billiards

billiards	bilyard	בִּילְיַארְד (ז)
billiard room, hall	'χeder bilyard	חֶדֶר בִּילְיַארְד (ז)
ball (snooker, etc.)	kadur bilyard	כַּדוּר בִּילְיַארְד (ז)
to pocket a ball	lehaχnis kadur lekis	לְהַכְנִיס כַּדוּר לְכִּיס
cue	makel bilyard	מַקֵל בִּילְיַארְד (ז)
pocket	kis	כִּיס (ז)

135. Games. Playing cards

diamonds	yahalom	יַהֲלוֹם (ז)
spades	ale	עָלֶה (ז)
hearts	lev	לֵב (ז)
clubs	tiltan	תִלְתָן (ז)
ace	as	אָס (ז)
king	'meleχ	מֶלֶך (ז)
queen	malka	מַלְכָּה (נ)
jack, knave	nasiχ	נָסִיך (ז)
playing card	klaf	קְלָף (ז)
cards	klafim	קְלָפִים (ז"ר)
trump	klaf nitsaχon	קְלָף נִיצָחוֹן (ז)
deck of cards	χafisat klafim	חֲפִיסַת קְלָפִּים (נ)
point	nekuda	נְקוּדָה (נ)
to deal (vi, vt)	leχalek klafim	לְחַלֵק קְלָפִים
to shuffle (cards)	litrof	לִטְרוֹף
lead, turn (n)	tor	תוֹר (ז)
cardsharp	noχel klafim	נוֹכֵל קְלָפִים (ז)

136. Rest. Games. Miscellaneous

to stroll (vi, vt)	letayel ba'regel	לְטַיֵּל בָּרֶגֶל
stroll (leisurely walk)	tiyul ragli	טִיוּל רַגְלִי (ז)
car ride	nesi'a bameҳonit	נְסִיעָה בָּמְכוֹנִית (נ)
adventure	harpatka	הַרְפַּתְקָה (נ)
picnic	'piknik	פִּיקְנִיק (ז)
game (chess, etc.)	misҳak	מִשְׂחָק (ז)
player	saҳkan	שַׂחְקָן (ז)
game (one ~ of chess)	misҳak	מִשְׂחָק (ז)
collector (e.g., philatelist)	asfan	אַסְפָן (ז)
to collect (stamps, etc.)	le'esof	לָאֱסוֹף
collection	'osef	אוֹסֵף (ז)
crossword puzzle	taʃbets	תַשְבֵּץ (ז)
racetrack (horse racing venue)	hipodrom	הִיפּוֹדְרוֹם (ז)
disco (discotheque)	diskotek	דִיסְקוֹטֶק (ז)
sauna	'sa'una	סָאוּנָה (נ)
lottery	'loto	לוֹטוֹ (ז)
camping trip	tiyul maҳana'ut	טִיוּל מַחֲנָאוּת (ז)
camp	maҳane	מַחֲנֶה (ז)
tent (for camping)	'ohel	אוֹהֶל (ז)
compass	matspen	מַצְפֵּן (ז)
camper	maҳnai	מַחֲנַאי (ז)
to watch (movie, etc.)	lir'ot	לִרְאוֹת
viewer	tsofe	צוֹפֶה (ז)
TV show (TV program)	toҳnit tele'vizya	תוֹכְנִית טֶלֶוִיזְיָה (נ)

137. Photography

camera (photo)	matslema	מַצְלֵמָה (נ)
photo, picture	tmuna	תמוּנָה (נ)
photographer	tsalam	צַלָם (ז)
photo studio	'studyo letsilum	סְטוּדְיוֹ לְצִילוּם (ז)
photo album	albom tmunot	אַלְבּוֹם תמוּנוֹת (ז)
camera lens	adaʃa	עֲדָשָה (נ)
telephoto lens	a'deʃet teleskop	עֲדָשֶת טֶלֶסְקוֹפ (נ)
filter	masnen	מַסְנֵן (ז)
lens	adaʃa	עֲדָשָה (נ)
optics (high-quality ~)	'optika	אוֹפְּטִיקָה (נ)
diaphragm (aperture)	tsamtsam	צַמְצַם (ז)

exposure time (shutter speed)	zman hahe'ara	זְמַן הַהָאָרָה (ז)
viewfinder	einit	עֵינִית (נ)
digital camera	matslema digi'talit	מַצְלֵמָה דִּיגִּיטָלִית (נ)
tripod	xatsuva	חֲצוּבָה (נ)
flash	mavzek	מַבְזֵק (ז)
to photograph (vt)	letsalem	לְצַלֵּם
to take pictures	letsalem	לְצַלֵּם
to have one's picture taken	lehitstalem	לְהִצְטַלֵּם
focus	moked	מוֹקֵד (ז)
to focus	lemaked	לְמַקֵּד
sharp, in focus (adj)	xad, memukad	חַד, מְמוּקָד
sharpness	xadut	חַדּוּת (נ)
contrast	nigud	נִיגוּד (ז)
contrast (as adj)	menugad	מְנוּגָד
picture (photo)	tmuna	תְּמוּנָה (נ)
negative (n)	taʃlil	תַשְׁלִיל (ז)
film (a roll of ~)	'seret	סֶרֶט (ז)
frame (still)	freim	פְרֵיים (ז)
to print (photos)	lehadpis	לְהַדְפִּיס

138. Beach. Swimming

beach	xof yam	חוֹף יָם (ז)
sand	xol	חוֹל (ז)
deserted (beach)	ʃomem	שׁוֹמֵם
suntan	ʃizuf	שִׁיזוּף (ז)
to get a tan	lehiʃtazef	לְהִשְׁתַּזֵּף
tan (adj)	ʃazuf	שָׁזוּף
sunscreen	krem hagana	קְרֶם הֲגָנָה (ז)
bikini	bi'kini	בִּיקִינִי (ז)
bathing suit	'beged yam	בֶּגֶד יָם (ז)
swim trunks	'beged yam	בֶּגֶד יָם (ז)
swimming pool	brexa	בְּרֵיכָה (נ)
to swim (vi)	lisxot	לִשְׂחוֹת
shower	mik'laxat	מִקְלַחַת (נ)
to change (one's clothes)	lehaxlif bgadim	לְהַחְלִיף בְּגָדִים
towel	ma'gevet	מַגֶּבֶת (נ)
boat	sira	סִירָה (נ)
motorboat	sirat ma'no'a	סִירַת מָנוֹעַ (נ)
water ski	ski 'mayim	סְקִי מַיִם (ז)

paddle boat	sirat pe'dalim	סִירַת פֶּדָלִים (נ)
surfing	gliʃat galim	גלִישַת גַלִים
surfer	goleʃ	גוֹלֵש (ז)
scuba set	'skuba	סקוּבָּה (נ)
flippers (swim fins)	snapirim	סנַפִּירִים (ז״ר)
mask (diving ~)	maseχa	מַסֵכָה (נ)
diver	tsolelan	צוֹלְלָן (ז)
to dive (vi)	litslol	לִצלוֹל
underwater (adv)	mi'taχat lifnei ha'mayim	מִתַחַת לִפנֵי הַמַיִם
beach umbrella	ʃimʃiya	שִמשִיָה (נ)
sunbed (lounger)	kise 'noaχ	כִּיסֵא נוֹחַ (ז)
sunglasses	miʃkefei 'ʃemeʃ	מִשקְפֵי שֶמֶש (ז״ר)
air mattress	mizron mitna'peaχ	מִזרוֹן מִתנַפֵּחַ (ז)
to play (amuse oneself)	lesaχek	לְשַחֵק
to go for a swim	lehitraχets	לְהִתרַחֵץ
beach ball	kadur yam	כַּדוּר יָם (ז)
to inflate (vt)	lena'peaχ	לְנַפֵּחַ
inflatable, air (adj)	menupaχ	מְנוּפָּח
wave	gal	גַל (ז)
buoy (line of ~s)	matsof	מָצוֹף (ז)
to drown (ab. person)	lit'bo'a	לִטבּוֹעַ
to save, to rescue	lehatsil	לְהַצִיל
life vest	χagorat hatsala	חֲגוֹרַת הַצָלָה (נ)
to observe, to watch	litspot, lehaʃkif	לִצפּוֹת, לְהַשקִיף
lifeguard	matsil	מַצִיל (ז)

TECHNICAL EQUIPMENT. TRANSPORTATION

Technical equipment

139. Computer

computer	maxʃev	מַחְשֵׁב (ז)
notebook, laptop	maxʃev nayad	מַחְשֵׁב נַיָּיד (ז)
to turn on	lehadlik	לְהַדְלִיק
to turn off	lexabot	לְכַבּוֹת
keyboard	mik'ledet	מִקְלֶדֶת (נ)
key	makaʃ	מַקָּשׁ (ז)
mouse	axbar	עַכְבָּר (ז)
mouse pad	ʃa'tiax le'axbar	שָׁטִיחַ לְעַכְבָּר (ז)
button	kaftor	כַּפְתּוֹר (ז)
cursor	saman	סַמָּן (ז)
monitor	masax	מָסָךְ (ז)
screen	tsag	צַג (ז)
hard disk	disk ka'ʃiax	דִּיסְק קָשִׁיחַ (ז)
hard disk capacity	'nefax disk ka'ʃiax	נֶפַח דִּיסְק קָשִׁיחַ (ז)
memory	zikaron	זִיכָּרוֹן (ז)
random access memory	zikaron giʃa akra'it	זִיכָּרוֹן גִּישָׁה אַקְרָאִית (ז)
file	'kovets	קוֹבֶץ (ז)
folder	tikiya	תִּיקִייָה (נ)
to open (vt)	lif'toax	לִפְתּוֹחַ
to close (vt)	lisgor	לִסְגּוֹר
to save (vt)	liʃmor	לִשְׁמוֹר
to delete (vt)	limxok	לִמְחוֹק
to copy (vt)	leha'atik	לְהַעְתִּיק
to sort (vt)	lemayen	לְמַיֵּן
to transfer (copy)	leha'avir	לְהַעֲבִיר
program	toxna	תּוֹכְנָה (נ)
software	toxna	תּוֹכְנָה (נ)
programmer	metaxnet	מְתַכְנֵת (ז)
to program (vt)	letaxnet	לְתַכְנֵת
hacker	'haker	הָאקֶר (ז)
password	sisma	סִיסְמָה (נ)

| virus | 'virus | וִירוּס (ז) |
| to find, to detect | limtso, le'ater | לִמְצוֹא, לְאַתֵּר |

| byte | bait | בַּייט (ז) |
| megabyte | megabait | מֶגָבַּייט (ז) |

| data | netunim | נְתוּנִים (ז"ר) |
| database | bsis netunim | בְּסִיס נְתוּנִים (ז) |

cable (USB, etc.)	'kevel	כֶּבֶל (ז)
to disconnect (vt)	lenatek	לְנַתֵּק
to connect (sth to sth)	leχaber	לְחַבֵּר

140. Internet. E-mail

Internet	'internet	אִינְטֶרְנֶט (ז)
browser	dafdefan	דַפְדְפָן (ז)
search engine	ma'no'a χipus	מָנוֹעַ חִיפּוּשׂ (ז)
provider	sapak	סַפָּק (ז)

webmaster	menahel ha'atar	מְנַהֵל הָאֲתַר (ז)
website	atar	אֲתַר (ז)
webpage	daf 'internet	דַף אִינְטֶרְנֶט (ז)

| address (e-mail ~) | 'ktovet | כְּתוֹבֶת (נ) |
| address book | 'sefer ktovot | סֵפֶר כְּתוֹבוֹת (ז) |

mailbox	teivat 'do'ar	תֵיבַת דוֹאַר (נ)
mail	'do'ar, 'do'al	דוֹאַר (ז), דוֹאָ"ל (ז)
full (adj)	gaduʃ	גָדוּשׁ

message	hoda'a	הוֹדָעָה (נ)
incoming messages	hoda'ot niχnasot	הוֹדָעוֹת נִכְנָסוֹת (נ"ר)
outgoing messages	hoda'ot yots'ot	הוֹדָעוֹת יוֹצְאוֹת (נ"ר)
sender	ʃo'leaχ	שׁוֹלֵחַ (ז)
to send (vt)	liʃ'loaχ	לִשְׁלוֹחַ
sending (of mail)	ʃliχa	שְׁלִיחָה (נ)

| receiver | nim'an | נִמְעָן (ז) |
| to receive (vt) | lekabel | לְקַבֵּל |

| correspondence | hitkatvut | הִתְכַּתְבוּת (נ) |
| to correspond (vi) | lehitkatev | לְהִתְכַּתֵב |

file	'kovets	קוֹבֶץ (ז)
to download (vt)	lehorid	לְהוֹרִיד
to create (vt)	litsor	לִיצוֹר
to delete (vt)	limχok	לִמְחוֹק
deleted (adj)	maχuk	מָחוּק
connection (ADSL, etc.)	χibur	חִיבּוּר (ז)

speed	mehirut	מְהִירוּת (נ)
modem	'modem	מוֹדֶם (ז)
access	giʃa	גִּישָׁה (נ)
port (e.g., input ~)	port	פּוֹרט (ז)
connection (make a ~)	χibur	חִיבּוּר (ז)
to connect to ... (vi)	lehitχaber	לְהִתְחַבֵּר
to select (vt)	livχor	לִבְחוֹר
to search (for ...)	leχapes	לְחַפֵּשׂ

Transportation

141. Airplane

airplane	matos	מָטוֹס (ז)
air ticket	kartis tisa	כַּרְטִיס טִיסָה (ז)
airline	xevrat te'ufa	חֶבְרַת תְעוּפָה (נ)
airport	nemal te'ufa	נְמַל תְעוּפָה (ז)
supersonic (adj)	al koli	עַל קוֹלִי
captain	kabarnit	קַבַּרְנִיט (ז)
crew	'tsevet	צֶוֶת (ז)
pilot	tayas	טַיָיס (ז)
flight attendant (fem.)	da'yelet	דַייֶלֶת (נ)
navigator	navat	נַוָוט (ז)
wings	kna'fayim	כְּנָפַיִם (נ"ר)
tail	zanav	זָנָב (ז)
cockpit	'kokpit	קוֹקְפִּיט (ז)
engine	ma'no'a	מָנוֹעַ (ז)
undercarriage (landing gear)	kan nesi'a	כַּן נְסִיעָה (ז)
turbine	tur'bina	טוּרבִּינָה (נ)
propeller	madxef	מַדחֵף (ז)
black box	kufsa ʃxora	קוּפסָה שחוֹרָה (נ)
yoke (control column)	'hege	הֶגֶה (ז)
fuel	'delek	דֶלֶק (ז)
safety card	hora'ot betixut	הוֹרָאוֹת בְּטִיחוּת (נ"ר)
oxygen mask	masexat xamtsan	מַסֵיכַת חַמצָן (נ)
uniform	madim	מַדִים (ז"ר)
life vest	xagorat hatsala	חֲגוֹרַת הַצָלָה (נ)
parachute	mitsnax	מִצנָח (ז)
takeoff	hamra'a	הַמרָאָה (נ)
to take off (vi)	lehamri	לְהַמרִיא
runway	maslul hamra'a	מַסלוּל הַמרָאָה (ז)
visibility	re'ut	רְאוּת (נ)
flight (act of flying)	tisa	טִיסָה (נ)
altitude	'gova	גוֹבַה (ז)
air pocket	kis avir	כִּיס אֲוֹויר (ז)
seat	moʃav	מוֹשָב (ז)
headphones	ozniyot	אוֹזנִיוֹת (נ"ר)

folding tray (tray table)	magaʃ mitkapel	מַגָּשׁ מְתקַפֵּל (ז)
airplane window	tsohar	צוֹהַר (ז)
aisle	ma'avar	מַעֲבָר (ז)

142. Train

train	ra'kevet	רַכֶּבֶת (נ)
commuter train	ra'kevet parvarim	רַכֶּבֶת פַּרבָרִים (נ)
express train	ra'kevet mehira	רַכֶּבֶת מְהִירָה (נ)
diesel locomotive	katar 'dizel	קַטָר דִיזֶל (ז)
steam locomotive	katar	קַטָר (ז)
passenger car	karon	קָרוֹן (ז)
dining car	kron mis'ada	קרוֹן מִסעָדָה (ז)
rails	mesilot	מְסִילוֹת (נ"ר)
railroad	mesilat barzel	מְסִילַת בַּרזֶל (נ)
railway tie	'eden	אֶדֶן (ז)
platform (railway ~)	ratsif	רָצִיף (ז)
track (~ 1, 2, etc.)	mesila	מְסִילָה (נ)
semaphore	ramzor	רַמזוֹר (ז)
station	taxana	תַחֲנָה (נ)
engineer (train driver)	nahag ra'kevet	נַהָג רַכֶּבֶת (ז)
porter (of luggage)	sabal	סַבָּל (ז)
car attendant	sadran ra'kevet	סַדרָן רַכֶּבֶת (ז)
passenger	no'se'a	נוֹסֵעַ (ז)
conductor (ticket inspector)	bodek	בּוֹדֵק (ז)
corridor (in train)	prozdor	פּרוֹזדוֹר (ז)
emergency brake	ma'atsar xirum	מַעֲצָר חִירוּם (ז)
compartment	ta	תָא (ז)
berth	dargaʃ	דַרגָשׁ (ז)
upper berth	dargaʃ elyon	דַרגָשׁ עֶליוֹן (ז)
lower berth	dargaʃ taxton	דַרגָשׁ תַחתוֹן (ז)
bed linen, bedding	matsa'im	מַצָעִים (ז"ר)
ticket	kartis	כַּרטִיס (ז)
schedule	'luax zmanim	לוּחַ זמַנִים (ז)
information display	'ʃelet meida	שֶׁלֶט מֵידָע (ז)
to leave, to depart	latset	לָצֵאת
departure (of train)	yetsi'a	יְצִיאָה (נ)
to arrive (ab. train)	leha'gi'a	לְהַגִּיעַ
arrival	haga'a	הַגָעָה (נ)
to arrive by train	leha'gi'a bera'kevet	לְהַגִּיעַ בְּרַכֶּבֶת
to get on the train	la'alot lera'kevet	לַעֲלוֹת לְרַכֶּבֶת

to get off the train	la'redet mehara'kevet	לָרֶדֶת מֵהָרַכֶּבֶת
train wreck	hitraskut	הִתְרַסְקוּת (נ)
to derail (vi)	la'redet mipasei ra'kevet	לָרֶדֶת מִפַּסֵי רַכֶּבֶת
steam locomotive	katar	קַטָּר (ז)
stoker, fireman	masik	מַסִּיק (ז)
firebox	kivʃan	כִּבְשָׁן (ז)
coal	peχam	פֶּחָם (ז)

143. Ship

ship	sfina	סְפִינָה (נ)
vessel	sfina	סְפִינָה (נ)
steamship	oniyat kitor	אוֹנִיַּת קִיטוֹר (נ)
riverboat	sfinat nahar	סְפִינַת נָהָר (נ)
cruise ship	oniyat ta'anugot	אוֹנִיַּת תַּעֲנוּגוֹת (נ)
cruiser	sa'yeret	סַיֶּרֶת (נ)
yacht	'yaχta	יַכְטָה (נ)
tugboat	go'reret	גּוֹרֶרֶת (נ)
barge	arba	אַרְבָּה (נ)
ferry	ma'a'boret	מַעֲבוֹרֶת (נ)
sailing ship	sfinat mifras	סְפִינַת מִפְרָשׂ (נ)
brigantine	briganit	בְּרִיגָנִית (נ)
ice breaker	ʃo'veret 'keraχ	שׁוֹבֶרֶת קֶרַח (נ)
submarine	tso'lelet	צוֹלֶלֶת (נ)
boat (flat-bottomed ~)	sira	סִירָה (נ)
dinghy	sira	סִירָה (נ)
lifeboat	sirat hatsala	סִירַת הַצָּלָה (נ)
motorboat	sirat ma'no'a	סִירַת מָנוֹעַ (נ)
captain	rav χovel	רַב-חוֹבֵל (ז)
seaman	malaχ	מַלָּח (ז)
sailor	yamai	יַמַּאי (ז)
crew	'tsevet	צֶוֶת (ז)
boatswain	rav malaχim	רַב-מַלָּחִים (ז)
ship's boy	'na'ar sipun	נַעַר סִיפּוּן (ז)
cook	tabaχ	טַבָּח (ז)
ship's doctor	rofe ha'oniya	רוֹפֵא הָאוֹנִיָּה (ז)
deck	sipun	סִיפּוּן (ז)
mast	'toren	תּוֹרֶן (ז)
sail	mifras	מִפְרָשׂ (ז)
hold	'beten oniya	בֶּטֶן אוֹנִיָּה (נ)
bow (prow)	χartom	חַרְטוֹם (ז)

stern	yarketei hasfina	יַרְכְּתֵי הַסְּפִינָה (ז״ר)
oar	maʃot	מָשׁוֹט (ז)
screw propeller	madχef	מַדְחֵף (ז)

cabin	ta	תָּא (ז)
wardroom	mo'adon ktsinim	מוֹעֲדוֹן קְצִינִים (ז)
engine room	χadar meχonot	חֲדַר מְכוֹנוֹת (ז)
bridge	'geʃer hapikud	גֶּשֶׁר הַפִּיקוּד (ז)
radio room	ta alχutan	תָּא אַלְחוּטָן (ז)

| wave (radio) | 'teder | תֶּדֶר (ז) |
| logbook | yoman ha'oniya | יוֹמַן הָאֳנִיָּה (ז) |

spyglass	miʃ'kefet	מִשְׁקֶפֶת (נ)
bell	pa'amon	פַּעֲמוֹן (ז)
flag	'degel	דֶּגֶל (ז)

| hawser (mooring ~) | avot ha'oniya | עֲבוֹת הָאֳנִיָּה (נ) |
| knot (bowline, etc.) | 'keʃer | קֶשֶׁר (ז) |

| deckrails | ma'ake hasipun | מַעֲקֵה הַסִּיפּוּן (ז) |
| gangway | 'keveʃ | כֶּבֶשׁ (ז) |

| anchor | 'ogen | עוֹגֶן (ז) |
| to weigh anchor | leharim 'ogen | לְהָרִים עוֹגֶן |

| to drop anchor | la'agon | לַעֲגּוֹן |
| anchor chain | ʃar'ʃeret ha'ogen | שַׁרְשֶׁרֶת הָעוֹגֶן (נ) |

| port (harbor) | namal | נָמֵל (ז) |
| quay, wharf | 'mezaχ | מֶזַח (ז) |

| to berth (moor) | la'agon | לַעֲגּוֹן |
| to cast off | lehaflig | לְהַפְלִיג |

| trip, voyage | masa, tiyul | מַסָּע (ז), טִיּוּל (ז) |
| cruise (sea trip) | 'ʃayit | שַׁיִט (ז) |

| course (route) | kivun | כִּיוּוּן (ז) |
| route (itinerary) | nativ | נָתִיב (ז) |

fairway (safe water channel)	nativ 'ʃayit	נְתִיב שַׁיִט (ז)
shallows	sirton	שִׂרְטוֹן (ז)
to run aground	la'alot al hasirton	לַעֲלוֹת עַל הַשִּׂרְטוֹן

storm	sufa	סוּפָה (נ)
signal	ot	אוֹת (ז)
to sink (vi)	lit'bo'a	לִטְבּוֹעַ
Man overboard!	adam ba'mayim!	אָדָם בַּמַּיִם!
SOS (distress signal)	kri'at hatsala	קְרִיאַת הַצָּלָה
ring buoy	galgal hatsala	גַּלְגַּל הַצָּלָה (ז)

144. Airport

airport	nemal te'ufa	נְמַל תְּעוּפָה (ז)
airplane	matos	מָטוֹס (ז)
airline	xevrat te'ufa	חֶבְרַת תְּעוּפָה (נ)
air traffic controller	bakar tisa	בַּקָר תְּוּחָה (ז)
departure	hamra'a	הַמְרָאָה (נ)
arrival	nexita	נְחִיתָה (נ)
to arrive (by plane)	leha'gi'a betisa	לְהַגִיעַ בְּטִיסָה
departure time	zman hamra'a	זְמַן הַמְרָאָה (ז)
arrival time	zman nexita	זְמַן נְחִיתָה (ז)
to be delayed	lehit'akev	לְהִתְעַכֵּב
flight delay	ikuv hatisa	עִיכּוּב הַטִיסָה (ז)
information board	'luax meida	לוּחַ מֵידָע (ז)
information	meida	מֵידָע (ז)
to announce (vt)	leho'dia	לְהוֹדִיעַ
flight (e.g., next ~)	tisa	טִיסָה (נ)
customs	'mexes	מֶכֶס (ז)
customs officer	pakid 'mexes	פָּקִיד מֶכֶס (ז)
customs declaration	hatsharat mexes	הַצְהָרַת מֶכֶס (נ)
to fill out (vt)	lemale	לְמַלֵא
to fill out the declaration	lemale 'tofes hatshara	לְמַלֵא טוֹפֶס הַצהָרָה
passport control	bdikat darkonim	בְּדִיקַת דַרכּוֹנִים (נ)
luggage	kvuda	כְּבוּדָה (נ)
hand luggage	kvudat yad	כְּבוּדַת יָד (נ)
luggage cart	eglat kvuda	עֶגְלַת כְּבוּדָה (נ)
landing	nexita	נְחִיתָה (נ)
landing strip	maslul nexita	מַסלוּל נְחִיתָה (ז)
to land (vi)	linxot	לַנחוֹת
airstairs	'kevef	כֶּבֶש (ז)
check-in	tfek in	צֶ'ק אִין (ז)
check-in counter	dalpak tfek in	דַלפַּק צֶ'ק אִין (ז)
to check-in (vi)	leva'tse'a tfek in	לְבַצֵעַ צֶ'ק אִין
boarding pass	kartis aliya lematos	כַּרטִיס עָלָיָה לְמָטוֹס (ז)
departure gate	'fa'ar yetsi'a	שַעַר יְצִיאָה (ז)
transit	ma'avar	מַעֲבָר (ז)
to wait (vt)	lehamtin	לְהַמתִין
departure lounge	traklin tisa	טְרַקלִין טִיסָה (ז)
to see off	lelavot	לְלַווֹת
to say goodbye	lomar lehitra'ot	לוֹמַר לְהִתרָאוֹת

145. Bicycle. Motorcycle

bicycle	ofa'nayim	אוֹפַנַּיִים (ז"ר)
scooter	kat'no'a	קַטְנוֹעַ (ז)
motorcycle, bike	of'no'a	אוֹפְנוֹעַ (ז)
to go by bicycle	lirkov al ofa'nayim	לִרְכּוֹב עַל אוֹפַנַּיִים
handlebars	kidon	כִּידוֹן (ז)
pedal	davʃa	דַּווְשָׁה (נ)
brakes	blamim	בְּלָמִים (ז"ר)
bicycle seat (saddle)	ukaf	אוּכָּף (ז)
pump	maʃeva	מַשְׁאֵבָה (נ)
luggage rack	sabal	סַבָּל (ז)
front lamp	panas kidmi	פָּנָס קִדְמִי (ז)
helmet	kasda	קַסְדָּה (נ)
wheel	galgal	גַּלְגַּל (ז)
fender	kanaf	כָּנָף (נ)
rim	xiʃuk	חִישׁוּק (ז)
spoke	xiʃur	חִישׁוּר (ז)

Cars

146. Types of cars

automobile, car	meχonit	מְכוֹנִית (נ)
sports car	meχonit sport	מְכוֹנִית סְפּוֹרְט (נ)
limousine	limu'zina	לִימוּזִינָה (נ)
off-road vehicle	'reχev 'ʃetaχ	רֶכֶב שֶׁטַח (ז)
convertible (n)	meχonit gag niftaχ	מְכוֹנִית גַג נִפְתָח (נ)
minibus	'minibus	מִינִיבּוּס (ז)
ambulance	'ambulans	אַמְבּוּלַנְס (ז)
snowplow	maf'leset 'ʃeleg	מַפְלֶסֶת שֶׁלֶג (נ)
truck	masa'it	מַשָׂאִית (נ)
tanker truck	meχalit 'delek	מֵיכָלִית דֶלֶק (נ)
van (small truck)	masa'it kala	מַשָׂאִית קַלָה (נ)
road tractor (trailer truck)	gorer	גוֹרֵר (ז)
trailer	garur	גָרוּר (ז)
comfortable (adj)	'noaχ	נוֹחַ
used (adj)	meʃumaʃ	מְשׁוּמָשׁ

147. Cars. Bodywork

hood	miχse hama'no'a	מִכְסֶה הַמָנוֹעַ (ז)
fender	kanaf	כָּנָף (נ)
roof	gag	גַג (ז)
windshield	ʃimʃa kidmit	שִׁמְשָׁה קִדְמִית (נ)
rear-view mirror	mar'a aχorit	מַרְאָה אֲחוֹרִית (נ)
windshield washer	mataz	מַתָז (ז)
windshield wipers	magev	מַגֵב (ז)
side window	ʃimʃat tsad	שִׁמְשַׁת צַד (נ)
window lift (power window)	χalon χaʃmali	חַלוֹן חַשְׁמַלִי (ז)
antenna	an'tena	אַנְטֶנָה (נ)
sunroof	χalon gag	חַלוֹן גַג (ז)
bumper	pagoʃ	פָּגוֹשׁ (ז)
trunk	ta mit'an	תָא מִטְעָן (ז)
roof luggage rack	gagon	גָגוֹן (ז)
door	'delet	דֶלֶת (נ)

door handle	yadit	יָדִית (נ)
door lock	man'ul	מַנְעוּל (ז)
license plate	luxit riʃui	לוּחִית רִישׁוּי (נ)
muffler	am'am	עַמְעָם (ז)
gas tank	meixal 'delek	מֵיכָל דֶּלֶק (ז)
tailpipe	maflet	מַפְלֵט (ז)
gas, accelerator	gaz	גָז (ז)
pedal	davʃa	דַּוְושָׁה (נ)
gas pedal	davʃat gaz	דַּוְושַׁת גָז (נ)
brake	'belem	בֶּלֶם (ז)
brake pedal	davʃat hablamim	דַּוְושַׁת הַבְּלָמִים (נ)
to brake (use the brake)	livlom	לִבְלוֹם
parking brake	'belem xaniya	בֶּלֶם חֲנָיָה (ז)
clutch	matsmed	מַצְמֵד (ז)
clutch pedal	davʃat hamatsmed	דַּוְושַׁת הַמַּצְמֵד (נ)
clutch disc	luxit hamatsmed	לוּחִית הַמַּצְמֵד (נ)
shock absorber	bolem za'a'zu'a	בּוֹלֵם זַעֲזוּעִים (ז)
wheel	galgal	גַּלְגַּל (ז)
spare tire	galgal xilufi	גַּלְגַּל חִילּוּפִי (ז)
tire	tsmig	צְמִיג (ז)
hubcap	tsa'laxat galgal	צַלַּחַת גַּלְגַּל (נ)
driving wheels	galgalim meni'im	גַּלְגַּלִים מְנִיעִים (ז"ר)
front-wheel drive (as adj)	shel hana'a kidmit	שֶׁל הֲנָעָה קִדְמִית
rear-wheel drive (as adj)	shel hana'a axorit	שֶׁל הֲנָעָה אֲחוֹרִית
all-wheel drive (as adj)	shel hana'a male'a	שֶׁל הֲנָעָה מָלְאָה
gearbox	teivat hiluxim	תֵּיבַת הִילּוּכִים (נ)
automatic (adj)	oto'mati	אוֹטוֹמָטִי
mechanical (adj)	me'xani	מֶכָנִי
gear shift	yadit hiluxim	יָדִית הִילּוּכִים (נ)
headlight	panas kidmi	פָּנָס קִדְמִי (ז)
headlights	panasim	פָּנָסִים (ז"ר)
low beam	or namux	אוֹר נָמוּךְ (ז)
high beam	or ga'voha	אוֹר גָּבוֹהַּ (ז)
brake light	or 'belem	אוֹר בֶּלֶם (ז)
parking lights	orot xanaya	אוֹרוֹת חֲנָיָה (ז"ר)
hazard lights	orot xerum	אוֹרוֹת חֵירוּם (ז"ר)
fog lights	orot arafel	אוֹרוֹת עֲרָפֶל (ז"ר)
turn signal	panas itut	פָּנָס אִיתּוּת (ז)
back-up light	orot revers	אוֹרוֹת רֶבֶרְס (ז"ר)

148. Cars. Passenger compartment

car inside (interior)	ta hanos'im	תָּא הַנּוֹסְעִים (ז)
leather (as adj)	asui me'or	עָשׂוּי מֵעוֹר
velour (as adj)	ktifati	קְטִיפָתִי
upholstery	ripud	רִיפּוּד (ז)
instrument (gage)	maxven	מַכְוֵן (ז)
dashboard	'luax maxvenim	לוּחַ מַכְוֵנִים (ז)
speedometer	mad mehirut	מַד מְהִירוּת (ז)
needle (pointer)	'maxat	מָחַט (נ)
odometer	mad merxak	מַד מֶרְחָק (ז)
indicator (sensor)	xaiʃan	חַיְישָׁן (ז)
level	ramat mi'lui	רָמַת מִילוּי (נ)
warning light	nurat azhara	נוּרַת אַזְהָרָה (נ)
steering wheel	'hege	הֶגֶה (ז)
horn	tsofar	צוֹפָר (ז)
button	kaftor	כַּפְתּוֹר (ז)
switch	'meteg	מֶתֶג (ז)
seat	moʃav	מוֹשָׁב (ז)
backrest	miʃ'enet	מִשְׁעֶנֶת (נ)
headrest	miʃ'enet roʃ	מִשְׁעֶנֶת רֹאשׁ (נ)
seat belt	xagorat betixut	חֲגוֹרַת בְּטִיחוּת (נ)
to fasten the belt	lehadek xagora	לְהַדֵּק חֲגוֹרָה
adjustment (of seats)	kivnun	כִּיווּנוּן (ז)
airbag	karit avir	כָּרִית אֲווִיר (נ)
air-conditioner	mazgan	מַזְגָּן (ז)
radio	'radyo	רָדִיוֹ (ז)
CD player	'diskmen	דִיסְקְמֶן (ז)
to turn on	lehadlik	לְהַדְלִיק
antenna	an'tena	אַנְטֶנָה (נ)
glove box	ta kfafot	תָּא כְּפָפוֹת (ז)
ashtray	ma'afera	מַאֲפֵרָה (נ)

149. Cars. Engine

engine, motor	ma'no'a	מָנוֹעַ (ז)
diesel (as adj)	shel 'dizel	שֶׁל דִיזֶל
gasoline (as adj)	'delek	דֶלֶק
engine volume	'nefax ma'no'a	נֶפַח מָנוֹעַ (ז)
power	otsma	עוֹצְמָה (נ)
horsepower	'koax sus	כּוֹחַ סוּס (ז)
piston	buxna	בּוּכְנָה (נ)

| cylinder | tsi'linder | צִילִינְדֶר (ז) |
| valve | ʃastom | שַׁסְתּוֹם (ז) |

injector	mazrek	מַזְרֵק (ז)
generator (alternator)	meχolel	מְחוֹלֵל (ז)
carburetor	me'ayed	מְאַיֵּד (ז)
motor oil	'ʃemen mano'im	שֶׁמֶן מָנוֹעִים (ז)

radiator	matsnen	מַצְנֵן (ז)
coolant	nozel kirur	נוֹזֵל קִירוּר (ז)
cooling fan	me'avrer	מְאַוְרֵר (ז)

battery (accumulator)	matsber	מַצְבֵּר (ז)
starter	mat'ne'a	מַתְנֵעַ (ז)
ignition	hatsata	הַצָּתָה (נ)
spark plug	matset	מַצֵּת (ז)

terminal (of battery)	'hedek	הֶדֵק (ז)
positive terminal	'hedek χiyuvi	הֶדֵק חִיּוּבִי (ז)
negative terminal	'hedek ʃlili	הֶדֵק שְׁלִילִי (ז)
fuse	natiχ	נָתִיךְ (ז)

air filter	masnen avir	מַסְנֵן אֲוִויר (ז)
oil filter	masnen 'ʃemen	מַסְנֵן שֶׁמֶן (ז)
fuel filter	masnen 'delek	מַסְנֵן דֶּלֶק (ז)

150. Cars. Crash. Repair

car crash	te'una	תְּאוּנָה (נ)
traffic accident	te'unat draχim	תְּאוּנַת דְּרָכִים (נ)
to crash (into the wall, etc.)	lehitnageʃ	לְהִתְנַגֵּשׁ
to get smashed up	lehima'eχ	לְהִימָּעֵךְ
damage	'nezek	נֶזֶק (ז)
intact (unscathed)	ʃalem	שָׁלֵם

breakdown	takala	תַּקָּלָה (נ)
to break down (vi)	lehitkalkel	לְהִתְקַלְקֵל
towrope	'χevel grar	חֶבֶל גְּרָר (ז)

puncture	'teker	תֶּקֶר (ז)
to be flat	lehitpantʃer	לְהִתְפַּנְצֵ'ר
to pump up	lena'peaχ	לְנַפֵּחַ
pressure	'laχats	לַחַץ (ז)
to check (to examine)	livdok	לִבְדּוֹק

repair	ʃiputs	שִׁיפּוּץ (ז)
auto repair shop	musaχ	מוּסָךְ (ז)
spare part	'χelek χiluf	חֵלֶק חִילּוּף (ז)
part	'χelek	חֵלֶק (ז)

bolt (with nut)	'boreg	בּוֹרֶג (ז)
screw (fastener)	'boreg	בּוֹרֶג (ז)
nut	om	אוֹם (ז)
washer	diskit	דִיסקִית (נ)
bearing	mesav	מֵסָב (ז)
tube	tsinorit	צִינוֹרִית (נ)
gasket (head ~)	'etem	אֶטֶם (ז)
cable, wire	χut	חוּט (ז)
jack	dʒek	גֵ'ק (ז)
wrench	maf'teaχ bragim	מַפתֵחַ בּרָגִים (ז)
hammer	patiʃ	פַּטִיש (ז)
pump	maʃeva	מַשאֵבָה (נ)
screwdriver	mavreg	מַברֵג (ז)
fire extinguisher	mataf	מַטַף (ז)
warning triangle	meʃulaʃ χirum	מְשוּלַש חֵירוּם (ז)
to stall (vi)	ledomem	לְדוֹמֵם
stall (n)	hadmama	הַדמָמָה (נ)
to be broken	lihyot ʃavur	לִהיוֹת שָבוּר
to overheat (vi)	lehitχamem yoter midai	לְהִתחַמֵם יוֹתֵר מִדַי
to be clogged up	lehisatem	לְהִיסָתֵם
to freeze up (pipes, etc.)	likpo	לִקפּוֹא
to burst (vi, ab. tube)	lehitpa'ke'a	לְהִתפַּקֵעַ
pressure	'laχats	לַחַץ (ז)
level	ramat mi'lui	רָמַת מִילוּי (נ)
slack (~ belt)	rafe	רָפֶה
dent	dfika	דְפִיקָה (נ)
knocking noise (engine)	'ra'aʃ	רַעַש (ז)
crack	'sedek	סֶדֶק (ז)
scratch	srita	שׂרִיטָה (נ)

151. Cars. Road

road	'dereχ	דֶרֶך (נ)
highway	kviʃ mahir	כּבִיש מָהִיר (ז)
freeway	kviʃ mahir	כּבִיש מָהִיר (ז)
direction (way)	kivun	כִּיווּן (ז)
distance	merχak	מֶרחָק (ז)
bridge	'geʃer	גֶשֶר (ז)
parking lot	χanaya	חֲנָיָה (נ)
square	kikar	כִּיכָּר (נ)
interchange	meχlaf	מֶחלָף (ז)
tunnel	minhara	מִנהָרָה (נ)

gas station	taxanat 'delek	תַחֲנַת דֶלֶק (נ)
parking lot	migraʃ xanaya	מִגְרַשׁ חֲנָיָה (ז)
gas pump (fuel dispenser)	maʃevat 'delek	מַשְׁאֵבַת דֶלֶק (נ)
auto repair shop	musax	מוּסָךְ (ז)
to get gas (to fill up)	letadlek	לְתַדְלֵק
fuel	'delek	דֶלֶק (ז)
jerrycan	'dʒerikan	גֶ'רִיקָן (ז)
asphalt	asfalt	אַסְפַלְט (ז)
road markings	simun	סִימוּן (ז)
curb	sfat midraxa	שְׂפַת מִדְרָכָה (נ)
guardrail	ma'ake betixut	מַעֲקֶה בְּטִיחוּת (ז)
ditch	te'ala	תְעָלָה (נ)
roadside (shoulder)	ʃulei ha'derex	שׁוּלֵי הַדֶרֶךְ (ז"ר)
lamppost	amud te'ura	עַמוּד תְאוּרָה (ז)
to drive (a car)	linhog	לִנְהוֹג
to turn (e.g., ~ left)	lifnot	לִפְנוֹת
to make a U-turn	leva'tse'a pniyat parsa	לְבַצֵעַ פְּנִיַת פַּרְסָה
reverse (~ gear)	hilux axori	הִילוּךְ אֲחוֹרִי (ז)
to honk (vi)	litspor	לִצְפּוֹר
honk (sound)	tsfira	צְפִירָה (נ)
to get stuck (in the mud, etc.)	lehitaka	לְהִיתָקַע
to spin the wheels	lesovev et hagalgal al rek	לְסוֹבֵב אֶת הַגַלְגַלִים עַל רֵיק
to cut, to turn off (vt)	ledomem	לְדוֹמֵם
speed	mehirut	מְהִירוּת (נ)
to exceed the speed limit	linhog bemehirut muf'rezet	לִנְהוֹג בְּמְהִירוּת מוּפְרֶזֶת
to give a ticket	liknos	לִקְנוֹס
traffic lights	ramzor	רַמְזוֹר (ז)
driver's license	riʃyon nehiga	רִשְׁיוֹן נְהִיגָה (ז)
grade crossing	ma'avar pasei ra'kevet	מַעֲבָר פַּסֵי רַכֶּבֶת (ז)
intersection	'tsomet	צוֹמֶת (ז)
crosswalk	ma'avar xatsaya	מַעֲבָר חֲצָיָה (ז)
bend, curve	pniya	פְּנִיָה (נ)
pedestrian zone	midrexov	מִדְרְחוֹב (ז)

PEOPLE. LIFE EVENTS

Life events

152. Holidays. Event

celebration, holiday	χagiga	חֲגִיגָה (נ)
national day	χag le'umi	חַג לְאוֹמִי (ז)
public holiday	yom χag	יוֹם חַג (ז)
to commemorate (vt)	laχgog	לַחגוֹג
event (happening)	hitraχaʃut	הִתרַחֲשׁוּת (נ)
event (organized activity)	ei'ru'a	אֵירוּעַ (ז)
banquet (party)	se'uda χagigit	סְעוּדָה חֲגִיגִית (נ)
reception (formal party)	ei'ruaχ	אֵירוּחַ (ז)
feast	miʃte	מִשׁתֶה (ז)
anniversary	yom haʃana	יוֹם הַשָׁנָה (ז)
jubilee	χag hayovel	חַג הַיוֹבֵל (ז)
to celebrate (vt)	laχgog	לַחגוֹג
New Year	ʃana χadaʃa	שָׁנָה חֲדָשָׁה (נ)
Happy New Year!	ʃana tova!	שָׁנָה טוֹבָה!
Santa Claus	'santa 'kla'us	סַנטָה קלָאוּס
Christmas	χag hamolad	חַג הַמוֹלָד (ז)
Merry Christmas!	χag hamolad sa'meaχ!	חַג הַמוֹלָד שָׂמֵחַ!
Christmas tree	ets χag hamolad	עֵץ חַג הַמוֹלָד (ז)
fireworks (fireworks show)	zikukim	זִיקוּקִים (ז"ר)
wedding	χatuna	חֲתוּנָה (נ)
groom	χatan	חָתָן (ז)
bride	kala	כַּלָה (נ)
to invite (vt)	lehazmin	לְהַזמִין
invitation card	hazmana	הַזמָנָה (נ)
guest	o'reaχ	אוֹרֵחַ (ז)
to visit	levaker	לְבַקֵר
(~ your parents, etc.)		
to meet the guests	lekabel orχim	לְקַבֵּל אוֹרחִים
gift, present	matana	מַתָנָה (נ)
to give (sth as present)	latet matana	לָתֵת מַתָנָה
to receive gifts	lekabel matanot	לְקַבֵּל מַתָנוֹת

bouquet (of flowers)	zer	זֵר (ז)
congratulations	braχa	בְּרָכָה (נ)
to congratulate (vt)	levareχ	לְבָרֵךְ

greeting card	kartis braχa	פַּרְטִיס בְּרָכָה (ז)
to send a postcard	liʃloaχ gluya	לִשְׁלוֹחַ גְלוּיָה
to get a postcard	lekabel gluya	לְקַבֵּל גְלוּיָה

toast	leharim kosit	לְהָרִים כּוֹסִית
to offer (a drink, etc.)	leχabed	לְכַבֵּד
champagne	ʃam'panya	שַׁמְפַּנְיָה (נ)

to enjoy oneself	lehanot	לֵיהָנוֹת
merriment (gaiety)	alitsut	עֲלִיצוּת (נ)
joy (emotion)	simχa	שִׂמְחָה (נ)

| dance | rikud | רִיקוּד (ז) |
| to dance (vi, vt) | lirkod | לִרְקוֹד |

| waltz | vals | וַלְס (ז) |
| tango | 'tango | טַנְגוֹ (ז) |

153. Funerals. Burial

cemetery	beit kvarot	בֵּית קְבָרוֹת (ז)
grave, tomb	'kever	קֶבֶר (ז)
cross	tslav	צְלָב (ז)
gravestone	matseva	מַצֵּבָה (נ)
fence	gader	גָדֵר (נ)
chapel	beit tfila	בֵּית תְּפִילָה (ז)

death	'mavet	מָוֶת (ז)
to die (vi)	lamut	לָמוּת
the deceased	niftar	נִפְטָר (ז)
mourning	'evel	אֵבֶל (ז)
to bury (vt)	likbor	לִקְבּוֹר
funeral home	beit levayot	בֵּית לְוָיוֹת (ז)
funeral	levaya	לְוָיָה (נ)

wreath	zer	זֵר (ז)
casket, coffin	aron metim	אֲרוֹן מֵתִים (ז)
hearse	kron hamet	קְרוֹן הַמֵּת (ז)
shroud	taχriχim	תַכְרִיכִים (ז"ר)

funeral procession	tahaluχat 'evel	תַהֲלוּכַת אֵבֶל (נ)
funerary urn	kad 'efer	כַּד אֵפֶר (ז)
crematory	misrafa	מִשְׂרָפָה (נ)
obituary	moda'at 'evel	מוֹדָעַת אֵבֶל (נ)
to cry (weep)	livkot	לִבְכּוֹת
to sob (vi)	lehitya'peaχ	לְהִתְיַיפֵּחַ

154. War. Soldiers

platoon	maxlaka	מַחלָקָה (נ)
company	pluga	פּלוּגָה (נ)
regiment	xativa	חֲטִיבָה (נ)
army	tsava	צָבָא (ז)
division	ugda	אוּגדָה (נ)
section, squad	kita	כִּיתָה (נ)
host (army)	'xayil	חַיִל (ז)
soldier	xayal	חַייָל (ז)
officer	katsin	קָצִין (ז)
private	turai	טוּרַאי (ז)
sergeant	samal	סַמָל (ז)
lieutenant	'segen	סֶגֶן (ז)
captain	'seren	סֶרֶן (ז)
major	rav 'seren	רַב־סֶרֶן (ז)
colonel	aluf miʃne	אַלוּף מִשנֶה (ז)
general	aluf	אַלוּף (ז)
sailor	yamai	יַמַאי (ז)
captain	rav xovel	רַב־חוֹבֵל (ז)
boatswain	rav malaxim	רַב־מַלָחִים (ז)
artilleryman	totxan	תוֹתחָן (ז)
paratrooper	tsanxan	צַנחָן (ז)
pilot	tayas	טַייָס (ז)
navigator	navat	נַווָט (ז)
mechanic	mexonai	מְכוֹנַאי (ז)
pioneer (sapper)	xablan	חַבּלָן (ז)
parachutist	tsanxan	צַנחָן (ז)
reconnaissance scout	iʃ modi'in kravi	אִיש מוֹדִיעִין קרָבִי (ז)
sniper	tsalaf	צַלָף (ז)
patrol (group)	siyur	סִיוּר (ז)
to patrol (vi)	lefatrel	לְפַטרֵל
sentry, guard	zakif	זָקִיף (ז)
warrior	loxem	לוֹחֵם (ז)
patriot	patriyot	פַּטרִיוֹט (ז)
hero	gibor	גִיבּוֹר (ז)
heroine	gibora	גִיבּוֹרָה (נ)
traitor	boged	בּוֹגֵד (ז)
to betray (vt)	livgod	לִבגוֹד
deserter	arik	עָרִיק (ז)
to desert (vi)	la'arok	לַעֲרוֹק
mercenary	sxir 'xerev	שֹׂכִיר חֶרֶב (ז)

| recruit | tiron | טִירוֹן (ז) |
| volunteer | mitnadev | מִתְנַדֵּב (ז) |

dead (n)	harug	הָרוּג (ז)
wounded (n)	pa'tsu'a	פָּצוּעַ (ז)
prisoner of war	ʃavui	שָׁבוּי (ז)

155. War. Military actions. Part 1

war	milχama	מִלְחָמָה (נ)
to be at war	lehilaχem	לְהִילָחֵם
civil war	mil'χemet ezraχim	מִלְחֶמֶת אֶזְרָחִים (נ)

treacherously (adv)	bogdani	בּוֹגְדָנִי
declaration of war	haχrazat milχama	הַכְרָזַת מִלְחָמָה (נ)
to declare (~ war)	lehaχriz	לְהַכְרִיז
aggression	tokfanut	תּוֹקְפָנוּת (נ)
to attack (invade)	litkof	לִתְקוֹף

to invade (vt)	liχboʃ	לִכְבּוֹשׁ
invader	koveʃ	כּוֹבֵשׁ (ז)
conqueror	koveʃ	כּוֹבֵשׁ (ז)

defense	hagana	הֲגָנָה (נ)
to defend (a country, etc.)	lehagen al	לְהָגֵן עַל
to defend (against ...)	lehitgonen	לְהִתְגּוֹנֵן

enemy	oyev	אוֹיֵב (ז)
foe, adversary	yariv	יָרִיב (ז)
enemy (as adj)	ʃel oyev	שֶׁל אוֹיֵב

| strategy | astra'tegya | אַסְטְרָטֶגְיָה (נ) |
| tactics | 'taktika | טַקְטִיקָה (נ) |

order	pkuda	פְּקוּדָה (נ)
command (order)	pkuda	פְּקוּדָה (נ)
to order (vt)	lifkod	לִפְקוֹד
mission	mesima	מְשִׂימָה (נ)
secret (adj)	sodi	סוֹדִי

| battle | ma'araχa | מַעֲרָכָה (נ) |
| combat | krav | קְרָב (ז) |

attack	hatkafa	הַתְקָפָה (נ)
charge (assault)	hista'arut	הִסְתָּעֲרוּת (נ)
to storm (vt)	lehista'er	לְהִסְתָּעֵר
siege (to be under ~)	matsor	מָצוֹר (ז)

| offensive (n) | mitkafa | מִתְקָפָה (נ) |
| to go on the offensive | latset lemitkafa | לָצֵאת לְמִתְקָפָה |

| retreat | nesiga | נְסִיגָה (נ) |
| to retreat (vi) | la'seget | לָסֶגֶת |

| encirclement | kitur | כִּיתּוּר (ז) |
| to encircle (vt) | leχater | לְכַתֵּר |

bombing (by aircraft)	haftsatsa	הַפְצָצָה (נ)
to drop a bomb	lehatil ptsatsa	לְהַטִּיל פְּצָצָה
to bomb (vt)	lehaftsits	לְהַפְצִיץ
explosion	pitsuts	פִּיצוּץ (ז)

shot	yeriya	יְרִייָה (נ)
to fire (~ a shot)	lirot	לִירוֹת
firing (burst of ~)	'yeri	יֶרִי (ז)

to aim (to point a weapon)	leχaven 'neʃek	לְכַוֵּון נֶשֶׁק
to point (a gun)	leχaven	לְכַוֵּון
to hit (the target)	lik'lo'a	לְקַלּוֹעַ

to sink (~ a ship)	lehat'bi'a	לְהַטְבִּיעַ
hole (in a ship)	pirtsa	פִּרְצָה (נ)
to founder, to sink (vi)	lit'bo'a	לִטְבּוֹעַ

front (war ~)	χazit	חֲזִית (נ)
evacuation	pinui	פִּינּוּי (ז)
to evacuate (vt)	lefanot	לְפַנּוֹת

trench	te'ala	תְעָלָה (נ)
barbwire	'tayil dokrani	תַּיִל דּוֹקְרָנִי (ז)
barrier (anti tank ~)	maχsom	מַחְסוֹם (ז)
watchtower	migdal ʃmira	מִגְדַּל שְׁמִירָה (ז)

military hospital	beit χolim tsva'i	בֵּית חוֹלִים צְבָאִי (ז)
to wound (vt)	lif'tso'a	לִפְצוֹעַ
wound	'petsa	פֶּצַע (ז)
wounded (n)	pa'tsu'a	פָּצוּעַ (ז)
to be wounded	lehipatsa	לְהִיפָּצַע
serious (wound)	kaʃe	קָשֶׁה

156. Weapons

weapons	'neʃek	נֶשֶׁק (ז)
firearms	'neʃek χam	נֶשֶׁק חַם (ז)
cold weapons (knives, etc.)	'neʃek kar	נֶשֶׁק קַר (ז)

chemical weapons	'neʃek 'χimi	נֶשֶׁק כִּימִי (ז)
nuclear (adj)	gar'ini	גַּרְעִינִי
nuclear weapons	'neʃek gar'ini	נֶשֶׁק גַּרְעִינִי (ז)
bomb	ptsatsa	פְּצָצָה (נ)

atomic bomb	ptsatsa a'tomit	פְּצָצָה אָטוֹמִית (נ)
pistol (gun)	ekdaχ	אֶקְדָּח (ז)
rifle	rove	רוֹבֶה (ז)
submachine gun	tat mak'le'a	תַּת־מַקְלֵעַ (ז)
machine gun	mak'le'a	מַקְלֵעַ (ז)
muzzle	kane	קָנֶה (ז)
barrel	kane	קָנֶה (ז)
caliber	ka'liber	קָלִיבֶּר (ז)
trigger	'hedek	הֶדֶק (ז)
sight (aiming device)	ka'venet	כַּוֶּנֶת (נ)
magazine	maχsanit	מַחְסָנִית (נ)
butt (shoulder stock)	kat	קַת (נ)
hand grenade	rimon	רִימוֹן (ז)
explosive	'χomer 'nefets	חוֹמֶר נֶפֶץ (ז)
bullet	ka'li'a	קְלִיעַ (ז)
cartridge	kadur	כַּדּוּר (ז)
charge	te'ina	טְעִינָה (נ)
ammunition	taχ'moʃet	תַחְמוֹשֶׁת (נ)
bomber (aircraft)	maftsits	מַפְצִיץ (ז)
fighter	metos krav	מָטוֹס קְרָב (ז)
helicopter	masok	מָסוֹק (ז)
anti-aircraft gun	totaχ 'neged metosim	תוֹתָח נֶגֶד מְטוֹסִים (ז)
tank	tank	טַנְק (ז)
tank gun	totaχ	תוֹתָח (ז)
artillery	arti'lerya	אַרְטִילֶרְיָה (נ)
gun (cannon, howitzer)	totaχ	תוֹתָח (ז)
to lay (a gun)	leχaven	לְכַוֵּון
shell (projectile)	pagaz	פָּגָז (ז)
mortar bomb	ptsatsat margema	פְּצָצַת מַרְגֵּמָה (נ)
mortar	margema	מַרְגֵּמָה (נ)
splinter (shell fragment)	resis	רְסִיס (ז)
submarine	tso'lelet	צוֹלֶלֶת (נ)
torpedo	tor'pedo	טוֹרְפֶּדוֹ (ז)
missile	til	טִיל (ז)
to load (gun)	lit'on	לִטְעוֹן
to shoot (vi)	lirot	לִירוֹת
to point at (the cannon)	leχaven	לְכַוֵּון
bayonet	kidon	כִּידוֹן (ז)
rapier	'χerev	חֶרֶב (נ)
saber (e.g., cavalry ~)	'χerev paraʃim	חֶרֶב פָּרָשִׁים (ז)
spear (weapon)	χanit	חֲנִית (נ)

bow	'keʃet	קֶשֶׁת (ז)
arrow	χets	חֵץ (ז)
musket	musket	מוּסְקֵט (ז)
crossbow	'keʃet metsu'levet	קֶשֶׁת מְצוּלֶבֶת (נ)

157. Ancient people

primitive (prehistoric)	kadmon	קַדְמוֹן
prehistoric (adj)	prehis'tori	פְּרֶהִיסְטוֹרִי
ancient (~ civilization)	atik	עַתִּיק
Stone Age	idan ha''even	עִידָן הָאֶבֶן (ז)
Bronze Age	idan ha'arad	עִידָן הָאָרָד (ז)
Ice Age	idan ha'keraχ	עִידָן הַקֶּרַח (ז)
tribe	'ʃevet	שֵׁבֶט (ז)
cannibal	oχel adam	אוֹכֵל אָדָם (ז)
hunter	tsayad	צַיָּיד (ז)
to hunt (vi, vt)	latsud	לָצוּד
mammoth	ma'muta	מָמוּטָה (נ)
cave	me'ara	מְעָרָה (נ)
fire	eʃ	אֵשׁ (נ)
campfire	medura	מְדוּרָה (נ)
cave painting	pet'roglif	פֶּטְרוֹגְלִיף (ז)
tool (e.g., stone ax)	kli	כְּלִי (ז)
spear	χanit	חֲנִית (נ)
stone ax	garzen ha'even	גַּרְזֶן הָאֶבֶן (ז)
to be at war	lehilaχem	לְהִילָּחֵם
to domesticate (vt)	levayet	לְבַיֵּית
idol	'pesel	פֶּסֶל (ז)
to worship (vt)	la'avod et	לַעֲבוֹד אֶת
superstition	emuna tfela	אֱמוּנָה תְּפֵלָה (נ)
rite	'tekes	טֶקֶס (ז)
evolution	evo'lutsya	אֵבוֹלוּצְיָה (נ)
development	hitpatχut	הִתְפַּתְּחוּת (נ)
disappearance (extinction)	he'almut	הֵיעָלְמוּת (נ)
to adapt oneself	lehistagel	לְהִסְתַּגֵּל
archeology	arχe'o'logya	אַרְכֵיאוֹלוֹגְיָה (נ)
archeologist	arχe'olog	אַרְכֵיאוֹלוֹג (ז)
archeological (adj)	arχe'o'logi	אַרְכֵיאוֹלוֹגִי
excavation site	atar χafirot	אֲתַר חֲפִירוֹת (ז)
excavations	χafirot	חֲפִירוֹת (נ"ר)
find (object)	mimtsa	מִמְצָא (ז)
fragment	resis	רְסִיס (ז)

158. Middle Ages

people (ethnic group)	am	עַם (ז)
peoples	amim	עַמִּים (ז״ר)
tribe	'ʃevet	שֵׁבֶט (ז)
tribes	ʃvatim	שְׁבָטִים (ז״ר)
barbarians	bar'barim	בַּרְבָּרִים (ז״ר)
Gauls	'galim	גָּאלִים (ז״ר)
Goths	'gotim	גּוֹתִים (ז״ר)
Slavs	'slavim	סְלָאבִים (ז״ר)
Vikings	'vikingim	וִיקִינְגִים (ז״ר)
Romans	roma'im	רוֹמָאִים (ז״ר)
Roman (adj)	'romi	רוֹמִי
Byzantines	bi'zantim	בִּיזַנְטִים (ז״ר)
Byzantium	bizantion, bizants	בִּיזַנְטִיוֹן, בִּיזַנְץ (נ)
Byzantine (adj)	bi'zanti	בִּיזַנְטִי
emperor	keisar	קֵיסָר (ז)
leader, chief (tribal ~)	manhig	מַנְהִיג (ז)
powerful (~ king)	rav 'koaχ	רַב־כּוֹחַ
king	'meleχ	מֶלֶךְ (ז)
ruler (sovereign)	ʃalit	שַׁלִּיט (ז)
knight	abir	אַבִּיר (ז)
feudal lord	fe'odal	פֵיאוֹדָל (ז)
feudal (adj)	fe'o'dali	פֵיאוֹדָלִי
vassal	vasal	וָסָל (ז)
duke	dukas	דּוּכָּס (ז)
earl	rozen	רוֹזֵן (ז)
baron	baron	בָּרוֹן (ז)
bishop	'biʃof	בִּישׁוֹף (ז)
armor	ʃiryon	שִׁרְיוֹן (ז)
shield	magen	מָגֵן (ז)
sword	'χerev	חֶרֶב (נ)
visor	magen panim	מָגֵן פָּנִים (ז)
chainmail	ʃiryon kaskasim	שִׁרְיוֹן קַשְׂקַשִּׂים (ז)
Crusade	masa tslav	מַסָּע צְלָב (ז)
crusader	tsalban	צַלְבָּן (ז)
territory	'ʃetaχ	שֶׁטַח (ז)
to attack (invade)	litkof	לִתְקוֹף
to conquer (vt)	liχboʃ	לִכְבּוֹש
to occupy (invade)	lehiʃtalet	לְהִשְׁתַּלֵּט
siege (to be under ~)	matsor	מָצוֹר (ז)
besieged (adj)	natsur	נָצוּר

to besiege (vt)	latsur	לָצוּר
inquisition	inkvi'zitsya	אִינקוִוידִיצִיָה (נ)
inquisitor	inkvi'zitor	אִינקוִוידִיטוֹר (ז)
torture	inui	עִינוּי (ז)
cruel (adj)	aχzari	אַכזָרִי
heretic	kofer	כּוֹפֵר (ז)
heresy	kfira	כּפִירָה (נ)
seafaring	haflaga bayam	הַפלָגָה בָּיָם (נ)
pirate	ʃoded yam	שוֹדֵד יָם (ז)
piracy	pi'ratiyut	פִּירָטִיוּת (נ)
boarding (attack)	la'alot al	לַעֲלוֹת עַל
loot, booty	ʃalal	שָלָל (ז)
treasures	otsarot	אוֹצָרוֹת (ז״ר)
discovery	taglit	תַגלִית (נ)
to discover (new land, etc.)	legalot	לְגַלוֹת
expedition	miʃlaχat	מִשלַחַת (נ)
musketeer	musketer	מוּסקֶטֵר (ז)
cardinal	χaʃman	חַשמָן (ז)
heraldry	he'raldika	הֶרַלדִיקָה (נ)
heraldic (adj)	he'raldi	הֶרַלדִי

159. Leader. Chief. Authorities

king	'meleχ	מֶלֶך (ז)
queen	malka	מַלכָּה (נ)
royal (adj)	malχuti	מַלכוּתִי
kingdom	mamlaχa	מַמלָכָה (נ)
prince	nasiχ	נָסִיך (ז)
princess	nesiχa	נְסִיכָה (נ)
president	nasi	נָשִיא (ז)
vice-president	sgan nasi	סגַן נָשִיא (ז)
senator	se'nator	סֶנָאטוֹר (ז)
monarch	'meleχ	מֶלֶך (ז)
ruler (sovereign)	ʃalit	שַלִיט (ז)
dictator	rodan	רוֹדָן (ז)
tyrant	aruts	עָרוּץ (ז)
magnate	eil hon	אַיל הוֹן (ז)
director	menahel	מְנַהֵל (ז)
chief	menahel, roʃ	מְנַהֵל (ז), רֹאש (ז)
manager (director)	menahel	מְנַהֵל (ז)
boss	bos	בּוֹס (ז)
owner	'ba'al	בַּעַל (ז)
leader	manhig	מַנהִיג (ז)

head (~ of delegation)	roʃ	רֹאשׁ (ז)
authorities	ʃiltonot	שִׁלְטוֹנוֹת (ז״ר)
superiors	memunim	מְמוּנִים (ז״ר)
governor	moʃel	מוֹשֵׁל (ז)
consul	'konsul	קוֹנְסוּל (ז)
diplomat	diplomat	דִיפְּלוֹמָט (ז)
mayor	roʃ ha'ir	רֹאשׁ הָעִיר (ז)
sheriff	ʃerif	שֶׁרִיף (ז)
emperor	keisar	קֵיסָר (ז)
tsar, czar	tsar	צָאר (ז)
pharaoh	par'o	פַּרְעֹה (ז)
khan	χan	חָאן (ז)

160. Breaking the law. Criminals. Part 1

bandit	ʃoded	שׁוֹדֵד (ז)
crime	'peʃa	פֶּשַׁע (ז)
criminal (person)	po'ʃe'a	פּוֹשֵׁעַ (ז)
thief	ganav	גַנָב (ז)
to steal (vi, vt)	lignov	לִגְנוֹב
stealing (larceny)	gneva	גְנֵיבָה (נ)
theft	gneva	גְנֵיבָה (נ)
to kidnap (vt)	laχatof	לַחְטוֹף
kidnapping	χatifa	חֲטִיפָה (נ)
kidnapper	χotef	חוֹטֵף (ז)
ransom	'kofer	כּוֹפֶר (ז)
to demand ransom	lidroʃ 'kofer	לִדְרוֹשׁ כּוֹפֶר
to rob (vt)	liʃdod	לִשְׁדוֹד
robbery	ʃod	שׁוֹד (ז)
robber	ʃoded	שׁוֹדֵד (ז)
to extort (vt)	lisχot	לִסְחוֹט
extortionist	saχtan	סַחְטָן (ז)
extortion	saχtanut	סַחְטָנוּת (נ)
to murder, to kill	lir'tsoaχ	לִרְצוֹחַ
murder	'retsaχ	רֶצַח (ז)
murderer	ro'tseaχ	רוֹצֵחַ (ז)
gunshot	yeriya	יְרִיָה (נ)
to fire (~ a shot)	lirot	לִירוֹת
to shoot to death	lirot la'mavet	לִירוֹת לַמָוֶת
to shoot (vi)	lirot	לִירוֹת
shooting	'yeri	יְרִי (ז)

incident (fight, etc.)	takrit	תַקְרִית (נ)
fight, brawl	ktata	קְטָטָה (נ)
Help!	ha'tsilu!	הַצִילוּ!
victim	nifga	נִפְגָע (ז)

to damage (vt)	lekalkel	לְקַלְקֵל
damage	'nezek	נֶזֶק (ז)
dead body, corpse	gufa	גוּפָה (נ)
grave (~ crime)	χamur	חָמוּר

to attack (vt)	litkof	לִתְקוֹף
to beat (to hit)	lehakot	לְהַכּוֹת
to beat up	lehakot	לְהַכּוֹת
to take (rob of sth)	la'kaχat be'koaχ	לָקַחַת בְּכוֹחַ
to stab to death	lidkor le'mavet	לִדְקוֹר לְמָוֶת
to maim (vt)	lehatil mum	לְהָטִיל מוּם
to wound (vt)	lif'tso'a	לִפְצוֹעַ

blackmail	saχtanut	סַחְטָנוּת (נ)
to blackmail (vt)	lisχot	לִסְחוֹט
blackmailer	saχtan	סַחְטָן (ז)

protection racket	dmei χasut	דְמֵי חָסוּת (ז"ר)
racketeer	gove χasut	גוֹבֶה חָסוּת (ז)
gangster	'gangster	גַנְגְסְטֶר (ז)
mafia, Mob	'mafya	מָאפְיָה (נ)

pickpocket	kayas	כַּיָס (ז)
burglar	porets	פוֹרֵץ (ז)
smuggling	havraχa	הַבְרָחָה (נ)
smuggler	mav'riaχ	מַבְרִיחַ (ז)

forgery	ziyuf	זִיוּף (ז)
to forge (counterfeit)	lezayef	לְזַיֵיף
fake (forged)	mezuyaf	מְזוּיָף

161. Breaking the law. Criminals. Part 2

rape	'ones	אוֹנֶס (ז)
to rape (vt)	le'enos	לֶאֱנוֹס
rapist	anas	אַנָס (ז)
maniac	'manyak	מַנְיָאק (ז)

prostitute (fem.)	zona	זוֹנָה (נ)
prostitution	znut	זְנוּת (נ)
pimp	sarsur	סַרְסוּר (ז)

drug addict	narkoman	נַרְקוֹמָן (ז)
drug dealer	soχer samim	סוֹחֵר סָמִים (ז)
to blow up (bomb)	lefotsets	לְפוֹצֵץ

explosion	pitsuts	פִּיצוּץ (ז)
to set fire	lehatsit	לְהַצִּית
arsonist	matsit	מַצִּית (ז)

terrorism	terorizm	טֶרוֹרִיזְם (ז)
terrorist	meχabel	מְחַבֵּל (ז)
hostage	ben aruba	בֶּן עֲרוּבָּה (ז)

to swindle (deceive)	lehonot	לְהוֹנוֹת
swindle, deception	hona'a	הוֹנָאָה (נ)
swindler	ramai	רַמַאי (ז)

to bribe (vt)	leʃaχed	לְשַׁחֵד
bribery	ʃoχad	שׁוֹחַד (ז)
bribe	ʃoχad	שׁוֹחַד (ז)

poison	'ra'al	רַעַל (ז)
to poison (vt)	lehar'il	לְהַרְעִיל
to poison oneself	lehar'il et atsmo	לְהַרְעִיל אֶת עַצְמוֹ
suicide (act)	hit'abdut	הִתְאַבְּדוּת (נ)
suicide (person)	mit'abed	מִתְאַבֵּד (ז)

to threaten (vt)	le'ayem	לְאַיֵּם
threat	iyum	אִיּוּם (ז)
to make an attempt	lehitnakeʃ	לְהִתְנַקֵּשׁ
attempt (attack)	nisayon hitnakʃut	נִיסָיוֹן הַתְנַקְשׁוּת (ז)

| to steal (a car) | lignov | לִגְנוֹב |
| to hijack (a plane) | laχatof matos | לַחֲטוֹף מָטוֹס |

| revenge | nekama | נְקָמָה (נ) |
| to avenge (get revenge) | linkom | לִנְקוֹם |

to torture (vt)	la'anot	לְעַנּוֹת
torture	inui	עִינּוּי (ז)
to torment (vt)	leyaser	לְיַיסֵר

pirate	ʃoded yam	שׁוֹדֵד יָם (ז)
hooligan	χuligan	חוּלִיגָאן (ז)
armed (adj)	mezuyan	מְזוּיָן
violence	alimut	אֲלִימוּת (נ)
illegal (unlawful)	'bilti le'gali	בִּלְתִּי לֶגָלִי

| spying (espionage) | rigul | רִיגוּל (ז) |
| to spy (vi) | leragel | לְרַגֵּל |

162. Police. Law. Part 1

| justice | 'tsedek | צֶדֶק (ז) |
| court (see you in ~) | beit miʃpat | בֵּית מִשְׁפָּט (ז) |

judge	ʃofet	שׁוֹפֵט (ז)
jurors	muʃba'im	מוּשׁבָּעִים (ז"ר)
jury trial	xaver muʃba'im	חֶבֶר מוּשׁבָּעִים (ז)
to judge (vt)	liʃpot	לִשׁפּוֹט

lawyer, attorney	orex din	עוֹרֵך דִין (ז)
defendant	omed lemiʃpat	עוֹמֵד לְמִשׁפָּט (ז)
dock	safsal ne'eʃamim	סַפסַל נֶאֱשָׁמִים (ז)

| charge | ha'aʃama | הַאֲשָׁמָה (נ) |
| accused | ne'eʃam | נֶאֱשָׁם (ז) |

| sentence | gzar din | גֹזֵר דִין (ז) |
| to sentence (vt) | lifsok | לִפסוֹק |

guilty (culprit)	aʃem	אָשֵׁם (ז)
to punish (vt)	leha'aniʃ	לְהַעֲנִישׁ
punishment	'oneʃ	עוֹנַשׁ (ז)

fine (penalty)	knas	קנָס (ז)
life imprisonment	ma'asar olam	מַאֲסַר עוֹלָם (ז)
death penalty	'oneʃ 'mavet	עוֹנַשׁ מָוֶות (ז)
electric chair	kise xaʃmali	כִּיסֵא חַשׁמַלִי (ז)
gallows	gardom	גַרדוֹם (ז)

| to execute (vt) | lehotsi la'horeg | לְהוֹצִיא לַהוֹרֵג |
| execution | hatsa'a le'horeg | הוֹצָאָה לְהוֹרֵג (נ) |

| prison, jail | beit 'sohar | בֵּית סוֹהַר (ז) |
| cell | ta | תָא (ז) |

escort	miʃmar livui	מִשׁמָר לִיווּי (ז)
prison guard	soher	סוֹהַר (ז)
prisoner	asir	אָסִיר (ז)

| handcuffs | azikim | אֲזִיקִים (ז"ר) |
| to handcuff (vt) | lixbol be'azikim | לִכבּוֹל בַּאֲזִיקִים |

prison break	brixa	בּרִיחָה (נ)
to break out (vi)	liv'roax	לִברוֹחַ
to disappear (vi)	lehe'alem	לְהֵיעָלֵם
to release (from prison)	leʃaxrer	לְשַׁחרֵר
amnesty	xanina	חֲנִינָה (נ)

police	miʃtara	מִשׁטָרָה (נ)
police officer	ʃoter	שׁוֹטֵר (ז)
police station	taxanat miʃtara	תַחֲנַת מִשׁטָרָה (נ)
billy club	ala	אַלָה (נ)
bullhorn	megafon	מֶגָפוֹן (ז)

| patrol car | na'yedet | נַייֶדֶת (נ) |
| siren | tsofar | צוֹפָר (ז) |

to turn on the siren	lehaf'il tsofar	לְהַפְעִיל צוֹפָר
siren call	tsfira	צְפִירָה (נ)
crime scene	zirat 'peʃa	זִירַת פָּשַע (נ)
witness	ed	עֵד (ז)
freedom	'χofeʃ	חוֹפֶש (ז)
accomplice	ʃutaf	שוּתָף (ז)
to flee (vi)	lehiχave	לְהֵיחָבֵא
trace (to leave a ~)	akev	עָקֵב (ז)

163. Police. Law. Part 2

search (investigation)	χipus	חִיפּוּש (ז)
to look for ...	leχapes	לְחַפֵּש
suspicion	χaʃad	חָשָד (ז)
suspicious (e.g., ~ vehicle)	χaʃud	חָשוּד
to stop (cause to halt)	la'atsor	לַעֲצוֹר
to detain (keep in custody)	la'atsor	לַעֲצוֹר
case (lawsuit)	tik	תִיק (ז)
investigation	χakira	חֲקִירָה (נ)
detective	balaʃ	בַּלָש (ז)
investigator	χoker	חוֹקֵר (ז)
hypothesis	haʃara	הַשעָרָה (נ)
motive	me'ni'a	מֵנִיעַ (ז)
interrogation	χakira	חֲקִירָה (נ)
to interrogate (vt)	laχkor	לַחקוֹר
to question (~ neighbors, etc.)	letaʃel	לְתַשאֵל
check (identity ~)	bdika	בּדִיקָה (נ)
round-up	matsod	מָצוֹד (ז)
search (~ warrant)	χipus	חִיפּוּש (ז)
chase (pursuit)	mirdaf	מִרדָף (ז)
to pursue, to chase	lirdof aχarei	לִרדוֹף אַחֲרֵי
to track (a criminal)	la'akov aχarei	לַעֲקוֹב אַחֲרֵי
arrest	ma'asar	מַאֲסָר (ז)
to arrest (sb)	le'esor	לֶאֱסוֹר
to catch (thief, etc.)	lilkod	לִלכּוֹד
capture	leχida	לְכִידָה (נ)
document	mismaχ	מִסמָך (ז)
proof (evidence)	hoχaχa	הוֹכָחָה (נ)
to prove (vt)	leho'χiaχ	לְהוֹכִיחַ
footprint	akev	עָקֵב (ז)
fingerprints	tvi'ot etsba'ot	טבִיעוֹת אֶצבָּעוֹת (נ"ר)
piece of evidence	re'aya	רְאָיָה (נ)
alibi	'alibi	אָלִיבִּי (ז)

innocent (not guilty)	χaf mi'peʃa	חַף מִפֶּשַׁע
injustice	i 'tsedek	אִי צֶדֶק (ז)
unjust, unfair (adj)	lo tsodek	לֹא צוֹדֵק

criminal (adj)	plili	פְּלִילִי
to confiscate (vt)	lehaχrim	לְהַחְרִים
drug (illegal substance)	sam	סַם (ז)
weapon, gun	'neʃek	נֶשֶׁק (ז)
to disarm (vt)	lifrok mi'neʃek	לִפְרוֹק מִנֶּשֶׁק
to order (command)	lifkod	לִפְקוֹד
to disappear (vi)	lehe'alem	לְהֵיעָלֵם

law	χok	חוֹק (ז)
legal, lawful (adj)	χuki	חוּקִי
illegal, illicit (adj)	'bilti χuki	בִּלְתִּי חוּקִי

| responsibility (blame) | aχrayut | אַחֲרָיוּת (נ) |
| responsible (adj) | aχrai | אַחְרַאי |

NATURE

The Earth. Part 1

164. Outer space

space	χalal	חָלָל (ז)
space (as adj)	ʃel χalal	שֶׁל חָלָל
outer space	χalal χitson	חָלָל חִיצוֹן (ז)
world	olam	עוֹלָם (ז)
universe	yekum	יְקוּם (ז)
galaxy	ga'laksya	גָלַקסִיָה (נ)
star	koχav	כּוֹכָב (ז)
constellation	tsvir koχavim	צְבִיר כּוֹכָבִים (ז)
planet	koχav 'leχet	כּוֹכָב לֶכֶת (ז)
satellite	lavyan	לַוְיָן (ז)
meteorite	mete'orit	מֶטֵאוֹרִיט (ז)
comet	koχav ʃavit	כּוֹכָב שָׁבִיט (ז)
asteroid	aste'ro'id	אַסטֵרוֹאִיד (ז)
orbit	maslul	מַסלוּל (ז)
to revolve (~ around the Earth)	lesovev	לסוֹבֵב
atmosphere	atmos'fera	אַטמוֹספֶרָה (נ)
the Sun	'ʃemeʃ	שֶׁמֶשׁ (נ)
solar system	ma'a'reχet ha'ʃemeʃ	מַעֲרֶכֶת הַשֶׁמֶשׁ (נ)
solar eclipse	likui χama	לִיקוּי חַמָה (ז)
the Earth	kadur ha''arets	כַּדוּר הָאָרֶץ (ז)
the Moon	ya'reaχ	יָרֵחַ (ז)
Mars	ma'adim	מַאֲדִים (ז)
Venus	'noga	נוֹגָה (ז)
Jupiter	'tsedek	צֶדֶק (ז)
Saturn	ʃabtai	שַׁבּתַאי (ז)
Mercury	koχav χama	כּוֹכָב חַמָה (ז)
Uranus	u'ranus	אוּרָנוּס (ז)
Neptune	neptun	נֶפּטוּן (ז)
Pluto	'pluto	פלוּטוֹ (ז)
Milky Way	ʃvil haχalav	שבִיל הֶחָלָב (ז)
Great Bear (Ursa Major)	duba gdola	דוּבָּה גדוֹלָה (נ)

North Star	koχav hatsafon	כּוֹכַב הַצָּפוֹן (ז)
Martian	toʃav ma'adim	תּוֹשָׁב מַאֲדִים (ז)
extraterrestrial (n)	χutsan	חוּצָן (ז)
alien	χaizar	חַייזָר (ז)
flying saucer	tsa'laχat me'o'fefet	צַלַחַת מְעוֹפֶפֶת (נ)
spaceship	χalalit	חֲלָלִית (נ)
space station	taχanat χalal	תַּחֲנַת חָלָל (נ)
blast-off	hamra'a	הַמרָאָה (נ)
engine	ma'no'a	מָנוֹעַ (ז)
nozzle	neχir	נָחִיר (ז)
fuel	'delek	דֶלֶק (ז)
cockpit, flight deck	'kokpit	קוֹקפִּיט (ז)
antenna	an'tena	אַנטֶנָה (נ)
porthole	eʃnav	אֶשׁנָב (ז)
solar panel	'luaχ so'lari	לוּחַ סוֹלָרִי (ז)
spacesuit	χalifat χalal	חֲלִיפַת חָלָל (נ)
weightlessness	'χoser miʃkal	חוֹסֶר מִשׁקָל (ז)
oxygen	χamtsan	חַמצָן (ז)
docking (in space)	agina	עֲגִינָה (נ)
to dock (vi, vt)	la'agon	לַעֲגוֹן
observatory	mitspe koχavim	מִצפֵּה כּוֹכָבִים (ז)
telescope	teleskop	טֶלֶסקוֹפּ (ז)
to observe (vt)	liʃpot, lehaʃkif	לִצפּוֹת, לְהַשׁקִיף
to explore (vt)	laχkor	לַחקוֹר

165. The Earth

the Earth	kadur ha''arets	כַּדוּר הָאָרֶץ (ז)
the globe (the Earth)	kadur ha''arets	כַּדוּר הָאָרֶץ (ז)
planet	koχav 'leχet	כּוֹכַב לֶכֶת (ז)
atmosphere	atmos'fera	אַטמוֹספֶרָה (נ)
geography	ge'o'grafya	גֵּיאוֹגרַפיָה (נ)
nature	'teva	טֶבַע (ז)
globe (table ~)	'globus	גלוֹבּוּס (ז)
map	mapa	מַפָּה (נ)
atlas	'atlas	אַטלָס (ז)
Europe	ei'ropa	אֵירוֹפָּה (נ)
Asia	'asya	אַסיָה (נ)
Africa	'afrika	אַפרִיקָה (נ)
Australia	ost'ralya	אוֹסטרַליָה (נ)
America	a'merika	אָמֶרִיקָה (נ)

North America	a'merika hatsfonit	אֲמֶרִיקָה הַצְּפוֹנִית (נ)
South America	a'merika hadromit	אֲמֶרִיקָה הַדְּרוֹמִית (נ)
Antarctica	ya'befet an'tarktika	יַבֶּשֶׁת אַנְטָארקְטִיקָה (נ)
the Arctic	'arktika	אַרקְטִיקָה (נ)

166. Cardinal directions

north	tsafon	צָפוֹן (ז)
to the north	tsa'fona	צָפוֹנָה
in the north	batsafon	בַּצָּפוֹן
northern (adj)	tsfoni	צְפוֹנִי
south	darom	דָּרוֹם (ז)
to the south	da'roma	דָּרוֹמָה
in the south	badarom	בַּדָּרוֹם
southern (adj)	dromi	דְּרוֹמִי
west	ma'arav	מַעֲרָב (ז)
to the west	ma'a'rava	מַעֲרָבָה
in the west	bama'arav	בַּמַּעֲרָב
western (adj)	ma'aravi	מַעֲרָבִי
east	mizraχ	מִזְרָח (ז)
to the east	miz'raχa	מִזְרָחָה
in the east	bamizraχ	בַּמִּזְרָח
eastern (adj)	mizraχi	מִזְרָחִי

167. Sea. Ocean

sea	yam	יָם (ז)
ocean	ok'yanos	אוֹקְיָאנוֹס (ז)
gulf (bay)	mifrats	מִפְרָץ (ז)
straits	meitsar	מֵיצַר (ז)
land (solid ground)	yabafa	יַבָּשָׁה (נ)
continent (mainland)	ya'befet	יַבֶּשֶׁת (נ)
island	i	אִי (ז)
peninsula	χatsi i	חֲצִי אִי (ז)
archipelago	arχipelag	אַרכִיפֶלָג (ז)
bay, cove	mifrats	מִפְרָץ (ז)
harbor	namal	נָמֵל (ז)
lagoon	la'guna	לָגוּנָה (נ)
cape	kef	כֵּף (ז)
atoll	atol	אָטוֹל (ז)
reef	funit	שׁוֹנִית (נ)

coral	almog	אַלְמוֹג (ז)
coral reef	ʃunit almogim	שׁוּנִית אַלְמוֹגִים (נ)
deep (adj)	amok	עָמוֹק
depth (deep water)	'omek	עוֹמֶק (ז)
abyss	tehom	תְּהוֹם (נ)
trench (e.g., Mariana ~)	maxtej	שֶׁקַע (ז)
current (Ocean ~)	'zerem	זֶרֶם (ז)
to surround (bathe)	lehakif	לְהַקִּיף
shore	χof	חוֹף (ז)
coast	χof yam	חוֹף יָם (ז)
flow (flood tide)	ge'ut	גֵּאוּת (נ)
ebb (ebb tide)	'ʃefel	שֵׁפֶל (ז)
shoal	sirton	שִׂרְטוֹן (ז)
bottom (~ of the sea)	karka'it	קַרְקָעִית (נ)
wave	gal	גַּל (ז)
crest (~ of a wave)	pisgat hagal	פְּסַגַּת הַגַּל (נ)
spume (sea foam)	'ketsef	קֶצֶף (ז)
storm (sea storm)	sufa	סוּפָה (נ)
hurricane	hurikan	הוֹרִיקָן (ז)
tsunami	tsu'nami	צוּנָאמִי (ז)
calm (dead ~)	'roga	רֹגַע (ז)
quiet, calm (adj)	ʃalev	שָׁלֵו
pole	'kotev	קוֹטֶב (ז)
polar (adj)	kotbi	קוֹטְבִּי
latitude	kav 'roχav	קַו רוֹחַב (ז)
longitude	kav 'oreχ	קַו אוֹרֶךְ (ז)
parallel	kav 'roχav	קַו רוֹחַב (ז)
equator	kav hamaʃve	קַו הַמַּשְׁוֶה (ז)
sky	ʃa'mayim	שָׁמַיִם (ז"ר)
horizon	'ofek	אוֹפֶק (ז)
air	avir	אֲוִיר (ז)
lighthouse	migdalor	מִגְדַּלּוֹר (ז)
to dive (vi)	litslol	לִצְלוֹל
to sink (ab. boat)	lit'bo'a	לִטְבּוֹעַ
treasures	otsarot	אוֹצָרוֹת (ז"ר)

168. Mountains

| mountain | har | הַר (ז) |
| mountain range | 'reχes harim | רֶכֶס הָרִים (ז) |

173

mountain ridge	'reχes har	רֶכֶס הַר (ז)
summit, top	pisga	פִּסְגָּה (נ)
peak	pisga	פִּסְגָּה (נ)
foot (~ of the mountain)	margelot	מַרְגְּלוֹת (נ"ר)
slope (mountainside)	midron	מִדְרוֹן (ז)
volcano	har 'ga'aʃ	הַר גַּעַשׁ (ז)
active volcano	har 'ga'aʃ pa'il	הַר גַּעַשׁ פָּעִיל (ז)
dormant volcano	har 'ga'aʃ radum	הַר גַּעַשׁ רָדוּם (ז)
eruption	hitparʦut	הִתְפָּרְצוּת (נ)
crater	lo'a	לוֹעַ (ז)
magma	megama	מַגְמָה (נ)
lava	'lava	לָאבָה (נ)
molten (~ lava)	lohet	לוֹהֵט
canyon	kanyon	קַנְיוֹן (ז)
gorge	gai	גַּיְא (ז)
crevice	'beka	בֶּקַע (ז)
abyss (chasm)	tehom	תְּהוֹם (נ)
pass, col	ma'avar harim	מַעֲבַר הָרִים (ז)
plateau	rama	רָמָה (נ)
cliff	ʦuk	צוּק (ז)
hill	giv'a	גִּבְעָה (נ)
glacier	karχon	קַרְחוֹן (ז)
waterfall	mapal 'mayim	מַפַּל מַיִם (ז)
geyser	'geizer	גֵּיְזֶר (ז)
lake	agam	אֲגַם (ז)
plain	miʃor	מִישׁוֹר (ז)
landscape	nof	נוֹף (ז)
echo	hed	הֵד (ז)
alpinist	metapes harim	מְטַפֵּס הָרִים (ז)
rock climber	metapes sla'im	מְטַפֵּס סְלָעִים (ז)
to conquer (in climbing)	liχboʃ	לִכְבּוֹשׁ
climb (an easy ~)	tipus	טִיפּוּס (ז)

169. Rivers

river	nahar	נָהָר (ז)
spring (natural source)	ma'ayan	מַעֲיָן (ז)
riverbed (river channel)	afik	אָפִיק (ז)
basin (river valley)	agan nahar	אֲגַן נָהָר (ז)
to flow into ...	lehiʃapeχ	לְהִישָׁפֵּךְ
tributary	yuval	יוּבַל (ז)
bank (of river)	χof	חוֹף (ז)

current (stream)	'zerem	זֶרֶם (ז)
downstream (adv)	bemorad hanahar	בְּמוֹרַד הַנָּהָר
upstream (adv)	bema'ale hanahar	בְּמַעֲלֵה הַזֶּרֶם
inundation	hatsafa	הֲצָפָה (נ)
flooding	ʃitafon	שִׁיטָפוֹן (ז)
to overflow (vi)	la alot al guotav	לַעֲלוֹת עַל גְּדוֹתָיו
to flood (vt)	lehatsif	לְהָצִיף
shallow (shoal)	sirton	שִׂרְטוֹן (ז)
rapids	'eʃed	אֶשֶׁד (ז)
dam	'seχer	סֶכֶר (ז)
canal	te'ala	תְּעָלָה (נ)
reservoir (artificial lake)	ma'agar 'mayim	מַאֲגַר מַיִם (ז)
sluice, lock	ta 'ʃayit	תָּא שַׁיִט (ז)
water body (pond, etc.)	ma'agar 'mayim	מַאֲגַר מַיִם (ז)
swamp (marshland)	bitsa	בִּיצָה (נ)
bog, marsh	bitsa	בִּיצָה (נ)
whirlpool	me'ar'bolet	מְעַרְבּוֹלֶת (נ)
stream (brook)	'naχal	נַחַל (ז)
drinking (ab. water)	ʃel ʃtiya	שֶׁל שְׁתִיָּה
fresh (~ water)	metukim	מְתוּקִים
ice	'keraχ	קֶרַח (ז)
to freeze over (ab. river, etc.)	likpo	לִקְפּוֹא

170. Forest

forest, wood	'ya'ar	יַעַר (ז)
forest (as adj)	ʃel 'ya'ar	שֶׁל יַעַר
thick forest	avi ha'ya'ar	עֲבִי הַיַּעַר (ז)
grove	χurʃa	חוּרְשָׁה (נ)
forest clearing	ka'raχat 'ya'ar	קָרַחַת יַעַר (נ)
thicket	svaχ	סְבַךְ (ז)
scrubland	'siaχ	שִׂיחַ (ז)
footpath (troddenpath)	ʃvil	שְׁבִיל (ז)
gully	'emek tsar	עֵמֶק צַר (ז)
tree	ets	עֵץ (ז)
leaf	ale	עָלֶה (ז)
leaves (foliage)	alva	עַלְוָה (נ)
fall of leaves	ʃa'leχet	שַׁלֶּכֶת (נ)
to fall (ab. leaves)	linʃor	לִנְשׁוֹר

top (of the tree)	tsa'meret	צַמֶרֶת (נ)
branch	anaf	עָנָף (ז)
bough	anaf ave	עָנָף עָבֶה (ז)
bud (on shrub, tree)	nitsan	נִיצָן (ז)
needle (of pine tree)	'maxat	מַחַט (נ)
pine cone	itstrubal	אִצטרוּבָּל (ז)

hollow (in a tree)	xor ba'ets	חוֹר בָּעֵץ (ז)
nest	ken	קֵן (ז)
burrow (animal hole)	mexila	מְחִילָה (נ)

trunk	'geza	גֶזַע (ז)
root	'foref	שוֹרֶש (ז)
bark	klipa	קלִיפָּה (נ)
moss	taxav	טַחַב (ז)

to uproot (remove trees or tree stumps)	la'akor	לַעֲקוֹר
to chop down	lixrot	לכרוֹת
to deforest (vt)	levare	לְבָרֵא
tree stump	'gedem	גֶדֶם (ז)

campfire	medura	מְדוּרָה (נ)
forest fire	srefa	שׂרֵיפָה (נ)
to extinguish (vt)	lexabot	לכבּוֹת

forest ranger	fomer 'ya'ar	שוֹמֵר יַעַר (ז)
protection	fmira	שמִירָה (נ)
to protect (~ nature)	lifmor	לשמוֹר
poacher	tsayad lelo refut	צַייָד לְלא רְשוּת (ז)
steel trap	mal'kodet	מַלכּוֹדֶת (נ)

| to gather, to pick (vt) | lelaket | לְלַקֵט |
| to lose one's way | lit'ot | לתעוֹת |

171. Natural resources

natural resources	otsarot 'teva	אוֹצְרוֹת טֶבַע (ז"ר)
minerals	mine'ralim	מִינֶרָלִים (ז"ר)
deposits	mirbats	מִרבָּץ (ז)
field (e.g., oilfield)	mirbats	מִרבָּץ (ז)

to mine (extract)	lixrot	לכרוֹת
mining (extraction)	kriya	כּרִייָה (נ)
ore	afra	עַפרָה (נ)
mine (e.g., for coal)	mixre	מִכרֶה (ז)
shaft (mine ~)	pir	פִּיר (ז)
miner	kore	כּוֹרֶה (ז)
gas (natural ~)	gaz	גָז (ז)
gas pipeline	tsinor gaz	צִינוֹר גָז (ז)

oil (petroleum)	neft	נֶפֶט (ז)
oil pipeline	tsinor neft	צִינוֹר נֶפֶט (ז)
oil well	be'er neft	בְּאֵר נֶפֶט (נ)
derrick (tower)	migdal ki'duaχ	מִגְדַל קִידוּחַ (ז)
tanker	meχalit	מֵיכָלִית (נ)
sand	χol	חוֹל (ז)
limestone	'even gir	אֶבֶן גִיר (נ)
gravel	χatsats	חָצָץ (ז)
peat	kavul	כָּבוּל (ז)
clay	tit	טִיט (ז)
coal	peχam	פֶּחָם (ז)
iron (ore)	barzel	בַּרְזֶל (ז)
gold	zahav	זָהָב (ז)
silver	'kesef	כֶּסֶף (ז)
nickel	'nikel	נִיקֶל (ז)
copper	ne'χoʃet	נְחוֹשֶׁת (נ)
zinc	avats	אָבָץ (ז)
manganese	mangan	מַנְגָן (ז)
mercury	kaspit	כַּסְפִּית (נ)
lead	o'feret	עוֹפֶרֶת (נ)
mineral	mineral	מִינֶרָל (ז)
crystal	gaviʃ	גָבִישׁ (ז)
marble	'ʃayiʃ	שַׁיִשׁ (ז)
uranium	u'ranyum	אוּרָנְיוּם (ז)

The Earth. Part 2

172. Weather

weather	'mezeg avir	מֶזֶג אֲוֹיר (ז)
weather forecast	taxazit 'mezeg ha'avir	תַּחֲזִית מֶזֶג הָאֲוֹיר (נ)
temperature	tempera'tura	טֶמפֶּרָטוּרָה (נ)
thermometer	madxom	מַדחוֹם (ז)
barometer	ba'rometer	בָּרוֹמֶטֶר (ז)
humid (adj)	lax	לַח
humidity	laxut	לַחוּת (נ)
heat (extreme ~)	xom	חוֹם (ז)
hot (torrid)	xam	חַם
it's hot	xam	חַם
it's warm	xamim	חָמִים
warm (moderately hot)	xamim	חָמִים
it's cold	kar	קַר
cold (adj)	kar	קַר
sun	'ʃemeʃ	שֶׁמֶשׁ (נ)
to shine (vi)	lizhor	לִזהוֹר
sunny (day)	ʃimʃi	שִׁמשִׁי
to come up (vi)	liz'roax	לִזרוֹחַ
to set (vi)	liʃ'ko'a	לִשׁקוֹעַ
cloud	anan	עָנָן (ז)
cloudy (adj)	meʿunan	מְעוּנָן
rain cloud	av	עָב (ז)
somber (gloomy)	sagriri	סַגרִירִי
rain	'geʃem	גֶשֶׁם (ז)
it's raining	yored 'geʃem	יוֹרֵד גֶשֶׁם
rainy (~ day, weather)	gaʃum	גָשׁוּם
to drizzle (vi)	letaftef	לְטַפטֵף
pouring rain	matar	מָטָר (ז)
downpour	mabul	מַבּוּל (ז)
heavy (e.g., ~ rain)	xazak	חָזָק
puddle	ʃlulit	שְׁלוּלִית (נ)
to get wet (in rain)	lehitratev	לְהִתרַטֵב
fog (mist)	arapel	עֲרָפֶּל (ז)
foggy	meʿurpal	מְעוּרפָּל

| snow | 'ʃeleg | שֶׁלֶג (ז) |
| it's snowing | yored 'ʃeleg | יוֹרֵד שֶׁלֶג |

173. Severe weather. Natural disasters

thunderstorm	sufat re'amim	סוּפַת רְעָמִים (נ)
lightning (~ strike)	barak	בָּרָק (ז)
to flash (vi)	livhok	לִבהוֹק
thunder	'ra'am	רַעַם (ז)
to thunder (vi)	lir'om	לִרעוֹם
it's thundering	lir'om	לִרעוֹם
hail	barad	בָּרָד (ז)
it's hailing	yored barad	יוֹרֵד בָּרָד
to flood (vt)	lehatsif	לְהָצִיף
flood, inundation	ʃitafon	שִׁיטָפוֹן (ז)
earthquake	re'idat adama	רְעִידַת אֲדָמָה (נ)
tremor, quake	re'ida	רְעִידָה (נ)
epicenter	moked	מוֹקֵד (ז)
eruption	hitpartsut	הִתפָּרצוּת (נ)
lava	'lava	לָאבָה (נ)
twister	hurikan	הוֹרִיקָן (ז)
tornado	tor'nado	טוֹרנָדוֹ (ז)
typhoon	taifun	טַייפוּן (ז)
hurricane	hurikan	הוֹרִיקָן (ז)
storm	sufa	סוּפָה (נ)
tsunami	tsu'nami	צוּנָאמִי (ז)
cyclone	tsiklon	צִיקלוֹן (ז)
bad weather	sagrir	סַגרִיר (ז)
fire (accident)	srefa	שׂרֵיפָה (נ)
disaster	ason	אָסוֹן (ז)
meteorite	mete'orit	מֶטֶאוֹרִיט (ז)
avalanche	ma'polet ʃlagim	מַפּוֹלֶת שְׁלָגִים (נ)
snowslide	ma'polet ʃlagim	מַפּוֹלֶת שְׁלָגִים (נ)
blizzard	sufat ʃlagim	סוּפַת שְׁלָגִים (נ)
snowstorm	sufat ʃlagim	סוּפַת שְׁלָגִים (נ)

Fauna

174. Mammals. Predators

predator	χayat 'teref	חַיַּת טֶרֶף (נ)
tiger	'tigris	טִיגְרִיס (ז)
lion	arye	אַרְיֵה (ז)
wolf	ze'ev	זְאֵב (ז)
fox	ʃu'al	שׁוּעָל (ז)
jaguar	yagu'ar	יָגוּאָר (ז)
leopard	namer	נָמֵר (ז)
cheetah	bardelas	בַּרְדְּלָס (ז)
black panther	panter	פַּנְתֵּר (ז)
puma	'puma	פּוּמָה (נ)
snow leopard	namer 'ʃeleg	נָמֵר שֶׁלֶג (ז)
lynx	ʃunar	שׁוּנָר (ז)
coyote	ze'ev ha'aravot	זְאֵב הָעֲרָבוֹת (ז)
jackal	tan	תַּן (ז)
hyena	tsa'vo'a	צָבוֹעַ (ז)

175. Wild animals

animal	'ba'al χayim	בַּעַל חַיִּים (ז)
beast (animal)	χaya	חַיָּה (נ)
squirrel	sna'i	סְנָאִי (ז)
hedgehog	kipod	קִיפּוֹד (ז)
hare	arnav	אַרְנָב (ז)
rabbit	ʃafan	שָׁפָן (ז)
badger	girit	גִּירִית (נ)
raccoon	dvivon	דְּבִיבוֹן (ז)
hamster	oger	אוֹגֵר (ז)
marmot	mar'mita	מַרְמִיטָה (נ)
mole	χafar'peret	חֲפַרְפֶּרֶת (נ)
mouse	aχbar	עַכְבָּר (ז)
rat	χulda	חוּלְדָּה (נ)
bat	atalef	עֲטַלֵּף (ז)
ermine	hermin	הֶרְמִין (ז)
sable	tsobel	צוֹבֶּל (ז)

marten	dalak	דָּלָק (ז)
weasel	χamus	חָמוֹס (ז)
mink	χorfan	חוֹרְפָן (ז)
beaver	bone	בּוֹנֶה (ז)
otter	lutra	לוּטְרָה (נ)
horse	sus	סוּס (ז)
moose	ayal hakore	אַיָּל הַקּוֹרֵא (ז)
deer	ayal	אַיָּל (ז)
camel	gamal	גָּמָל (ז)
bison	bizon	בִּיזוֹן (ז)
aurochs	bizon ei'ropi	בִּיזוֹן אֵירוֹפִי (ז)
buffalo	te'o	תְּאוֹ (ז)
zebra	'zebra	זֶבְּרָה (נ)
antelope	anti'lopa	אַנְטִילוֹפָה (ז)
roe deer	ayal hakarmel	אַיָּל הַכַּרְמֶל (ז)
fallow deer	yaχmur	יַחְמוּר (ז)
chamois	ya'el	יָעֵל (ז)
wild boar	χazir bar	חֲזִיר בָּר (ז)
whale	livyatan	לִוְיָתָן (ז)
seal	'kelev yam	כֶּלֶב יָם (ז)
walrus	sus yam	סוּס יָם (ז)
fur seal	dov yam	דּוֹב יָם (ז)
dolphin	dolfin	דּוֹלְפִין (ז)
bear	dov	דּוֹב (ז)
polar bear	dov 'kotev	דּוֹב קוֹטֶב (ז)
panda	'panda	פַּנְדָה (נ)
monkey	kof	קוֹף (ז)
chimpanzee	ʃimpanze	שִׁימְפַּנְזֶה (נ)
orangutan	orang utan	אוֹרַנְג-אוּטָן (ז)
gorilla	go'rila	גּוֹרִילָה (נ)
macaque	makak	מָקָק (ז)
gibbon	gibon	גִּיבּוֹן (ז)
elephant	pil	פִּיל (ז)
rhinoceros	karnaf	קַרְנַף (ז)
giraffe	dʒi'rafa	ג׳ִירָפָּה (נ)
hippopotamus	hipopotam	הִיפּוֹפּוֹטָם (ז)
kangaroo	'kenguru	קֶנְגּוּרוּ (ז)
koala (bear)	ko''ala	קוֹאָלָה (ז)
mongoose	nemiya	נְמִיָּה (נ)
chinchilla	tʃin'tʃila	צִ׳ינְצ׳ִילָה (נ)
skunk	bo'eʃ	בּוֹאֵשׁ (ז)
porcupine	darban	דַּרְבָּן (ז)

176. Domestic animals

cat	χatula	חֲתוּלָה (נ)
tomcat	χatul	חָתוּל (ז)
dog	'kelev	כֶּלֶב (ז)
horse	sus	סוּס (ז)
stallion (male horse)	sus harba'a	סוּס הַרְבָּעָה (ז)
mare	susa	סוּסָה (נ)
cow	para	פָּרָה (נ)
bull	ʃor	שׁוֹר (ז)
ox	ʃor	שׁוֹר (ז)
sheep (ewe)	kivsa	כִּבְשָׂה (נ)
ram	'ayil	אַיִל (ז)
goat	ez	עֵז (נ)
billy goat, he-goat	'tayiʃ	תַּיִשׁ (ז)
donkey	χamor	חֲמוֹר (ז)
mule	'pered	פֶּרֶד (ז)
pig, hog	χazir	חֲזִיר (ז)
piglet	χazarzir	חֲזַרְזִיר (ז)
rabbit	arnav	אַרְנָב (ז)
hen (chicken)	tarne'golet	תַּרְנְגֹלֶת (נ)
rooster	tarnegol	תַּרְנְגֹל (ז)
duck	barvaz	בַּרְוָז (ז)
drake	barvaz	בַּרְוָז (ז)
goose	avaz	אֲוָז (ז)
tom turkey, gobbler	tarnegol 'hodu	תַּרְנְגֹל הֹדוּ (ז)
turkey (hen)	tarne'golet 'hodu	תַּרְנְגֹלֶת הֹדוּ (נ)
domestic animals	χayot 'bayit	חַיּוֹת בַּיִת (נ"ר)
tame (e.g., ~ hamster)	mevuyat	מְבוּיָת
to tame (vt)	levayet	לְבַיֵּת
to breed (vt)	lehar'bi'a	לְהַרְבִּיעַ
farm	χava	חַוָּה (נ)
poultry	ofot 'bayit	עוֹפוֹת בַּיִת (נ"ר)
cattle	bakar	בָּקָר (ז)
herd (cattle)	'eder	עֵדֶר (ז)
stable	urva	אוּרְוָה (נ)
pigpen	dir χazirim	דִּיר חֲזִירִים (ז)
cowshed	'refet	רֶפֶת (נ)
rabbit hutch	arnaviya	אַרְנָבִיָּה (נ)
hen house	lul	לוּל (ז)

177. Dogs. Dog breeds

dog	'kelev	כֶּלֶב (ז)
sheepdog	'kelev ro'e	כֶּלֶב רוֹעֶה (ז)
German shepherd	ro'e germani	רוֹעֶה גֶּרְמָנִי (ז)
poodle	'pudel	פּוּדֶל (ז)
dachshund	'taxaʃ	תַחַשׁ (ז)
bulldog	buldog	בּוּלְדוֹג (ז)
boxer	'bokser	בּוֹקְסֶר (ז)
mastiff	mastif	מָסְטִיף (ז)
Rottweiler	rot'vailer	רוֹטְוַיְילָר (ז)
Doberman	'doberman	דוֹבֶּרְמָן (ז)
basset	'baset 'ha'und	בָּאסֶט-הָאוּנְד (ז)
bobtail	bobteil	בּוֹבְטֵייל (ז)
Dalmatian	dal'mati	דַלְמָטִי (ז)
cocker spaniel	'koker 'spani'el	קוֹקֶר סְפָּנִיאֶל (ז)
Newfoundland	nyu'fa'undlend	נְיוּפָאוּנְדְלָנְד (ז)
Saint Bernard	sen bernard	סֶן בֶּרְנַרד (ז)
husky	'haski	הָאסְקִי (ז)
Chow Chow	'tʃa'u 'tʃa'u	צַ'אוּ צַ'אוּ (ז)
spitz	ʃpits	שְׁפִּיץ (ז)
pug	pag	פָּאג (ז)

178. Sounds made by animals

barking (n)	nevixa	נְבִיחָה (נ)
to bark (vi)	lin'boax	לִנְבּוֹחַ
to meow (vi)	leyalel	לְיַלֵל
to purr (vi)	legarger	לְגַרְגֵּר
to moo (vi)	lig'ot	לִגְעוֹת
to bellow (bull)	lig'ot	לִגְעוֹת
to growl (vi)	linhom	לִנְהוֹם
howl (n)	yelala	יְלָלָה (נ)
to howl (vi)	leyalel	לְיַלֵל
to whine (vi)	leyabev	לְיַבֵּב
to bleat (sheep)	lif'ot	לִפְעוֹת
to oink, to grunt (pig)	lexarxer	לְחַרְחֵר
to squeal (vi)	lits'voax	לִצְווֹחַ
to croak (vi)	lekarker	לְקַרְקֵר
to buzz (insect)	lezamzem	לְזַמְזֵם
to chirp (crickets, grasshopper)	letsartser	לְצַרְצֵר

179. Birds

bird	tsipor	צִיפּוֹר (נ)
pigeon	yona	יוֹנָה (נ)
sparrow	dror	דְרוֹר (ז)
tit (great tit)	yargazi	יַרְגָזִי (ז)
magpie	orev neχalim	עוֹרֵב נְחָלִים (ז)

raven	orev ʃaχor	עוֹרֵב שָחוֹר (ז)
crow	orev afor	עוֹרֵב אָפוֹר (ז)
jackdaw	ka'ak	קָאק (ז)
rook	orev hamizra	עוֹרֵב הַמִזְרָע (ז)

duck	barvaz	בַּרְוָז (ז)
goose	avaz	אַוָז (ז)
pheasant	pasyon	פַסְיוֹן (ז)

eagle	'ayit	עַיִט (ז)
hawk	nets	נֵץ (ז)
falcon	baz	בַּז (ז)
vulture	ozniya	עוֹזְנִיָה (ז)
condor (Andean ~)	kondor	קוֹנְדוֹר (ז)

swan	barbur	בַּרְבּוּר (ז)
crane	agur	עָגוּר (ז)
stork	χasida	חֲסִידָה (נ)

parrot	'tuki	תוּכִּי (ז)
hummingbird	ko'libri	קוֹלִיבְּרִי (ז)
peacock	tavas	טַוָוס (ז)

ostrich	bat ya'ana	בַּת יַעֲנָה (נ)
heron	anafa	אֲנָפָה (נ)
flamingo	fla'mingo	פְלָמִינְגוֹ (ז)
pelican	saknai	שַׂקְנַאי (ז)

| nightingale | zamir | זָמִיר (ז) |
| swallow | snunit | סְנוּנִית (נ) |

thrush	kiχli	קִיכְלִי (ז)
song thrush	kiχli mezamer	קִיכְלִי מְזַמֵר (ז)
blackbird	kiχli ʃaχor	קִיכְלִי שָחוֹר (ז)

swift	sis	סִיס (ז)
lark	efroni	עֶפְרוֹנִי (ז)
quail	slav	שְׂלָיו (ז)

woodpecker	'neker	נַקָר (ז)
cuckoo	kukiya	קוּקִיָה (נ)
owl	yanʃuf	יַנְשוּף (ז)
eagle owl	'oaχ	אוֹחַ (ז)

wood grouse	seχvi 'ya'ar	שְׂכְוִוי יַעַר (ז)
black grouse	seχvi	שְׂכְוִוי (ז)
partridge	χogla	חוֹגְלָה (נ)
starling	zarzir	זַרְזִיר (ז)
canary	ka'narit	קָנָרִית (נ)
hazel grouse	seχvi haya'arot	שְׂכְוִוי הַיְעָרוֹת (ז)
chaffinch	paroʃ	פָּרוֹשׁ (ז)
bullfinch	admonit	אַדְמוֹנִית (נ)
seagull	'ʃaχaf	שַׁחַף (ז)
albatross	albatros	אַלְבַּטְרוֹס (ז)
penguin	pingvin	פִּינְגּוִֹין (ז)

180. Birds. Singing and sounds

to sing (vi)	laʃir	לָשִׁיר
to call (animal, bird)	lits'ok	לִצְעוֹק
to crow (rooster)	lekarker	לְקַרְקֵר
cock-a-doodle-doo	kuku'riku	קוּקוּרִיקוּ
to cluck (hen)	lekarker	לְקַרְקֵר
to caw (vi)	lits'roaχ	לִצְרוֹחַ
to quack (duck)	lega'a'ge'a	לְגַעֲגֵעַ
to cheep (vi)	letsayets	לְצַיֵּץ
to chirp, to twitter	letsaftsef, letsayets	לְצַפְצֵף, לְצַיֵּץ

181. Fish. Marine animals

bream	avroma	אַבְרוֹמָה (נ)
carp	karpiyon	קַרְפְּיוֹן (ז)
perch	'okunus	אוֹקוּנוּס (ז)
catfish	sfamnun	שְׂפַמְנוּן (ז)
pike	ze'ev 'mayim	זְאֵב מַיִם (ז)
salmon	'salmon	סַלְמוֹן (ז)
sturgeon	χidkan	חִדְקָן (ז)
herring	ma'liaχ	מָלִיחַ (ז)
Atlantic salmon	iltit	אִילְתִּית (נ)
mackerel	makarel	מַקָרֵל (ז)
flatfish	dag moʃe ra'benu	דַּג מֹשֶׁה רַבֵּנוּ (ז)
zander, pike perch	amnun	אַמְנוּן (ז)
cod	ʃibut	שִׁיבּוּט (ז)
tuna	'tuna	טוּנָה (נ)
trout	forel	פּוֹרֵל (ז)

eel	tslofaχ	צְלוֹפָח (ז)
electric ray	trisanit	תְּרִיסָנִית (נ)
moray eel	mo'rena	מוֹרֶנָה (נ)
piranha	pi'ranya	פִּירַנְיָה (נ)

shark	kariʃ	כָּרִיש (ז)
dolphin	dolfin	דוֹלְפִין (ז)
whale	livyatan	לִוְיָתָן (ז)

crab	sartan	סַרְטָן (ז)
jellyfish	me'duza	מְדוּזָה (נ)
octopus	tamnun	תַּמְנוּן (ז)

starfish	koχav yam	כּוֹכַב יָם (ז)
sea urchin	kipod yam	קִיפּוֹד יָם (ז)
seahorse	suson yam	סוּסוֹן יָם (ז)

oyster	tsidpa	צִדְפָּה (נ)
shrimp	χasilon	חָסִילוֹן (ז)
lobster	'lobster	לוֹבּסְטֶר (ז)
spiny lobster	'lobster kotsani	לוֹבּסְטֶר קוֹצָנִי (ז)

182. Amphibians. Reptiles

| snake | naχaʃ | נָחָש (ז) |
| venomous (snake) | arsi | אַרְסִי |

| viper | 'tsefa | צֶפַע (ז) |
| cobra | 'peten | פֶּתֶן (ז) |

| python | piton | פִּיתוֹן (ז) |
| boa | χanak | חֲנָק (ז) |

grass snake	naχaʃ 'mayim	נָחָש מַיִם (ז)
rattle snake	ʃfifon	שְׁפִיפוֹן (ז)
anaconda	ana'konda	אֲנָקוֹנְדָה (נ)

lizard	leta'a	לְטָאָה (נ)
iguana	igu''ana	אִיגוּאָנָה (נ)
monitor lizard	'koaχ	כּוֹחַ (ז)
salamander	sala'mandra	סָלָמַנְדְרָה (נ)

| chameleon | zikit | זִיקִית (נ) |
| scorpion | akrav | עַקְרָב (ז) |

| turtle | tsav | צָב (ז) |
| frog | tsfar'de'a | צְפַרְדֵעַ (נ) |

| toad | karpada | קַרְפָּדָה (נ) |
| crocodile | tanin | תַּנִין (ז) |

183. Insects

insect, bug	χarak	חָרָק (ז)
butterfly	parpar	פַּרְפַּר (ז)
ant	nemala	נְמָלָה (נ)
fly	zvuv	זְבוּב (ז)
mosquito	yatuʃ	יַתּוּשׁ (ז)
beetle	χipuʃit	חִיפּוּשִׁית (נ)

wasp	tsir'a	צִרְעָה (נ)
bee	dvora	דבוֹרָה (נ)
bumblebee	dabur	דַבּוּר (ז)
gadfly (botfly)	zvuv hasus	זְבוּב הַסוּס (ז)

| spider | akaviʃ | עַכָּבִישׁ (ז) |
| spiderweb | kurei akaviʃ | קוּרֵי עַכָּבִישׁ (ז"ר) |

dragonfly	ʃapirit	שַׁפִּירִית (נ)
grasshopper	χagav	חָגָב (ז)
moth (night butterfly)	aʃ	עָשׁ (ז)

cockroach	makak	מָקָק (ז)
tick	kartsiya	קַרְצִיָה (נ)
flea	par'oʃ	פַּרְעוֹשׁ (ז)
midge	yavχuʃ	יַבחוּשׁ (ז)

locust	arbe	אַרְבֶּה (ז)
snail	χilazon	חִילָזוֹן (ז)
cricket	tsartsar	צַרְצַר (ז)
lightning bug	gaχlilit	גַחְלִילִית (נ)
ladybug	parat moʃe ra'benu	פָּרַת מֹשֶׁה רַבֵּנוּ (נ)
cockchafer	χipuʃit aviv	חִיפּוּשִׁית אָבִיב (נ)

leech	aluka	עֲלוּקָה (נ)
caterpillar	zaχal	זַחַל (ז)
earthworm	to'la'at	תוֹלַעַת (נ)
larva	'deren	דֶרֶן (ז)

184. Animals. Body parts

beak	makor	מָקוֹר (ז)
wings	kna'fayim	כְּנָפַיים (נ"ר)
foot (of bird)	'regel	רֶגֶל (נ)
feathers (plumage)	pluma	פְּלוּמָה (נ)
feather	notsa	נוֹצָה (נ)
crest	tsitsa	צִיצָה (נ)

| gills | zimim | זִימִים (ז"ר) |
| spawn | beitsei dagim | בֵּיצֵי דָגִים (נ"ר) |

larva	'deren	דֶרֶן (ז)
fin	snapir	סְנַפִּיר (ז)
scales (of fish, reptile)	kaskasim	קַשְׂקַשִׂים (ז״ר)

fang (canine)	niv	נִיב (ז)
paw (e.g., cat's ~)	'regel	רֶגֶל (נ)
muzzle (snout)	partsuf	פַּרְצוּף (ז)
mouth (of cat, dog)	lo'a	לוֹעַ (ז)
tail	zanav	זָנָב (ז)
whiskers	safam	שָׂפָם (ז)

| hoof | parsa | פַּרְסָה (נ) |
| horn | 'keren | קֶרֶן (נ) |

carapace	ʃiryon	שִׁרְיוֹן (ז)
shell (of mollusk)	konχiya	קוֹנְכִיָּה (נ)
eggshell	klipa	קְלִיפָּה (נ)

| animal's hair (pelage) | parva | פַּרְוָה (נ) |
| pelt (hide) | or | עוֹר (ז) |

185. Animals. Habitats

| habitat | beit gidul | בֵּית גִּידוּל (ז) |
| migration | hagira | הַגִּירָה (נ) |

mountain	har	הַר (ז)
reef	ʃunit	שׁוּנִית (נ)
cliff	'sela	סֶלַע (ז)

forest	'ya'ar	יַעַר (ז)
jungle	'dʒungel	ג׳וּנְגֶל (ז)
savanna	sa'vana	סָוָונָה (נ)
tundra	'tundra	טוּנְדְרָה (נ)

steppe	arava	עֲרָבָה (נ)
desert	midbar	מִדְבָּר (ז)
oasis	neve midbar	נְוֵה מִדְבָּר (ז)

sea	yam	יָם (ז)
lake	agam	אֲגַם (ז)
ocean	ok'yanos	אוֹקְיָאנוֹס (ז)

swamp (marshland)	bitsa	בִּיצָה (נ)
freshwater (adj)	ʃel 'mayim metukim	שֶׁל מַיִם מְתוּקִים
pond	breχa	בְּרֵיכָה (נ)
river	nahar	נָהָר (ז)

| den (bear's ~) | me'ura | מְאוּרָה (נ) |
| nest | ken | קֵן (ז) |

hollow (in a tree)	χor ba'ets	חוֹר בָּעֵץ (ז)
burrow (animal hole)	meχila	מְחִילָה (נ)
anthill	kan nemalim	קַן נְמָלִים (ז)

Flora

186. Trees

tree	ets	עֵץ (ז)
deciduous (adj)	naʃir	נָשִׁיר
coniferous (adj)	maxtani	מַחְטָנִי
evergreen (adj)	yarok ad	יָרוֹק עַד
apple tree	ta'puax	תַּפּוּחַ (ז)
pear tree	agas	אַגָּס (ז)
sweet cherry tree	gudgedan	גּוּדְגְּדָן (ז)
sour cherry tree	duvdevan	דּוּבְדְּבָן (ז)
plum tree	ʃezif	שְׁזִיף (ז)
birch	ʃadar	שְׁדָר (ז)
oak	alon	אַלּוֹן (ז)
linden tree	'tilya	טִילְיָה (נ)
aspen	aspa	אַסְפָּה (נ)
maple	'eder	אֶדֶר (ז)
spruce	a'ʃuax	אֲשׁוּחַ (ז)
pine	'oren	אוֹרֶן (ז)
larch	arzit	אַרְזִית (נ)
fir tree	a'ʃuax	אֲשׁוּחַ (ז)
cedar	'erez	אֶרֶז (ז)
poplar	tsaftsefa	צַפְצֶפָה (נ)
rowan	ben xuzrar	בֶּן־חוּזְרָר (ז)
willow	arava	עֲרָבָה (נ)
alder	alnus	אַלְנוּס (ז)
beech	aʃur	אָשׁוּר (ז)
elm	bu'kitsa	בּוּקִיצָה (נ)
ash (tree)	mela	מֵילָה (נ)
chestnut	armon	עַרְמוֹן (ז)
magnolia	mag'nolya	מַגְנוֹלְיָה (נ)
palm tree	'dekel	דֶּקֶל (ז)
cypress	broʃ	בְּרוֹשׁ (ז)
mangrove	mangrov	מַנְגְּרוֹב (ז)
baobab	ba'obab	בָּאוֹבָּב (ז)
eucalyptus	eika'liptus	אִיקָלִיפְּטוּס (ז)
sequoia	sek'voya	סֶקְווֹיָה (נ)

187. Shrubs

bush	'siaχ	שִׂיחַ (ז)
shrub	'siaχ	שִׂיחַ (ז)
grapevine	'gefen	גֶּפֶן (נ)
vineyard	'kerem	כֶּרֶם (ז)
raspberry bush	'petel	פֶּטֶל (ז)
blackcurrant bush	'siaχ dumdemaniyot ʃχorot	שִׂיחַ דּוּמְדְּמָנִיּוֹת שְׁחוֹרוֹת (ז)
redcurrant bush	'siaχ dumdemaniyot adumot	שִׂיחַ דּוּמְדְּמָנִיּוֹת אֲדוּמּוֹת (ז)
gooseberry bush	χazarzar	חֲזַרְזַר (ז)
acacia	ʃita	שִׁיטָה (נ)
barberry	berberis	בֶּרְבֶּרִיס (ז)
jasmine	yasmin	יַסְמִין (ז)
juniper	ar'ar	עַרְעָר (ז)
rosebush	'siaχ vradim	שִׂיחַ וְרָדִים (ז)
dog rose	'vered bar	וֶרֶד בָּר (ז)

188. Mushrooms

mushroom	pitriya	פִּטְרִיָּה (נ)
edible mushroom	pitriya ra'uya lema'aχal	פִּטְרִיָּה רְאוּיָה לְמַאֲכָל
poisonous mushroom	pitriya ra'ila	פִּטְרִיָּה רְעִילָה (נ)
cap (of mushroom)	kipat pitriya	כִּיפַּת פִּטְרִיָּה (נ)
stipe (of mushroom)	'regel	רֶגֶל (נ)
cep (Boletus edulis)	por'tʃini	פּוֹרְצִ'ינִי (ז)
orange-cap boletus	pitriyat 'kova aduma	פִּטְרִיַּת כּוֹבַע אֲדוּמָה (נ)
birch bolete	pitriyat 'ya'ar	פִּטְרִיַּת יַעַר (נ)
chanterelle	gvi'onit ne'e'χelet	גְבִיעוֹנִית נֶאֱכֶלֶת (נ)
russula	χarifit	חָרִיפִית (נ)
morel	gamtsuts	גַמְצוּץ (ז)
fly agaric	zvuvanit	זְבוּבָנִית (נ)
death cap	pitriya ra'ila	פִּטְרִיָּה רְעִילָה (נ)

189. Fruits. Berries

fruit	pri	פְּרִי (ז)
fruits	perot	פֵּירוֹת (ז"ר)
apple	ta'puaχ	תַּפּוּחַ (ז)
pear	agas	אַגָס (ז)
plum	ʃezif	שְׁזִיף (ז)

strawberry (garden ~)	tut sade	תּוּת שָׂדֶה (ז)
sour cherry	duvdevan	דּוּבְדְּבָן (ז)
sweet cherry	gudgedan	גֻּדְגְּדָן (ז)
grape	anavim	עֲנָבִים (ז"ר)
raspberry	'petel	פֶּטֶל (ז)
blackcurrant	dumdemanit ʃχora	דֻּמְדְּמָנִית שְׁחוֹרָה (נ)
redcurrant	dumdemanit aduma	דֻּמְדְּמָנִית אֲדֻמָּה (נ)
gooseberry	χazarzar	חֲזַרְזַר (ז)
cranberry	χamutsit	חֲמוּצִית (נ)
orange	tapuz	תַּפּוּז (ז)
mandarin	klemen'tina	קְלֶמֶנְטִינָה (נ)
pineapple	'ananas	אֲנָנָס (ז)
banana	ba'nana	בַּנָנָה (נ)
date	tamar	תָּמָר (ז)
lemon	limon	לִימוֹן (ז)
apricot	'miʃmeʃ	מִשְׁמֵשׁ (ז)
peach	afarsek	אֲפַרְסֵק (ז)
kiwi	'kivi	קִיוִוי (ז)
grapefruit	eʃkolit	אֶשְׁכּוֹלִית (נ)
berry	garger	גַּרְגֵּר (ז)
berries	gargerim	גַּרְגְּרִים (ז"ר)
cowberry	uχmanit aduma	אוּכְמָנִית אֲדֻמָּה (נ)
wild strawberry	tut 'ya‘ar	תּוּת יַעַר (ז)
bilberry	uχmanit	אוּכְמָנִית (נ)

190. Flowers. Plants

flower	'peraχ	פֶּרַח (ז)
bouquet (of flowers)	zer	זֵר (ז)
rose (flower)	'vered	וֶרֶד (ז)
tulip	tsiv‘oni	צִבְעוֹנִי (ז)
carnation	tsi'poren	צִיפּוֹרֶן (ז)
gladiolus	glad'yola	גְּלַדְיוֹלָה (נ)
cornflower	dganit	דְּגָנִית (נ)
harebell	pa‘amonit	פַּעֲמוֹנִית (נ)
dandelion	ʃinan	שִׁינָן (ז)
camomile	kamomil	קָמוֹמִיל (ז)
aloe	alvai	אַלְוַוי (ז)
cactus	'kaktus	קַקְטוּס (ז)
rubber plant, ficus	'fikus	פִיקוּס (ז)
lily	ʃoʃana	שׁוֹשַׁנָּה (נ)
geranium	ge'ranyum	גֶּרָנְיוּם (ז)

hyacinth	yakinton	יָקִינְטוֹן (ז)
mimosa	mi'moza	מִימוֹזָה (נ)
narcissus	narkis	נַרְקִיס (ז)
nasturtium	'kova hanazir	כּוֹבַע הַנָּזִיר (ז)
orchid	saxlav	סַחְלָב (ז)
peony	admonit	אַדְמוֹנִית (נ)
violet	sigalit	סִיגָּלִית (נ)

pansy	amnon vetamar	אַמְנוֹן וְתָמָר (ז)
forget-me-not	zix'rini	זִכְרִינִי (ז)
daisy	marganit	מַרְגָּנִית (נ)

poppy	'pereg	פֶּרֶג (ז)
hemp	ka'nabis	קָנַאבִּיס (ז)
mint	'menta	מֶנְתָּה (נ)

lily of the valley	zivanit	זִיוָנִית (נ)
snowdrop	ga'lantus	גָּלַנְטוּס (ז)
nettle	sirpad	סִרְפָּד (ז)
sorrel	xum'a	חוּמְעָה (נ)
water lily	nufar	נוּפָר (ז)
fern	ʃarax	שָׁרָךְ (ז)
lichen	xazazit	חֲזָזִית (נ)

greenhouse (tropical ~)	xamama	חֲמָמָה (נ)
lawn	midʃa'a	מִדְשָׁאָה (נ)
flowerbed	arugat praxim	עֲרוּגַת פְּרָחִים (נ)

plant	'tsemax	צֶמַח (ז)
grass	'deʃe	דֶּשֶׁא (ז)
blade of grass	giv'ol 'esev	גִּבְעוֹל עֵשֶׂב (ז)

leaf	ale	עָלֶה (ז)
petal	ale ko'teret	עָלֶה כּוֹתֶרֶת (ז)
stem	giv'ol	גִּבְעוֹל (ז)
tuber	'pka'at	פְּקַעַת (נ)

| young plant (shoot) | 'nevet | נֶבֶט (ז) |
| thorn | kots | קוֹץ (ז) |

to blossom (vi)	lif'roax	לִפְרוֹחַ
to fade, to wither	linbol	לִנְבּוֹל
smell (odor)	'reax	רֵיחַ (ז)
to cut (flowers)	ligzom	לִגְזוֹם
to pick (a flower)	liktof	לִקְטוֹף

191. Cereals, grains

| grain | tvu'a | תְּבוּאָה (נ) |
| cereal crops | dganim | דְּגָנִים (ז"ר) |

ear (of barley, etc.)	ʃi'bolet	שִׁיבּוֹלֶת (נ)
wheat	χita	חִיטָה (נ)
rye	ʃifon	שִׁיפוֹן (ז)
oats	ʃi'bolet ʃu'al	שִׁיבּוֹלֶת שׁוּעָל (נ)
millet	'doχan	דּוֹחַן (ז)
barley	se'ora	שְׂעוֹרָה (נ)
corn	'tiras	תִּירָס (ז)
rice	'orez	אוֹרֶז (ז)
buckwheat	ku'semet	כּוּסֶמֶת (נ)
pea plant	afuna	אֲפוּנָה (נ)
kidney bean	ʃu'it	שְׁעוּעִית (נ)
soy	'soya	סוֹיָה (נ)
lentil	adaʃim	עֲדָשִׁים (נ״ר)
beans (pulse crops)	pol	פּוֹל (ז)

REGIONAL GEOGRAPHY

Countries. Nationalities

192. Politics. Government. Part 1

politics	po'litika	פּוֹלִיטִיקָה (נ)
political (adj)	po'liti	פּוֹלִיטִי
politician	politikai	פּוֹלִיטִיקָאִי (ז)
state (country)	medina	מְדִינָה (נ)
citizen	ezrax	אֶזְרָח (ז)
citizenship	ezraxut	אֶזְרָחוּת (נ)
national emblem	'semel le'umi	סֶמֶל לְאוּמִי (ז)
national anthem	himnon le'umi	הִמְנוֹן לְאוּמִי (ז)
government	memʃala	מֶמְשָׁלָה (נ)
head of state	roʃ medina	רֹאש מְדִינָה (ז)
parliament	parlament	פַּרְלָמֶנְט (ז)
party	miflaga	מִפְלָגָה (נ)
capitalism	kapitalizm	קַפִּיטָלִיזם (ז)
capitalist (adj)	kapita'listi	קַפִּיטָלִיסטִי
socialism	sotsyalizm	סוֹצִיאָלִיזם (ז)
socialist (adj)	sotsya'listi	סוֹצִיאָלִיסטִי
communism	komunizm	קוֹמוּנִיזם (ז)
communist (adj)	komu'nisti	קוֹמוּנִיסטִי
communist (n)	komunist	קוֹמוּנִיסט (ז)
democracy	demo'kratya	דֶמוֹקְרַטְיָה (נ)
democrat	demokrat	דֶמוֹקְרָט (ז)
democratic (adj)	demo'krati	דֶמוֹקְרָטִי
Democratic party	miflaga demo'kratit	מִפְלָגָה דֶמוֹקְרָטִית (נ)
liberal (n)	libe'rali	לִיבֶּרָלִי (ז)
liberal (adj)	libe'rali	לִיבֶּרָלִי
conservative (n)	ʃamran	שַׁמְרָן (ז)
conservative (adj)	ʃamrani	שַׁמְרָנִי
republic (n)	re'publika	רֶפּוּבְּלִיקָה (נ)
republican (n)	republi'kani	רֶפּוּבְּלִיקָנִי (ז)
Republican party	miflaga republi'kanit	מִפְלָגָה רֶפּוּבְּלִיקָנִית (נ)

elections	bxirot	בְּחִירוֹת (נ״ר)
to elect (vt)	livxor	לִבְחוֹר
elector, voter	mats'bi'a	מַצְבִּיעַ (ז)
election campaign	masa bxirot	מַסָּע בְּחִירוֹת (ז)
voting (n)	hatsba'a	הַצְבָּעָה (נ)
to vote (vi)	lehats'bi'a	לְהַצְבִּיעַ
suffrage, right to vote	zxut hatsba'a	זְכוּת הַצְבָּעָה (נ)
candidate	mu'amad	מוּעֲמָד (ז)
to be a candidate	lehatsig mu'amadut	לְהַצִּיג מוּעֲמָדוּת
campaign	masa	מַסָּע (ז)
opposition (as adj)	opozitsyoni	אוֹפּוֹזִיצְיוֹנִי
opposition (n)	opo'zitsya	אוֹפּוֹזִיצְיָה (נ)
visit	bikur	בִּיקוּר (ז)
official visit	bikur rifmi	בִּיקוּר רִשְׁמִי (ז)
international (adj)	benle'umi	בֵּינְלְאוּמִי
negotiations	masa umatan	מַשָׂא וּמַתָּן (ז)
to negotiate (vi)	laset velatet	לָשֵׂאת וְלָתֵת

193. Politics. Government. Part 2

society	xevra	חֶבְרָה (נ)
constitution	xuka	חוּקָה (נ)
power (political control)	filton	שִׁלְטוֹן (ז)
corruption	fxitut	שְׁחִיתוּת (נ)
law (justice)	xok	חוֹק (ז)
legal (legitimate)	xuki	חוּקִי
justice (fairness)	'tsedek	צֶדֶק (ז)
just (fair)	tsodek	צוֹדֵק
committee	'va'ad	וַעַד (ז)
bill (draft law)	hatsa'at xok	הַצָּעַת חוֹק (נ)
budget	taktsiv	תַּקְצִיב (ז)
policy	mediniyut	מְדִינִיּוּת (נ)
reform	re'forma	רֶפוֹרְמָה (נ)
radical (adj)	radi'kali	רָדִיקָלִי
power (strength, force)	otsma	עוֹצְמָה (נ)
powerful (adj)	rav 'koax	רַב־כּוֹחַ
supporter	tomex	תּוֹמֵךְ (ז)
influence	hafpa'a	הַשְׁפָּעָה (נ)
regime (e.g., military ~)	miftar	מִשְׁטָר (ז)
conflict	sixsux	סִכְסוּךְ (ז)

conspiracy (plot)	'keʃer	קֶשֶׁר (ז)
provocation	provo'katsya, hitgarut	פְּרוֹבוֹקַצְיָה, הִתְגָּרוּת (נ)
to overthrow (regime, etc.)	leha'diax	לְהַדִּיחַ
overthrow (of government)	hadaxa mikes malxut	הֲדָחָה מֶקֶס מַלְכוּת (נ)
revolution	mahapexa	מַהְפֵּכָה (נ)
coup d'état	hafixa	הֲפִיכָה (נ)
military coup	mahapax tsva'i	מַהְפָּךְ צְבָאִי (ז)
crisis	maʃber	מַשְׁבֵּר (ז)
economic recession	mitun kalkali	מִיתוּן כַּלְכָּלִי (ז)
demonstrator (protester)	mafgin	מַפְגִּין (ז)
demonstration	hafgana	הַפְגָּנָה (נ)
martial law	miʃtar tsva'i	מִשְׁטָר צְבָאִי (ז)
military base	basis tsva'i	בָּסִיס צְבָאִי (ז)
stability	yatsivut	יַצִּיבוּת (נ)
stable (adj)	yatsiv	יַצִּיב
exploitation	nitsul	נִיצוּל (ז)
to exploit (workers)	lenatsel	לְנַצֵּל
racism	giz'anut	גִּזְעָנוּת (נ)
racist	giz'ani	גִּזְעָנִי (ז)
fascism	faʃizm	פָשִׁיזְם (ז)
fascist	faʃist	פָשִׁיסְט (ז)

194. Countries. Miscellaneous

foreigner	zar	זָר (ז)
foreign (adj)	zar	זָר
abroad (in a foreign country)	bexul	בְּחוּ"ל
emigrant	mehager	מְהַגֵּר (ז)
emigration	hagira	הֲגִירָה (נ)
to emigrate (vi)	lehager	לְהַגֵּר
the West	ma'arav	מַעֲרָב (ז)
the East	mizrax	מִזְרָח (ז)
the Far East	hamizrax haraxok	הַמִּזְרָח הָרָחוֹק (ז)
civilization	tsivili'zatsya	צִיבִילִיזַצְיָה (נ)
humanity (mankind)	enoʃut	אֱנוֹשׁוּת (נ)
the world (earth)	olam	עוֹלָם (ז)
peace	ʃalom	שָׁלוֹם (ז)
worldwide (adj)	olami	עוֹלָמִי
homeland	mo'ledet	מוֹלֶדֶת (נ)
people (population)	am	עַם (ז)

population	oxlusiya	אוּכְלוּסִיָה (נ)
people (a lot of ~)	anaʃim	אֲנָשִׁים (ז״ר)
nation (people)	uma	אוּמָה (נ)
generation	dor	דוֹר (ז)
territory (area)	ʃetax	שֶׁטַח (ז)
region	ezor	אֵזוֹר (ז)
state (part of a country)	medina	מְדִינָה (נ)
tradition	ma'soret	מָסוֹרֶת (נ)
custom (tradition)	minhag	מִנְהָג (ז)
ecology	eko'logya	אֶקוֹלוֹגְיָה (נ)
Indian (Native American)	ind'yani	אִינְדִיאָנִי (ז)
Gypsy (masc.)	tso'ani	צוֹעֲנִי (ז)
Gypsy (fem.)	tso'aniya	צוֹעֲנִיָה (נ)
Gypsy (adj)	tso'ani	צוֹעֲנִי
empire	im'perya	אִימְפֶּרְיָה (נ)
colony	ko'lonya	קוֹלוֹנְיָה (נ)
slavery	avdut	עַבְדוּת (נ)
invasion	pliʃa	פְּלִישָׁה (נ)
famine	'ra'av	רָעָב (ז)

195. Major religious groups. Confessions

religion	dat	דָת (נ)
religious (adj)	dati	דָתִי
faith, belief	emuna	אֱמוּנָה (נ)
to believe (in God)	leha'amin	לְהַאֲמִין
believer	ma'amin	מַאֲמִין
atheism	ate'izm	אָתֵאִיזְם (ז)
atheist	ate'ist	אָתֵאִיסְט (ז)
Christianity	natsrut	נַצְרוּת (נ)
Christian (n)	notsri	נוֹצְרִי (ז)
Christian (adj)	notsri	נוֹצְרִי
Catholicism	ka'toliyut	קָתוֹלִיוּת (נ)
Catholic (n)	ka'toli	קָתוֹלִי (ז)
Catholic (adj)	ka'toli	קָתוֹלִי
Protestantism	protes'tantiyut	פְּרוֹטֶסְטַנְטִיוּת (נ)
Protestant Church	knesiya protes'tantit	כְּנֵסִיָה פְּרוֹטֶסְטַנְטִית (נ)
Protestant (n)	protestant	פְּרוֹטֶסְטַנְט (ז)
Orthodoxy	natsrut orto'doksit	נַצְרוּת אוֹרתוֹדוֹקסִית (נ)
Orthodox Church	knesiya orto'doksit	כְּנֵסִיָה אוֹרתוֹדוֹקסִית (נ)

Orthodox (n)	orto'doksi	אוֹרְתוֹדוֹקְסִי
Presbyterianism	presbiteryanizm	פְּרֶסְבִּיטֶרְיָאנִיזם (ז)
Presbyterian Church	knesiya presviteri''anit	כְּנֵסִיָּה פְּרֶסְבִּיטֶרְיָאנִית (נ)
Presbyterian (n)	presbiter'yani	פְּרֶסְבִּיטֶרְיָאנִי (ז)

| Lutheranism | knesiya lute'ranit | כְּנֵסִיָּה לוּתֶרָנִית (נ) |
| Lutheran (n) | lute'rani | לוּתֶרָנִי (ז) |

| Baptist Church | knesiya bap'tistit | כְּנֵסִיָּה בַּפְּטִיסְטִית (נ) |
| Baptist (n) | baptist | בַּפְּטִיסט (ז) |

Anglican Church	knesiya angli'kanit	כְּנֵסִיָּה אַנגלִיקָנִית (נ)
Anglican (n)	angli'kani	אַנגלִיקָנִי (ז)
Mormonism	mor'monim	מוֹרמוֹנִים (ז)
Mormon (n)	mormon	מוֹרמוֹן (ז)

| Judaism | yahadut | יַהֲדוּת (נ) |
| Jew (n) | yehudi, yehudiya | יְהוּדִי (ז), יְהוּדִיָּה (נ) |

| Buddhism | budhizm | בּוּדהִיזם (ז) |
| Buddhist (n) | budhist | בּוּדהִיסט (ז) |

| Hinduism | hindu'izm | הִינדוּאִיזם (ז) |
| Hindu (n) | 'hindi | הִינדִי (ז) |

Islam	islam	אִיסלָאם (ז)
Muslim (n)	'muslemi	מוּסלְמִי (ז)
Muslim (adj)	'muslemi	מוּסלְמִי

Shiah Islam	islam 'ʃi'i	אִסלָאם שִיעִי (ז)
Shiite (n)	'ʃi'i	שִיעִי (ז)
Sunni Islam	islam 'suni	אִסלָאם סוּנִי (ז)
Sunnite (n)	'suni	סוּנִי (ז)

196. Religions. Priests

| priest | 'komer | כּוֹמֶר (ז) |
| the Pope | apifyor | אַפִּיפיוֹר (ז) |

monk, friar	nazir	נָזִיר (ז)
nun	nazira	נְזִירָה (נ)
pastor	'komer	כּוֹמֶר (ז)

abbot	roʃ minzar	רֹאש מִנזָר (ז)
vicar (parish priest)	'komer hakehila	כּוֹמֶר הַקְהִילָה (ז)
bishop	'biʃof	בִּישוֹף (ז)
cardinal	χaʃman	חַשמָן (ז)

| preacher | matif | מַטִיף (ז) |
| preaching | hatafa, draʃa | הַטָּפָה, דְרָשָה (נ) |

parishioners	χaver kehila	חָבֵר קְהִילָה (ז)
believer	ma'amin	מַאֲמִין (ז)
atheist	ate'ist	אָתֵאִיסְט (ז)

197. Faith. Christianity. Islam

| Adam | adam | אָדָם |
| Eve | χava | חַוָּה |

God	elohim	אֱלוֹהִים
the Lord	adonai	אֲדוֹנָי
the Almighty	kol yaχol	כָּל יָכוֹל

sin	χet	חֵטְא (ז)
to sin (vi)	laχato	לַחֲטוֹא
sinner (masc.)	χote	חוֹטֵא (ז)
sinner (fem.)	χo'ta'at	חוֹטֵאת (נ)

| hell | gehinom | גֵּיהִינוֹם (ז) |
| paradise | gan 'eden | גַּן עֵדֶן (ז) |

| Jesus | 'yeʃu | יֵשׁוּ |
| Jesus Christ | 'yeʃu hanotsri | יֵשׁוּ הַנּוֹצְרִי |

the Holy Spirit	'ruaχ ha'kodeʃ	רוּחַ הַקּוֹדֶשׁ (נ)
the Savior	mo'ʃi'a	מוֹשִׁיעַ (ז)
the Virgin Mary	'miryam hakdoʃa	מִרְיָם הַקְּדוֹשָׁה

the Devil	satan	שָׂטָן (ז)
devil's (adj)	stani	שְׂטָנִי
Satan	satan	שָׂטָן (ז)
satanic (adj)	stani	שְׂטָנִי

angel	mal'aχ	מַלְאָךְ (ז)
guardian angel	mal'aχ ʃomer	מַלְאָךְ שׁוֹמֵר (ז)
angelic (adj)	mal'aχi	מַלְאָכִי

apostle	ʃa'liaχ	שָׁלִיחַ (ז)
archangel	arχimalaχ	אַרְכִימַלְאָךְ (ז)
the Antichrist	an'tikrist	אַנְטִיכְרִיסְט (ז)

Church	knesiya	כְּנֵסִיָּה (נ)
Bible	tanaχ	תַּנַ"ךְ (ז)
biblical (adj)	tanaχi	תַּנַ"כִי
Old Testament	habrit hayeʃana	הַבְּרִית הַיְשָׁנָה (נ)
New Testament	habrit haχadaʃa	הַבְּרִית הַחֲדָשָׁה (נ)
Gospel	evangelyon	אֱוַונְגֶלְיוֹן (ז)
Holy Scripture	kitvei ha'kodeʃ	כִּתְבֵי הַקּוֹדֶשׁ (ז"ר)
Heaven	malχut ʃa'mayim, gan 'eden	מַלְכוּת שָׁמַיִם (נ), גַּן עֵדֶן (ז)

Commandment	mitsva	מִצְוָה (נ)
prophet	navi	נָבִיא (ז)
prophecy	nevu'a	נְבוּאָה (נ)
Allah	'alla	אַלְלָה
Mohammed	mu'ɣamad	מוּחַמַד
the Koran	kur'an	קוּרְאָן (ז)
mosque	misgad	מִסְגָד (ז)
mullah	'mula	מוֹלָא (ז)
prayer	tfila	תְפִילָה (נ)
to pray (vi, vt)	lehitpalel	לְהִתְפַלֵל
pilgrimage	aliya le'regel	עֲלָיָה לָרֶגֶל (נ)
pilgrim	tsalyan	צַלְיָן (ז)
Mecca	'meka	מֶכָּה (נ)
church	knesiya	כְּנֵסִייָה (נ)
temple	mikdaʃ	מִקְדָש (ז)
cathedral	kated'rala	קָתֶדְרָלָה (נ)
Gothic (adj)	'goti	גוֹתִי
synagogue	beit 'kneset	בֵּית כְּנֶסֶת (ז)
mosque	misgad	מִסְגָד (ז)
chapel	beit tfila	בֵּית תְפִילָה (ז)
abbey	minzar	מִנְזָר (ז)
convent	minzar	מִנְזָר (ז)
monastery	minzar	מִנְזָר (ז)
bell (church ~s)	pa'amon	פַעֲמוֹן (ז)
bell tower	migdal pa'amonim	מִגְדַל פַעֲמוֹנִים (ז)
to ring (ab. bells)	letsaltsel	לְצַלְצֵל
cross	tslav	צְלָב (ז)
cupola (roof)	kipa	כִּיפָּה (נ)
icon	ikonin	אִיקוֹנִין (ז)
soul	neʃama	נְשָמָה (נ)
fate (destiny)	goral	גוֹרָל (ז)
evil (n)	'ro'a	רוֹעַ (ז)
good (n)	tuv	טוּב (ז)
vampire	arpad	עַרְפָּד (ז)
witch (evil ~)	maxʃefa	מַכְשֵפָה (נ)
demon	ʃed	שֵד (ז)
spirit	'ruax	רוּחַ (נ)
redemption (giving us ~)	kapara	כַּפָּרָה (נ)
to redeem (vt)	lexaper al	לְכַפֵּר עַל
church service, mass	'misa	מִיסָה (נ)
to say mass	la'arox 'misa	לַעֲרוֹך מִיסָה

confession	vidui	וִידוּי (ז)
to confess (vi)	lehitvadot	לְהִתְוַודוֹת
saint (n)	kadoʃ	קָדוֹשׁ (ז)
sacred (holy)	mekudaʃ	מְקוּדָשׁ
holy water	'mayim kdoʃim	מַיִם קְדוֹשִׁים (ז"ר)
ritual (n)	'tekes	טֶקֶס (ז)
ritual (adj)	ʃel 'tekes	שֶׁל טֶקֶס
sacrifice	korban	קוֹרבָּן (ז)
superstition	emuna tfela	אֱמוּנָה תְּפֵלָה (נ)
superstitious (adj)	ma'amin emunot tfelot	מַאֲמִין אֱמוּנוֹת תְּפֵלוֹת
afterlife	ha'olam haba	הָעוֹלָם הַבָּא (ז)
eternal life	χayei olam, χayei 'netsaχ	חַיֵי עוֹלָם (ז"ר), חַיֵי נֶצַח (ז"ר)

MISCELLANEOUS

198. Various useful words

background (green ~)	'reka	רֶקַע (ז)
balance (of situation)	izun	אִיזוּן (ז)
barrier (obstacle)	miχʃol	מִכְשׁוֹל (ז)
base (basis)	basis	בָּסִיס (ז)
beginning	hatχala	הַתְחָלָה (נ)
category	kate'gorya	קָטֶגוֹרְיָה (נ)
cause (reason)	siba	סִיבָּה (נ)
choice	bχina	בְּחִינָה (נ)
coincidence	hat'ama	הַתְאָמָה (נ)
comfortable (~ chair)	'noaχ	נוֹחַ
comparison	haʃva'a	הַשׁוָואָה (נ)
compensation	pitsui	פִּיצוּי (ז)
degree (extent, amount)	darga	דַרְגָה (נ)
development	hitpatχut	הִתְפַּתְחוּת (נ)
difference	'ʃoni	שׁוֹנִי (ז)
effect (e.g., of drugs)	efekt	אֶפֶקְט (ז)
effort (exertion)	ma'amats	מַאֲמָץ (ז)
element	element	אֶלֶמֶנְט (ז)
end (finish)	sof	סוֹף (ז)
example (illustration)	dugma	דוּגמָה (נ)
fact	uvda	עוּבְדָה (נ)
frequent (adj)	tadir	תָדִיר
growth (development)	gidul	גִידוּל (ז)
help	ezra	עֶזְרָה (נ)
ideal	ide'al	אִידֵיאָל (ז)
kind (sort, type)	sug	סוּג (ז)
labyrinth	mavoχ	מָבוֹך (ז)
mistake, error	ta'ut	טָעוּת (נ)
moment	'rega	רֶגַע (ז)
object (thing)	'etsem	עֶצֶם (ז)
obstacle	maχsom	מַחְסוֹם (ז)
original (original copy)	makor	מָקוֹר (ז)
part (~ of sth)	'χelek	חֵלֶק (ז)
particle, small part	χelkik	חֶלְקִיק (ז)
pause (break)	hafuga	הֲפוּגָה (נ)

position	emda	עֶמְדָּה (נ)
principle	ikaron	עִיקָרוֹן (ז)
problem	be'aya	בְּעָיָה (נ)
process	tahaliχ	תַּהֲלִיךְ (ז)
progress	kidma	קִדְמָה (נ)
property (quality)	tχuna, sgula	תְּבוּנָה, סְגוּלָה (נ)
reaction	tguva	תְּגוּבָה (נ)
risk	sikun	סִיכּוּן (ז)
secret	sod	סוֹד (ז)
series	sidra	סִדְרָה (נ)
shape (outer form)	tsura	צוּרָה (נ)
situation	matsav	מַצָּב (ז)
solution	pitaron	פִּיתָרוֹן (ז)
standard (adj)	tikni	תִּקְנִי
standard (level of quality)	'teken	תֶּקֶן (ז)
stop (pause)	hafsaka	הַפְסָקָה (נ)
style	signon	סִגְנוֹן (ז)
system	ʃita	שִׁיטָה (נ)
table (chart)	tavla	טַבְלָה (נ)
tempo, rate	'ketsev	קֶצֶב (ז)
term (word, expression)	musag	מוּשָׂג (ז)
thing (object, item)	'χefets	חֵפֶץ (ז)
truth (e.g., moment of ~)	emet	אֱמֶת (נ)
turn (please wait your ~)	tor	תּוֹר (ז)
type (sort, kind)	min	מִין (ז)
urgent (adj)	daχuf	דָּחוּף
urgently (adv)	bidχifut	בִּדְחִיפוּת
utility (usefulness)	to''elet	תּוֹעֶלֶת (נ)
variant (alternative)	girsa	גִּירְסָה (נ)
way (means, method)	'ofen	אוֹפֶן (ז)
zone	ezor	אֵזוֹר (ז)